THE WARTIME HOUSE

HOME LIFE IN WARTIME
BRITAIN 1939–1945

MIKE BROWN & CAROL HARRIS

First Published in 2001 by
Sutton Publishing Limited · Phoenix Mill
Thrupp · Stroud · Gloucestershire ·GL5 2BU

This paperback edition first published in 2005

British Library Cataloguing in Publication Data
A catalogue record for this book is available from the British Library

ISBN 0 7509 4212 6

Typeset in 10.5/13.5 Photina
Typesetting and origination by
Sutton Publishing Limited.
Printed in Great Britain by
J.H. Haynes & Co. Ltd, Sparkford, England.

CONTENTS

ACKNOWLEDGEMENTS

We would like to take this opportunity to thank the following people whose help has proved invaluable in the production of this book:

John Davis of Manchester Metropolitan University; Ramesh Rajadurai; Clare Bishop, Catherine Watson, Kirsty Steadman and Jonathan Falconer from Sutton Publishing; William and Ralph.

Photographs are from the following sources:

Bromley Local Studies Unit; Daily Express; Daily Mail; Design Council; Hallmark Cards (Holdings) Ltd; Geo Harrap; Imperial War Museum; Lewisham Local History Centre; Osbert Lancaster, *Homes Sweet Homes* (1938); John Murray (Publishers) Ltd; Odhams Press; Vinmag Archives Ltd.

CONVERSION
TABLES

MONEY

The currency used during the war was, like today, based on the pound. But under the old system, known as pounds, shillings and pence, the pound was divided into 20 shillings, each of which was worth 12 pennies. An amount would be written in the form of £3 17s 10d, or three pounds, seventeen shillings and tenpence. Smaller amounts might be written in the form of 12/6d or twelve shillings and sixpence. The guinea, worth £1 1s, was rather old fashioned by the late thirties, but continued to be used for more expensive items. Items priced in guineas were therefore implicitly of better quality.

1d = 1 old penny = 0.4p
1s = 1 shilling = 5p
1gn = 1 guinea = £1.05

RELATIVE VALUE OF THE POUND

It is difficult to understand how much something was actually worth in the past. A house might cost £800 pounds in 1932, but people earned a lot less too; so, is it relatively more or less expensive than a house today? The following conversion table shows the relative value of £1 using today's values; so £1 in 1900 would be worth £55.36 today.

1900	=	£55.39	1939	=	£30.12
1905	=	£53.66	1940	=	£26.02
1910	=	£50.50	1941	=	£23.85
1914	=	£47.69	1942	=	£23.85
1918	=	£22.01	1943	=	£23.85
1920	=	£19.08	1944	=	£23.85
1925	=	£26.83	1945	=	£23.52
1930	=	£30.12	1950	=	£20.44
1935	=	£33.02			

Source: National Statistical Office

COOKING

Weight

1 pound = 1 lb = 453 g
½ lb = 227 g
¼ pound = 113 g
1 ounce = 1 oz = 28 g

Measures

1 tablespoon = 3 teaspoons
1 tablespoon = 15 ml
1 teaspoon = 5 ml

Liquid

1 pint = 568 ml
½ pint = 284 ml
¼ pint = 142 ml

The Cup

Another measure commonly used was the cup – 'take one cupful of breadcrumbs'. This referred to a standard tea-cup (not a mug). It was an approximate measure, different from the precise US measure, also called a cup.

Oven Temperatures

Most wartime recipes have oven settings that are described rather than given as a figure; for example: 'Bake in a moderately hot oven for fifteen minutes.' The following table gives modern equivalents for these.

Description	Degrees C	Gas number
very slow	110–120	¼–½
slow	140–150	1–2
moderate	160–180	3–4
moderately hot	190–200	5–6
hot	220–230	7–8
very hot	240	9

INTRODUCTION

One of the greatest social revolutions of the last two centuries has been the massive and rapid expansion of what we would today call the middle classes. This group had its beginnings in the freemen of feudal England, the merchants and artisans, people whose skills and intelligence enabled them to rise above the 'common' people, without threatening the position of the ruling elite. The members of this group became the grease that allowed the wheels of society to turn smoothly. Those with ability and intelligence were plucked from the lowest rungs and put to good use in the evolving civil service, in the Church, and in commerce, running the country for those who ruled. This symbiotic relationship was nothing if not mercenary; the wealth created by the middle classes during the Industrial Revolution bought them marriages into the aristocracy, which by this time needed both money and fresh blood.

The middle classes excelled especially in the growing field of commerce, putting to good use the education that they valued so highly. So it was no coincidence that, as England became part of Great Britain, the middle classes spread throughout the towns and cities where most of that trade was conducted. This expansion was particularly obvious in the south-east of England, where much of the increasing Continental trade was based. Yet until the Industrial Revolution, the middle classes remained but a small sector of British society.

In 1867, the same year in which Karl Marx's *Das Kapital* was published, Dudley Baxter's book *National Income of the United Kingdom* quantified the size and distribution of the national income. As part of this process, Baxter attempted to sort the population into a number of groups or classes, creating a system that is still recognised today. He grouped the upper class with the upper middle class to make about half a per cent of the population. Next came the middle and lower middle classes, who together made up 20 per cent. Finally, skilled, 'less skilled' and unskilled labour, plus agricultural workers, made up the rest. So, by the second half of the nineteenth century, the middle classes had become a significant group and their numbers continued to rise.

But income was not the only identifying characteristic. Education was important, as was religion. Middle class morality, so despised by Alfred Doolittle in George Bernard Shaw's play *Pygmalion*, was a definable set of values unique to the class. Retrospectively, it became synonymous with the values of the Victorians, and, as Dickens demonstrated time and again, the hypocrisy of a society which often paid little more than lip service to them. Its morality was rooted in a genteel lifestyle fuelled by salaries earned by predominantly clerical and professional workers.

With this new morality came a new way of life, unique to those living in the suburbs, totally alien to manual labourers living in the inner cities, or on farms for whom domestic life, with its earth closets, standpipes, slums, poverty and disease, had changed little since their grandparents' time. In the twentieth century, the success of Suburbia was such that the enduring image of the inter-war period is of their cosy, semi-detached world.

This is the story of a typical British suburban house and the lives of those who might have inhabited it during the Second World War: it is representative of millions who, from their beginnings in the middle of the nineteenth century, grew rapidly to become the dominant feature of twentieth-century British society.

ONE

THE SUBURBAN DREAM

THE BEGINNINGS OF SUBURBIA

The nineteenth century witnessed a huge expansion of Britain's towns and cities. The Industrial Revolution had followed a distinct pattern: workers were packed into tenements that had been quickly thrown up around the factories. The lack of public transport and the long hours they worked meant that the people had to live near to their workplaces, and this gave rise to overcrowded slums, close to the smoke, grime and dirt created by these industries.

The towns grew quickly as the move from countryside to town gathered pace. In 1851 about half the population of England and Wales lived in urban areas; by 1901 this had risen to three-quarters, and by 1939 to four-fifths. At this time, Greater London alone encompassed one-fifth of the entire population of the two countries. The rate of expansion continued into the twentieth century. In 1900 London's Charing Cross was about 8 miles from the countryside, north or south; by 1939 this had almost doubled to about 15 miles in a new outward surge.

As the population of workers in the slum areas of the industrial towns grew, those with higher paid positions who could afford transport lived on the outskirts of the town, or the suburban areas – the suburbs. Here they were on the edge of the countryside, and could enjoy fresh air and peaceful surroundings.

In 1898 Ebenezer Howard's book *Garden Cities of Tomorrow* compared urban and rural living. His 'Garden City' concept combined the pleasant aspects of living in the country with the ability to work in the town, while keeping commuting time to an acceptable minimum. He proposed that a series of new towns be established around London, each surrounded by its own 'Green Belt' of land. With private funding, Howard began building at Letchworth in 1903, and Welwyn Garden City in 1920. His ideas were very popular, and were copied in such schemes as the Hampstead Garden Suburb, begun in 1907. His ideas and influence also contributed to the fashion for nostalgia in designs, with Elizabethan and other historic styles predominating.

AN ENGLISHMAN'S HOME IS . . .

The typical seven-room semi contained (average sizes are given): three bedrooms: 14 ft 6 in x 11 ft (4.35 m x 3.3 m); 13 ft x 11 ft 6 in (3.9 m x 3.5 m); and 8 ft x 7 ft 6 in (2.4 m x 2.25 m); a drawing-room: 14 ft 6 in x 12 ft 6 in (4.35 m x 3.75 m); a dining-room: 14 ft x 11 ft (4.2 m x 3.3 m); a kitchen or kitchenette: 10 ft x 7 ft 6 in (3 m x 2.25 m); and a bathroom, of a similar size to the kitchen.

An Edwardian 'Tyrolean' semi with rendered Tyrolean finish, half timbering, leaded lights, decorative back chimney pots and a rather strange small fence by the front door with MacIntosh style cut-outs.

The late Victorian and Edwardian suburbs had typically comprised rows of neat, brick-built terraced houses, but the ease of movement (and consequent expansion of the suburbs) provided by improved transport systems meant that houses could be built far less densely, with front and back gardens. This led to the shift away from terraced to detached, or at least semi-detached construction, and the inter-war suburb – the period during which growth was most marked – was typified by the three-bedroomed semi-detached house, or 'semi'. The single family semi was a determined move from the typical Victorian tenement lifestyle, where many generations of the same family lived squashed together, everyone knowing everyone else's business; the suburban semi, with its garden (front and back) and its (partial) insularity, was the embodiment of a desire for genteel privacy.

Initially, however, few could afford to move out to the suburbs; while the houses were not particularly expensive, they were still beyond the reach of the lowest paid. The cost of commuting also had to be considered. Transport in the form of the horse, with or without carriage, was pricey. Even the earliest horse-drawn omnibuses were relatively expensive, although the arrival of passenger trains, with their cheap, early morning, workman's tickets eased the situation. These factors tended to make the suburbs the domain of the rapidly growing lower middle classes.

TRANSPORT

By the beginning of the twentieth century, public transport services were being rapidly improved, with the result that more people could live further away from their places of work. Allied to this was the move to shorter working hours, which gave people more time to be able to travel to and from work. These changes, in turn, created a new outward spurt of suburban house building.

Electric trams had been introduced at the turn of the century, and soon replaced the horse-drawn versions. Motor buses were also introduced; although at first they were noisy, smelly, and inclined to break down, by 1910 new models such as the London General Omnibus Company's B type – sometimes called the 'Old Bill' – had solved most of the problems. The omnibus, which could cover new routes without needing new tracks or cables, became the preferred mode of transport for town dwellers, putting most of the tram companies out of business.

In the larger cities, where longer distances between the centre and the outskirts made travel by bus less viable, railways met the demand for public transport. The sheer size of London meant that the scale of the problem was far greater and needed a different solution. The first underground electric line had opened in London in 1890, then the Metropolitan and District Underground Railway Companies began replacing their steam trains with electric versions. In 1900 a new company, the Central London Railway, opened its first line, running from the Bank to Shepherd's Bush. It proved a great success, carrying 100,000 passengers a day, and was followed by several others: the Bakerloo line in 1906 (Baker Street to Waterloo); the Piccadilly line, also in 1906 (Finsbury Park to Hammersmith); and the Hampstead line in 1907 (later integrated into the Northern line).

The Hampstead line is an excellent example of the symbiotic relationship between transport and housing development at the time. The line terminated at the cross-roads in Golders Green and for a short while the station was the only building in the area. But within months, builders were putting up houses all around it. Such was the demand for housing in these locations that house-builders themselves put money towards the cost of constructing stations.

After the First World War, the underground lines continued to expand, and in 1933 the various companies were brought together into the London Passenger Transport Board (LPTB). Buses linked the stations to the new estates, allowing easy access to the centre from the suburbs, facilitating the movement outwards. Between 1921 and 1937 the population of outer London rose by 1,400,000, while that of central London fell by 400,000.

Underground posters encouraged this outward move, with many extolling the peace and beauty of suburban life. The first of these, 'Golders Green', produced in 1908, shows a neat timber-gabled house with an equally neat garden; a middle-class man in his shirtsleeves is watering his flowers, while his wife sits winding wool in a deck-chair on the lawn, with their young daughter at her feet.

The Metropolitan Railway produced an annual guidebook, *Metro-land*, from 1915, which described the country districts served by the line. One of the main sections, and the purpose of the booklet, was the 'House Seekers' section, with pages of advertisements for houses, usually newly built, in the area. The term 'Metro-land' became synonymous with districts north-west of London in Middlesex, Hertfordshire and Buckinghamshire, which were served by the line. The booklet continued to be issued until 1932, after which the Metropolitan line disappeared into the LPTB.

Two Underground posters promoting Metro-land. The first depicts its rural delights, while the second shows how convenient it was for the city's attractions.

The road network too had seen expansion. By-passes, such as that at Kingston in Surrey and the North Circular Road, as well as new fast routes, such as the Western and Eastern Avenues, were signs that cities were becoming more accessible to the rapidly expanding car-owning

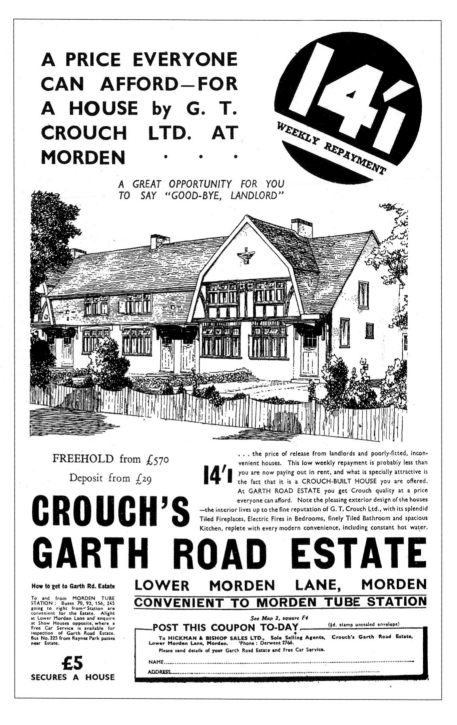

A house advert from the mid-thirties. Rather than being sold as exclusive, the main thrust of the advert is that anyone can afford to buy these houses and become a homeowner – 'Say Good-bye, Landlord'. 'Convenient to Morden Tube Station' is an added temptation.

public who could commute greater distances. Houses, factories and shops sprang up along these and other main roads because services (gas, water, electricity and sewage) were immediately accessible so there was no need for new and expensive pipework. This meant that houses could be built far more cheaply. However, ribbon development, as this became known, marred the whole point of these new roads, as what were supposed to be fast access roads became clogged with local traffic; ribbon development was prohibited by an Act of Parliament in 1935 but by then the damage had been done.

SOCIAL TRENDS

In 1909 C.F.G. Masterman, in *The Condition of England*, delineated the class structure in Britain as: the Conquerors; the Suburbans; and the Multitude. He described the Suburbans as 'practically the product of the last half century'. Masterman's description of suburban life was just as valid in 1939 (and, apart from its sexual stereotyping, is still recognisable today):

its male population is engaged in all its working hours in small, crowded offices, under artificial light, doing immense sums, adding up other men's accounts, writing other men's letters. It is sucked into the City at daybreak and scattered again as darkness falls. It finds itself towards evening in its own territory in the miles and miles of little red houses in little, silent streets, in number defying imagination. Each boasts its pleasant drawing room, its bow window, its little front garden, its high-sounding title – 'Acacia Villa' or 'Camperdown Lodge' – attesting unconquerable human aspiration.

The aspiration again stems from the Industrial Revolution. Previously, knowing one's place and its immutability, set at birth, had been the cornerstone of society. During the Industrial Revolution, men like Richard Arkwright had literally gone from rags to immense riches and, in doing so, had taken on the trappings of traditional 'Lord of the Manor'. Upward mobility became the aim of many, even on a modest scale. And upward mobility most easily defined itself in the manner exemplified by Arkwright and other successful magnates, who themselves took a traditional approach to displaying their success. Therefore, it is no coincidence that much suburban housing of the twenties and thirties had the feel of minor baronial halls, with their half-timbered finishes, their bow windows

This aerial shot of an estate in Streatham Vale between the wars shows how it was arranged around one of the centres of the community — the school. The school was also used by an Evening Institute and by the local Sports and Social Club for dances and other Saturday evening entertainment. Road access is good and the houses, in short terraces, all have a garden. Rows of white washing are hanging 'out back'; perhaps the photograph was taken on a Monday. (Courtesy of Patrick Loobey)

Tudor-style housing in Twickenham. Special features include the 'Brick Inglenook Fireplace', wood block floors, and fitted electric fires.

with stained glass and latticed panes, and their Gothic front doors. This feeling of rural selectivity was aided by the naming of roads as Drives, Lanes and Avenues. Indeed, many houses were marketed as 'Baronial Halls', or 'Cosy Palaces', and a big selling point was that 'Every one different', even though the differences were usually minuscule.

The numbers of those in 'blackcoat' jobs – in government offices, banks, trade and commerce – raced up, reaching 3 million in 1939. Besides these, there were the professionals, or salaried workers – lawyers, teachers, doctors, clergymen and so on – whose numbers doubled to

1½ million between 1911 and 1921. By the late thirties, most of these men were earning good salaries and could afford to pay for good houses. These new salary-workers swelled the ranks of the lower middle classes, who demonstrated this newly improved status by moving out of the city centres and into more genteel surroundings. To move from a terrace to a detached or semi-detached villa, and better still, from renting a property to buying one, was the ultimate way to show one's transition from worker to professional. By 1939 over a quarter of all houses were owner occupied; a remarkable change in just four decades.

Yet this affluence did not remain exclusively the reserve of the middle class; the living standards of the working classes, especially the skilled craftsmen, foremen and supervisors, also gradually improved during the last quarter of the nineteenth century. The average purchasing power of the working classes increased by almost 50 per cent. In 1900 the average wage for a skilled craftsman was about 37s. a week. By the end of 1919, wages had increased by about 120 per cent over pre-war levels, but the cost of living had increased by a similar amount, wiping out any advantages. Over the next ten years, both wages and the cost of living fell, with wages slightly ahead. By the early thirties, unemployment was high, reaching 22 per cent. Yet paradoxically, those still in full-time employment in 1933 had a purchasing power that had increased by over 10 per cent since 1930 – their wages had fallen but prices had fallen even more.

After 1933, the world began to ease its way out of the slump and the cost of living began to rise again and by the outbreak of the Second World War wages were 15 per cent higher in real terms than they had been in 1924. One result of this was that many of the better paid manual workers were able to make the move to suburbia; by 1939 over 30 per cent of all those taking out mortgages were wage earning as opposed to salaried workers.

This move towards house-ownership was completely new. Few Victorians owned the houses they lived in, mainly because renting made

A job advertisement from the *Bath Chronicle and Herald*, May 1942.

COMPARATIVE COSTS

Date	number of private cars	cost of semi	cost of family saloon
1904	8,465		
1907	32,000		Rover 8hp £250
1910	53,196		
1914	132,110	£450–£600	Singer 10 £195
1918	77,707	£1,000–£1,200	
1919	109,000		
1921	242,500	£1,000–£1,400	Austin 7 £165 (first produced 1922)
1929	980,886		Morris Minor £130 (first produced 1928)
1932	1,127,681	£800–£600	Austin 7 £130
1938	1,944,394	£600–£400	Austin 7 Ruby £125

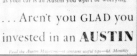

Advice about the blackout, featuring an Austin car.

Lloyd George, Prime Minister during the First World War, promised 'Homes Fit for Heroes' for returning servicemen; but these homes never materialised.

HOUSES TO BE SOLD

THE MIDLANDS, Leamington Spa, situated in best part of town in country surroundings, 2 reception rooms, kitchen, large garden, 5 bedrooms, bathroom, electric light and every convenience. Price £2,500. Vacant possession.—G. Orange, House Agent, 78 Warwick St., Leamington Spa. Tel. 953.
£3,250 FREEHOLD. 3 miles Glastonbury; bus service passes. Close to village. Interesting Character House of 13th and 15th Century, modernised and in excellent order; main electricity; Aga and gas cookers; 3 reception, 2 bathrooms, 5 bedrooms (h. and c.), 2 garages; useful outbuildings; inexpensive gardens; walled kitchen garden, orchard about 4 acres.—Tresidder and Co., 77, South Audley St., London, W.1.
TORQUAY.—Gentleman's charming detached freehold residence with possession (£3,500).—Particulars Kenny Smith and Co., Solicitors, Torquay.

APARTMENTS.

TO LET, Furnished, 3 BEDROOMS, sitting-room, joint use of kitchen, daily maid; use of sun-parlour in absence of owner.—Eves, Hilltop, Blagdon.
ACCOMMODATION suitable semi-invalids; terms according to requirements.—F40, Chronicle, Bath.
BOARD RESIDENCE.—Large Country House, 11 miles from Shrewsbury.—The Grange, Church Preen, Leebotwood, Salop.
HOME for elderly people has vacancy for Lady or Gentleman; special care taken, from 3½ gns.—Harper, Deane House, Carlton, near Bedford. Phone Harrold 250.
FURNISHED BEDROOM, use of kitchen; electric and lounge.—Linda Vista, Berrow, Burnham-on-Sea.
FURNISHED ACCOMMODATION required by young married couple. Both working. Careful tenants.—Write M46, Chronicle, Bath.

FURNISHED HOUSES

FURNISHED HOUSES to let in Evesham and District.—Detached riverside Residence containing 5 bedrooms, 3 rec. rooms; 8 gns. per week. Detached Residence with nice gardens, 4 bedrooms, etc.; 4 gns. per week. Residence in Evesham 6 bedrooms, etc.; 6 gns. and rates per week. Detached House in village, 3 bedrooms, etc. 5 gns. per week.—Further particulars apply E. G. Righton and Son, Estate Agents, Evesham.
TO LET, FURNISHED, small modern House near sea; every convenience, lovely country.—Apply, Isherwood, Tor Cross, Kingsbridge, S. Devon. Anon. £20; Mrs R. Tabor, £1; A. BUNGALOW; electric light, indoor sanitation and everything for your use; 3 bedrooms; garage.—Store and Cafe, Gwithian Towans, Near Hayle, Cornwall.

Houses and apartments for sale or rent, advertised in the *Bath Chronicle and Herald*, May 1942.

far more sense in a society which was far more economically mobile than today. Also, the size of a Victorian household could fluctuate wildly; a young family would expand rapidly. The average family had five or six children, and almost 20 per cent of families had ten or more. On the other hand, a family could, even more rapidly, shrink at a time when child mortality rates were high and epidemics of measles, chicken pox, diphtheria and other viruses could rage unchecked. Additionally, the typical Victorian family could be expected to care for aged, infirm, or less fortunate relatives, as even a cursory glance at Dickens' works can tell us. Most of the advice to those looking for a home in the late nineteenth century recommended taking out a lease of no more than three years.

Before the First World War, the most prolific year for house building was 1906, when about 150,000 houses were constructed. The ever-increasing demands for manpower during the war meant house building effectively stopped; afterwards, in the election of December 1918, Lloyd George's coalition promised soldiers that they would return to 'Homes Fit for Heroes', but the costs were huge. The war had created runaway inflation – in 1919 it cost four times as much to build a house than it had in 1914.

During the war, rent strikes by militant workers had led to the Government imposing a rent freeze on poorer dwellings. This was extended to all housing after the war in response to the acute shortage of houses for rent, and the consequent profiteering by landlords who realised they could charge ever higher rents. In responding to the necessity to keep available housing affordable, the Government found itself facing a worsening shortage that it could do little to remedy.

Before the war, it had been common for people to buy houses as a form of investment, either outright or as part of a syndicate. The owners would receive a regular income in the form of rent, and the capital (the house) could be realised (sold) fairly easily at any point. The best investments could be said to be 'as safe as houses', but rent freezes meant that they ceased to be such an attractive proposition, and few people were prepared to invest their money in them.

Not only were no new houses built for the four years of the war, but there appeared to be little hope of any more being built at all, especially at a time of rapidly spiralling costs for raw materials. The promises of Lloyd George started to ring hollow.

This was also a time when the rulers and governments of Europe had been shaken to their foundations by the Russian Revolution of 1917, which had resulted in the overthrow of one of the most powerful dynasties in Europe. The ruling classes of this country were not a little concerned at the prospect of men, trained and experienced in the use of arms, returning to find that their promised 'Homes fit for Heroes' were, in reality, the same stinking tenements and slums they had left behind.

Partly to pre-empt this, the British Government passed what was to become known as the Addison Act, after Dr Christopher Addison, the then Minister of Health. Under this act, for the first time government money was put into public housing. This was done in the form of large grants to local councils towards the cost of building houses. Not surprisingly, this led to a massive increase in the building of local

St.Meryl

THE MAGNIFICENT

Is an estate that will be a permanent joy to those wh are tired of the squalor of the towns and the dingines of the inner suburbs.

It is absolutely and entirely surrounded by wooded rollin hills and is part of the Green Belt. St. Meryl is 350 f above sea level, has an Underground Station on th estate and is only 30 minutes from town.

These attractive bungalows each have 2 bedrooms, sitting room, kitchen, tiled bathroom, constant hot water, etc. From 13/7 weekly.

HOW TO GET THERE
Book (via Underground) from the Elephant & Castle and intermediate stations on the Bakerloo or L.M.S. Electric, Oxford Circus, Baker Street, Paddington, etc., direct to Carpenders Park Station, which is actually on the estate. Travelling by road to Oxhey Lane, Oxhey, Herts

BUNGALOWS
Bungalow Specialists from
£550 ~ £1000 Freehold
MAGNIFICENT

Please send me further particulars.
To St. Meryl Estates, Ltd., Carpenders Park, Watford.
Phone : Hatch End 612.

NAME ....

ADDRESS ....

Only 30 minutes from LONDON

The 'St Meryl the Magnificent' estate was actually in Carpenders Park. The modern-style two-bedroomed bungalows are advertised as being 'part of the Green Belt' and promise escape from the 'dinginess of the inner suburbs'.

authority housing between 1919 and 1921. Sixty per cent of all the houses erected in this period were council houses – a ten-fold increase of pre-war figures. But in 1921 a severe economic slump brought all this to an end; inevitable cuts in public spending included the cessation of grants created by the Addison Act. In 1919, in an effort to stimulate the building trade, the Government had also introduced grants to private builders to put up cheap semis either for rent or sale. This practice continued, and was extended in 1923 when the grants were raised.

THE RISE OF THE BUILDING SOCIETY

As the market for investing in houses collapsed in the 1920s, so the end of the war, the Communist uprisings in central Europe and the re-drawing of the political map by the Treaty of Versailles, which ended the First World War, and other treaties brought such uncertainty in the world that overseas investments also became risky. One domestic solution was the building society. Instead of directly investing in a house, people put their money into these societies. This was further encouraged by a deal worked out between the societies and the Inland Revenue which allowed investors to pay tax at source. Soon the societies had far more money to lend.

Further, the uncertainties of the 1920s, which began with the slump and ended with the Depression, made the middle classes worried about their investments. So, once again the idea of investing in property in the form of buying your own house (if only on a mortgage) seemed very attractive. These factors both stimulated the building of new houses, and dictated that most of them would be sold rather than rented, creating a different kind of social revolution from that which was happening in Russia. More and more, people bought their own houses and owner-occupation began to filter down the social scale. Soon the proportion of houses built by the local authorities began to shrink back towards pre-war figures.

Building societies had been around on a small scale since the act of 1836. Now they began to grow. For example, in 1913 the building societies advanced £9 million to those wanting to buy their own homes; by 1938 this had risen to £137 million. Mortgage repayments became very favourable compared with rents and there were few disincentives to buying; repayments were made over (usually) twenty to twenty-five years,

'Why pay more?' Suntrap semis in Swanley – no road or legal charges, garage space, large gardens, and all for 68p a week!

the average repayment being around £1 a week. However, for many prospective home-buyers the down-payment demanded by the building society was often difficult to find. Frequently set at 20 per cent of the purchase price of the house, it was well beyond most first-time buyers' pockets – and most people, at this time, were first-time buyers. So the building societies worked with the building trade to set up 'Builders' Pools'. Under this scheme, the developer of an estate would pay some of the down-payment demanded by the building society, so that the down-payment for the buyer was able to fall to a far more reasonable average of 5 per cent of the purchase price.

An added impetus for house-buying was the steep drop in prices; in the immediate post-war period, a typical three-bedroomed semi might cost around £1,000 to £1,200. In the early thirties, this had tumbled to £600 to £800 for a similar house in Greater London. By the outbreak of war, this had dropped to £400 to £600 (£100 less in provincial towns). There were many reasons for this fall. In the building trade, wages remained low because of high unemployment in other areas of industry. Costs were further held down by the standardisation of house design. A simple plan, which could be adjusted in size, meant that costly architects were not needed.

'Buy your house through the Prudential and dispense with rent', April 1933. Mortgage schemes like this one included an insurance element giving added security 'should the borrower die'.

THE BUILDING BOOM

As mortgages were growing in popularity during the later 1920s, renting was becoming more and more difficult. Most of the middle-classes, and even the better paid manual workers, were therefore more or less forced to buy their own properties, spending a greater proportion of their earnings on property than ever before. House advertising began to emphasise the comparative advantages of ownership; slogans such as 'Why pay rent?' became common.

Agriculture was depressed so, increasingly, land-owners sold off parcels of land cheaply to the builders. Many of these land-owners tried to control the type of housing, or more accurately, the type of tenants who would occupy the land. They would often do this by stipulating, as part of the deal, that the land could only be used for a certain type of high quality housing, thus ensuring that the value of the rest of their land did not plummet. These caveats usually took the form of an agreement to limit the size and number of buildings per acre. These demands were often supported by the local councils, who had no wish to see city slums, or slum-dwellers for that matter, appearing in their area.

PROSPEROUS PROPERTY

The 1921 census recorded a total of just over 9 million houses in Britain, and the next two decades were to see an incredible boom, with 4 million new houses being built altogether. Each year, more and more houses were constructed, the number rising from 93,000 in 1923/4 to 261,000 in 1927/8. Almost three-quarters of these were private, rather than council, houses and by far the majority of these were for sale rather than to rent. Thousands of seven-room semis were built; by the mid-thirties, over 360,000 homes were being built each year, although this figure tailed off after 1937.

On the signboard in the image:
HEATHS PARK ESTA
MODERN   FREE HOLD   HO
£490   NO ROAD CHARGES
FREE CONV
SMALL CASH DEPOSITS - MORTGAGES A
FOR FURTHER PARTICULARS APPLY
L & C SIT
BUILDERS
Northend R
15'10

A building crew outside an unfinished semi-detached house. The workers are typically dressed in flat caps and trilbys; the seventh from the left has his trousers tied up below the knees. The large number of men reveals the labour-intensive nature of house-building in the inter-war period.

So there was an upturn in house building. Builders were quick to respond to this new demand. 'Spec-building' – building houses to be sold when finished, rather than building them to order – became the normal practice. Most building was carried out by small businesses; in 1930, over 80 per cent of all building firms employed fewer than ten workers.

Various methods were employed to make what were essentially the same, formula houses appear slightly more unique. Some were given a fascia of white plaster and black-painted timber to create the Tudor cottage look, referred to derisively as 'Stockbroker Tudor' – a term coined by the cartoonist and satirist Osbert Lancaster; in others, the exterior walls often had cement render over the bricks; small gravel was thrown on to the wet cement to create a new effect called 'pebble-dash'. Purchasers had a choice of stained glass designs for front windows and doors ranging from the traditional to the pictorial, and the ultra-modern, Art Deco geometric. Individuality was further ensured by choices of styles for front doors and porches.

ROGUE TRADERS?

Standards of building varied enormously. It is an indication of how poorly some houses were built that some were actually advertised as having 'concrete foundations, double slate damp courses and lead flashings' –

things that would be taken for granted today. One case that made the news was that of Mrs Elsie Borders, who became known as the 'Tenants' K.C.'

Mrs Borders bought a house in West Wickham in Kent, with a mortgage from a building society. The house cost £633 and Mrs Borders moved in with her family in 1934. The shoddy workmanship soon became evident as damp and infestation by beetles took hold, wallpaper peeled away from the walls, cracks appeared and the floorboards shrank. Mrs Borders stopped her mortgage payments, arguing that the building society's assurances that the house was sound were clearly a misrepresentation. The builder, not untypically, had gone into liquidation so Mrs Borders also claimed that the building society had therefore lent money on inadequate security. The building society sued for repossession. Mrs Borders, by now fast becoming a nationally known figure, counterclaimed for the return of her money as well as for an additional £1,000 to represent the cost of repairs to the property.

The press was not slow to realise this homeowner's fight against poor building standards struck a chord with many others on similar estates and developments throughout the country. National newspapers ran pictures showing the family in the front porch of their crumbling house, with its name, 'Insanity', picked out neatly in white letters beside the front door. Mrs Borders became a *cause célèbre* and fought her case until 1941, when the House of Lords, the highest court in the land, finally ruled in favour of the building society. But if her seven-year battle had eventually been lost in the courts, the war against poor standards was, by 1941, largely won.

Tenants' Defence Leagues, guarantees of workmanship from builders and other initiatives to allay the fears of the aspiring suburbanites became prominent selling features as those building houses tried to distance themselves from the perils of jerry-building – a nineteenth-century term, incidentally, and nothing to do with the First World War. One consequence of the continuing furore was that many builders began offering one- or two-year guarantees on materials and workmanship. In 1937 the National Housebuilders' Registration Council was set up, offering registration of companies prepared to work to a certain standard, and offer a two-year warranty. Over a thousand companies registered in the first year, and many used this membership as part of their advertising.

Inevitably, all this building created a buyers' market, and builders had to work hard to sell their properties. Advertising boomed and the practice of producing a furnished show house on an estate became common. Houses were offered with lawns and gardens planted free, one-year's free season ticket on the railway, free furniture or kitchen fittings. Radio or film stars were hired to promote the launch of an estate, as were firework displays and concerts. As the Second World War approached, even the threat of aerial bombardments in the inner-cities was used to sell suburban houses in safer surroundings.

BUILDING A NEW LIFE

For those who did not have the means to buy a new house yet longed to own a house out of the city, one solution was to buy a plot of land (average cost £5) and build your own home, travelling to the plot at weekends and during holidays to do some work on the project. Farmers were only too

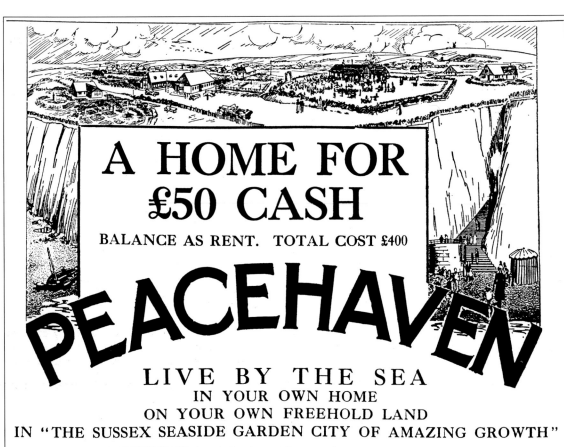

A HOME FOR £50 CASH

BALANCE AS RENT.   TOTAL COST £400

PEACEHAVEN

LIVE BY THE SEA
IN YOUR OWN HOME
ON YOUR OWN FREEHOLD LAND
IN "THE SUSSEX SEASIDE GARDEN CITY OF AMAZING GROWTH"

FREEHOLD LAND AS AN INVESTMENT ON THE VALLEY ESTATES.

WHAT undoubtedly is the finest proposition ever placed within your reach is that now being offered on the Valley Estates which form part of the great Peacehaven section of the South Downs.

The Valley Estate commands magnificent views of the Ouse Valley, adjoins the Brighton Road passing through the Estate, and is within a few minutes of the Golf Links. Freehold Land on the original Peacehaven Estate close by has increased 300 per cent. in value during the past eighteen months, and those fortunate enough to acquire plots in the Valley Estate, will undoubtedly reap a substantial benefit from their property owing to our scheme of quick development.

SIZE OF PLOTS.

The Freehold Land in our Valley Estate is sold in quarter, half, and one Acre Plots. Every plot offered for sale is properly surveyed. You are under no obligation to build until you desire to do so, but Ideal Homes can be built when you are ready from materials on the spot at minimum prices. Free deeds, no legal charges, and no other expenses.

PRICES OF PLOTS vary according to size and position.

THE FERTILITY OF THE SOIL is wonderful—a rich, natural possession. The flavour and size of the vegetables and other produce grown on the Estate are remarkable, and some magnificent results have been obtained. Success depends entirely upon your own individual effort and inclinations, and whether you go in for Small Fruit Growing, Poultry and Bee-keeping, or Small Holdings, you can easily make a secure income a certainty, besides which your investment will bring you a handsome return for your capital outlay. Brighton, Lewes, Seaford and Newhaven markets are within easy distance, and London is only 58 miles from the Estate.

THE AIR is invigorating, health promoting, and you get the maximum of sunshine.

FREEHOLD LAND ON THE HARBOUR HEIGHTS ESTATE.

Freehold Land on the Harbour Heights Estate will treble and quadruple in value. Here you can secure, for £25, plots of building land absolutely Freehold, which is not less than 2,500 superficial feet in extent. Owing to its elevation the plots are particularly valuable on this Estate for building purposes, and command magnificent views over the Sea and Downs. You have maximum sunshine in one of the sunniest spots on the South Coast.

THE EXTENT OF PEACEHAVEN.

Although not yet three years old, the Peacehaven Estates extend over an area of nearly five square miles and have a frontage of almost five miles in length. They stretch from the right bank of the River Ouse, in the neighbourhood of Newhaven, up to the quaint old village of Rottingdean, close to Brighton. Peace-

haven is the outcome of the greatest Seaside land development scheme ever undertaken in this country.

What SIR JOHN FOSTER FRASER says about PEACEHAVEN.

In a recent issue of the "Daily Chronicle" Sir John said:—" . . . It struck me that everything is done to retain the beauty of the Downs. The Bungalows are mostly detached, and rest contentedly on the uplands, with their bits of gardens, and in many cases with Cornish rustic slate, so that the colours seem to blend with the landscape. . . . Yes, Peacehaven, the garden city by the sea, is one of the most remarkable places in the world. . . . I found the Peacehaveners a happy, jolly community, very proud of their infant prodigy of a garden city."

UNPRECEDENTED OPPORTUNITY TO SECURE YOUR COMPLETE HOME ON YOUR OWN FREEHOLD LAND FOR A £50 CASH DEPOSIT. THE BALANCE CAN BE PAID AS RENT UNTIL YOUR PURCHASE IS COMPLETE. ONLY SIX HOUSES ARE AT PRESENT AVAILABLE UNDER THIS OFFER.

"Good Housekeeping" is intimately associated with the ideal home, because the latest labour-saving devices make it more easily possible under the best conditions.

Peacehaven abounds in such homes, which are so plentiful that the famous Garden City of the South Coast has come to be known as the Home of Ideal Homes.

Peacehaven homes are snug and cosy. They will all be supplied with Electric light and water by Peacehaven Companies, and are in very great demand. Standing on their own Freehold Land, some of these delightful Peacehaven homes are ready for immediate

occupation, and, provided with modern conveniences, can be purchased for as low as £400 inclusive.

A £50 cash deposit will secure you one of the available charming Seaside Homes, and, if more convenient, you can pay the balance monthly according to arrangement, just as if you were paying rent, but with this difference, that the Home will be your own property all the time.

PEACEHAVEN'S POTENT POINTS.

1. **EXCELLENT SANITATION,** fulfilling all local Council Requirements.

2. **WONDERFUL CHALK CLIFFS** rise to a height of from 50 to 150 feet above sea-level.

3. **STEPS** have been cut through the great cliffs to the Beach, where there are caves and sands for bathing.

4. **MANY FACILITIES FOR SPORT** in the Parks, already provided, or in course of preparation. There are also Tennis Courts, and the Peacehaven Golf Course will shortly be available for play.

5. **BUSINESS OPPORTUNITIES** await enterprising tradesmen, business people, and all professional men.

HOTEL PEACEHAVEN.—During your visit stay at the Hotel Peacehaven, the loveliest hotel on the South Coast. Beautiful Italian Gardens, Excellent Cuisine. Fully licensed. Terms moderate.

HOW TO GET TO PEACEHAVEN.

1. Travel by train from Victoria or London Bridge to Brighton, and thence by bus from the Aquarium to Peacehaven : or

2. Travel by train from Victoria or London Bridge to Newhaven Town Station, where the Company's motor cars will meet you by request, or where you can take a bus to Peacehaven.

---

keen to sell of areas of poor quality agricultural land. Councils in seaside locations were more willing to allow developments on unused land than their suburban and metropolitan equivalents. On the whole, they were also less concerned about preserving the existing character of the locality, if such existed and, while they might not have liked the more radical designs, they welcomed the income that such developments inevitably brought.

Ideal Home magazine produced a series of books throughout the twenties and thirties, *The Ideal Home Book of Plans*, each of which contained sets of (very basic) plans for houses and bungalows. They tempted readers with: 'Dreams of that "Home of your own". . . of that haven of comfort which you hope will soon come true? Not the ready-made "creation" of someone else – but a distinctive dwelling place which will express your own personality.'

The second *Book of Plans* contained a doom-laden warning to those foolish enough to buy unserviced land:

> In the course of the last few years many estates have been cleverly exploited by people having capital whose sole object is to sell land and houses and make money. Again and again people have bought land with the promise that roads, sewers, water, light would be forthcoming very soon. Having bought and paid for the land they find that they own a small freehold in the middle of a field, without access, and with no facilities for building. It is clearly impossible to build unless water is laid on and for that one may have to wait for years.

Various building acts brought in over the period set down minimum standards for self-built or commercial premises. These concerned safety and covered fire-proofing, sanitation (including plumbing and drainage), and the fabric of the building, including a law to make a damp-proof course compulsory on every building. These regulations, to some extent, added to the uniformity of buildings produced but this was far outweighed by the general improvements in standards.

It is often said that 'They don't build them like they used to!' A brief inspection of a late Victorian terraced house can reveal inadequate or non-existent footings, cheap materials and poor workmanship which would lead most to agree with the words of the statement – if not the usual implication.

'A PLACE OF ONE'S OWN'

The suburban semi, epitomising the lower middle classes, has long been the butt of jokes. Even while they were being built, they were scorned by architects and writers. Osbert Lancaster famously differentiated semis

---

HOME SWEET HOME

Away from the patronage of leading architects, so-called shanty towns sprang up. A popular song, recorded by Les Allen in 1932, celebrated the joys or otherwise of this type of living:

A Shanty in Old Shanty Town

It's only a shanty in an old shanty town,
Where the roof is so slanty it touches the ground.
Just a tumbledown shack
By an old railroad track,
Like a millionaire's mansion,
It's calling me back.
I'd give up my palace,
If I were a king,
It's more than a palace, it's my everything.
There's a queen waiting there with a silvery crown
In a shanty in old shanty town.

In the period after the Second World War, many of these developments were cleared away by the local authorities who had welcomed them just as enthusiastically a couple of decades earlier.

Opposite: An advertisement for Peacehaven, one of the most famous 'plotlands' where plots could be bought for self-build or with houses ready-built. These areas were often unregulated and became shambolic shanty towns.

The Downham estate,
Lewisham, under construction.
Besides the car – probably
belonging to the architect – the
only piece of machinery visible
is a cement mixer. The pile of
sleepers and rails (front left) are
the remains of a rail system that
had been connected to the
nearby main-line railway so that
goods trucks containing
materials could be delivered to,
and manually pushed around
the site. (Lewisham Local
Studies Library)

under the headings: 'Stockbrokers' Tudor'; 'Wimbledon Transitional'; and
'By-pass Variegated'. Heath Robinson, whose illustrations lampooned all
aspects of modern life, certainly included suburban dwellers and their
mores among his targets. But the suburban developments had tapped into
a deep current; they allowed many who could not otherwise have
afforded to do so to purchase 'a place of their own', to have their own bit
of garden, and to live in quiet respectability. Today, this seems a fairly
modest ambition, but just a century ago it would have been an impossible
pipe-dream for many people.

In 1939, however, the building of new houses slowed once more,
coming to a complete halt in 1940, as another war shook the world.

HOUSE BEAUTIFUL

STYLES AND DESIGN

The Arts and Crafts Influence

There was no single identifiable 'wartime' house. No houses were built during the Second World War, so suburban houses were mainly those built before or during the inter-war years. Furnishings and fittings were in short supply, if they could be obtained at all, and furniture was rationed. So throughout the war, the average wartime house in the suburbs was built, decorated and furnished in thirties' style.

Houses built between the beginning of the twentieth century and the outbreak of the First World War were still usually built in terraces, had long sash windows and were mainly of brick, although the use of cement render was increasing. The influence of the Arts and Crafts movement of the late nineteenth century was also beginning to spread. The style,

This 1920s terrace has an interesting blend of styles, using traditional bricks and tiles with rendered areas, curved bays and faience-tiled entrances.

A 1920s block of flats. A notable building, again combining more traditional materials with a contemporary albeit understated Art Deco influence in the horizontal barred windows, the Egyptian influence door surrounds and the stepped parapets.

which was linked to the similarly popular Art Nouveau, looked for its inspiration to a bygone, idealised rustic age – a reaction to the machines and factories of the Industrial Revolution. Overall, the Arts and Crafts movement was lighter in style than the fashions of the Victorian age, its followers choosing woods such as light oak in preference to mahogany and ebony. Its designers and architects, among them Voysey and Lutyens, were influenced by William Morris and Charles Rennie Mackintosh.

The English Rural House

After the First World War, the successor to the Arts and Crafts style was known as English Rural. Arts and Crafts houses had been influenced by traditional English designs to produce a style that was at once both reassuringly familiar yet refreshingly new. But 'English Rural' was a pastiche of an idealised English architectural past. Its main influences were Elizabethan, Jacobean and, to a lesser extent, Georgian; it was satirically referred to as Jacobethan, Tudoresque, or Olde Worlde by the writers and cartoonists of the day.

English Rural houses were inspired by pre-war Arts and Crafts houses that had been created by leading architects and designers. But the speculation-built semis of the post-war period were mainly planned without the benefit of advice from either profession, and so were cheaper and more prosaic than their expensive, commissioned ancestors.

The main features of English Rural, which we recognise today, were black half-timbering filled with, usually, white painted rendering or red bricks, sometimes laid in a herringbone style. Other popular features included gabled ends with deep eaves; red tiled roofs often enclosing dormer windows; mullioned windows, often with diamond-latticed leaded lights; and traditional oak doors, sometimes with a bottle glass panel,

An illustration from *The Home of Today*, showing a 'Jacobethan'-style wood-panelled living-room with mock beams on the ceiling, wide fireplace, period-style furniture and leaded lights.

fitted with wrought iron hinges and door fittings. Regional variations took the form of the use of local materials such as thatch and flint.

Interiors often continued the English rural theme with parquet flooring, wood panelled walls, and red brick fireplaces, often with inglenooks. The theme might be completed by the furnishing: imitation period furniture, reproduction period pictures and English pewter knick-knacks.

A brick-built fireplace, advertised in *Good Housekeeping* in the 1930s; the Ideal Home Exhibition is also mentioned.

The Modern Movement

At the other end of the aesthetic scale were the designs of the Modern Movement, which believed that architecture should be primarily functional. One of its leading exponents was the French architect Le Corbusier, who declared that a house should be 'a machine for living'. In 1923 he published *Vers Une Architecture*, in which he argued that a house should be designed as functionally as a ship, an aeroplane or a motorcar, and the book became compulsory reading for a new generation of architects.

Modern Movement houses, as the name suggests, made full use of new materials, especially reinforced concrete walls, which could contain large areas of glass. Other innovations included flat roofs and glass bricks. The overall effect was of geometric shapes, a nod towards Cubism, with little adornment. Internal doors rarely had the traditional panelling and would be fitted flush with their equally plain, or stepped frames. Modernist tastes for reinforced concrete shells, glass panels and flat roofs were perfect for blocks of flats but apart from London and a

A Modernist house in Silver End, Essex. This is part of an estate built by the Crittal Glass Company for its staff. The Cubist design is emphasised in the corner-spanning suntrap windows and the white rendered finish.

Opposite, above: This 1930s semi is very much a blend of the Modernist style – suntrap windows and white rendering – and the more traditional house – pitched roof and angled bay – of the 1920s. Many houses of the period were of a similar blend, modern yet familiar.

Opposite: A 1930s advert for bathroom fittings, available in white or colour and created to give an atmosphere of 'beauty combined with utility'. (*Good Housekeeping*)

few coastal resorts, where they were usually designed for bachelors or childless couples, these flats were unpopular.

Modernist designs were more successful in large buildings like Odeon cinemas, factories, such as the Hoover factory by Gilbert Scott and Partners; airports, for example that at Croydon, and underground stations including Arnos Grove on the Piccadilly line.

In the suburbs, Modernist housing generally failed to catch on. Perhaps it was because we have the wrong climate for flat roofs and glass walls but most probably, the British at the time were just too conservative (we probably still are). A few entirely Modernist houses were built but far more common was the standard semi with some Modernist influences. The overall plan of the average pair of semis was derived from the two-winged Tudor manor-house. Of a style usually called Sun House, the Sunshine House or Suntrap, they were usually of cement render on brick, sometimes with flat roofs, but more often with a pitched roof disguised by high parapet walls. They often included wide metal-framed windows, sectioned horizontally, a bay extending up to the roof, some containing curved windows, geometric front doors and stained glass panels. The geometric theme was often continued in the ubiquitous sunburst design on the gate, front door, gable or window. Internal doors were panelled, yet painted and fitted with plastic handles.

Inside, functionalism and the Modernist influence were most often seen in the kitchen, bathroom, and WC, where cleanliness and functionality was welcome. Many homes, even those otherwise in English Rural style, had a Modernist-inspired bathroom.

Other types of low-cost housing included bungalows, which were very popular. Variations, such as bungaloids, included the semi-detached

bungalow with one room in the roof, and the chalet, which had two. Looking like small detached houses, these were usually built in areas such as coastal resorts, where land costs were low. The cheapest of all were the 'semi-terraces', a type of expanded semi or shortened terrace incorporating four, six, or eight houses, often with gable ends, and bay windows in the centre two houses.

Structural Changes

One of the greatest changes in house construction over the last quarter of the nineteenth century was the introduction of integral bathrooms and inside toilets. As late as 1875, the majority of houses were still built without a bathroom, and it was only from this time that water closets, the forerunner of the modern toilet, were regularly included in new middle-class housing.

Bathrooms for all were a new concept in the twentieth century; none but the best Victorian homes had one but they were standard in just about every house built commercially after the First World War. Design and fittings had developed rapidly; at first, baths looked more like a piece of furniture than a fitting, standing unenclosed on clawed feet; taps and fittings in brass, sanitary ware in white, and wooden cupboards, shelves, toilet seats in mahogany or some other dark wood were standard in Edwardian times. Within thirty years baths were enclosed, fittings were in chrome, sanitary ware in a wide range of colours, and glass, aluminium and plastic had all but replaced wood.

Windows changed completely, from the long, vertical wooden-framed sash style predominant in the Victorian terrace to the wide, horizontal casement with metal frame, usually split by horizontal bars. This change was principally the result of the introduction of reinforced concrete lintels, a step on from the timber sort used by earlier builders.

A spacious, half-timbered semi with an integral garage. It has a pebble-dash finish to the upper storey, chain link fencing and the original hydrant sign (H) on the fence post.

Other structural improvements included concrete foundations, breeze blocks for internal walls and the 11-inch cavity wall. These all made houses warmer and cheaper to heat. A wide range of cement preparations was developed including coloured, quick-setting and aluminous cements. White Portland cement was especially attractive in Modernist buildings. Concrete was widely used for rendering, either flat, inlaid with small pieces of gravel – pebbledash – or mixed in with gravel to give a more textured finish in a style known as roughcast or Tyrolean.

MATERIALS

Along with new styles and designs, the inter-war years also saw the introduction and increased use of many new materials. Materials first used and accepted for use during the period included: bituminous sheeted flat roofing; glazed panels in bathrooms and kitchens; rubber- and lead-sheathed flexible electric cables; plywood; copper pipes and cylinders. Chrome and stainless steel were widely used, the latter mainly for kitchen sinks and draining-boards, although porcelain, enamelled and hardwood – usually teak – versions were used too.

Teak sinks were sold as grease proof, absorbing grease from the water, with the added selling point that fewer plates were broken in them, but they did not really catch on.

The development of plastics, first invented in the nineteenth century, had progressed to the stage where their use in houses was continually increasing. Most of us associate wood-finish brown Bakelite with this period, although it was first produced by the Belgian chemist Leo Baekeland in 1909. By the 1930s, however, Bakelite was also produced in red, blue, white, black and green, and other plastics such as urea-formaldehyde (invented 1924), cast phenolic, melamine resin and Perspex (1935) were popular, allowing a rapidly increasing range of colours and uses. Door furniture, electric switches and fittings, electric cable and flex sheathing, table-tops, work surfaces, toilet seats and bath surrounds were all ideally suited to the new plastics.

The inter-war period was witness to many changes in the style of, and materials used for, housing built for the general population. However, many of the changes went far deeper than building styles or materials; they reflected the great upheavals that were taking place in the social order, with the introduction of new technology, and in the very function of the house itself.

THE CENTRE OF FAMILY LIFE

The First World War had led to a relaxation of rigid Victorian formality across society, which also encouraged less rigid social structures within the family. Previously, different members of the family had, during various parts of the day, occupied their own sections of the house. Now, middle-class children were no longer kept apart from adults in the charge of a nurse, nanny or governess, so rooms allocated to day and night nurseries were not required. Wives and daughters no longer had their own rooms in the house, such as the morning-room and the drawing-room, for entertaining their guests, while husbands and sons met their visitors in the study or the library. Now the living-room was used by the whole family for many purposes; receiving friends, family entertainment, and listening to the radio. The radio itself sometimes replaced the hearth as the centre-piece of the room around which seating was arranged.

The post-First World War suburban home became the centre of family life, an idea that was quite revolutionary at the time. The Victorians, or at least the middle classes, had held that the *family* was at the centre of society. In their ideal world, the house had been a base for the family, and as such should be comfortable and well managed, with a complement of servants to make sure the whole thing ran smoothly. Yet the house itself remained outside what was thought of as the family.

In the world of the Suburbans, by contrast, the *house* or family home was at the very core of family life, from its building or selection to its furnishing, decoration, maintenance and improvement. All these aspects were the focus of much of the family's time and income. A contemporary description from the mid-thirties highlights the importance that was now placed on the home itself:

It is the centre of interest, not only in the immediate family life, but equally in the wider bustling world of trade and commerce, for its influence is far-reaching and all-important.

For the average British man and woman, each day begins and ends in the family centre. The influence of a happy, harmonious home is therefore a national asset.

The early morning family contact will have its reaction on business life throughout the day; the return to the home at night will bring rest and peace and a laying aside of worries and care.

The Ideal Home Exhibition, 1925. This advert lists features including the 'All-Electric' House and the 'All-Gas' House, as well as sections on hobbies and pastimes such as Wireless and Photography. (*Good Housekeeping*)

HAPPY FAMILIES

The size of the average family had been declining since the last decades of the nineteenth century. From the turn of the century to the mid-thirties, the average number of children per family fell from 3.5 to 2.2, with the figures even smaller among non-manual workers (1.9 in 1929). At the same time, the death rate fell. At the turn of the century, only about 7 per cent of the population was over sixty; this almost doubled to 13 per cent by the mid-thirties and was about 16 per cent after the Second World War.

SMALL IS BEAUTIFUL?

As well as differences in how people viewed the home, physical differences were also becoming apparent. New houses, on the whole, were smaller, lighter and more cheerful looking than their Gothic Victorian equivalents. The smaller houses reflected changes in society, especially the fact that households themselves were becoming smaller, and this was indeed the case. This contributed to a rapid increase in the numbers of households looking for accommodation, as well as a reduction in the size of accommodation needed.

A second factor that had a major impact on the size of new houses, not to mention on daily life generally after the First World War, was the sharp decline in the numbers of people working in service. Domestic work was dull and poorly paid and many domestic servants, especially women, were only too keen to move into well-paid jobs in munitions and industry which became available during the war. Most of these jobs either disappeared or were given to men at the end of the war but a large post-war expansion of better paid manual and clerical jobs attracted many who would previously have entered service.

The rapid increase in the number of middle-class households also had an effect on the number of servants a household could employ. Before the war, each of these households would have required both a maid and cook, which, in pre-war days, was probably quite achievable. However, as the number of middle-class households increased, for the reasons given in Chapter One, and the number of servants decreased, so more households were chasing fewer servants; in many books or plays from the period, at least one character says something along the lines of 'One just can't get the

Like many bungalows of the period – many of which were self-built – these in Jaywick are crammed into the smallest possible plots of land.

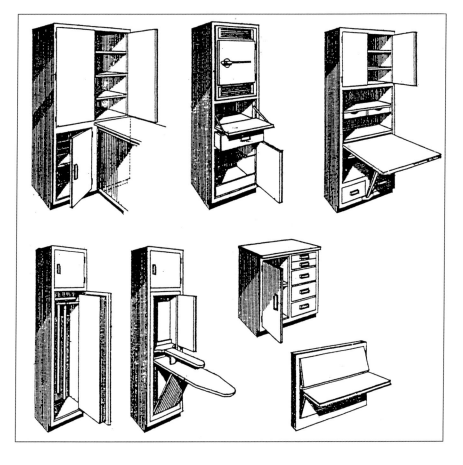

Illustrations from the Peerless Built-in Furniture catalogue. Built-in furniture evolved at this time in response to the smaller modern kitchen with features such as fold-down tables and ironing boards.

The *Home of Today* featured this 'delightful modern kitchen with a "novel" porthole window', fitted cupboards, extractor fans and a food mixer.

staff these days!' This situation was especially marked among the middle class; the old landed gentry could still manage to get together a staff, but few below the upper middle class could afford even a maid, and the effect on the design of housing was marked. First, servants' quarters were no longer required and, secondly, the design of the middle-class kitchen changed completely.

Previously the kitchen had been a huge room with many work areas leading off it, and was often windowless to protect the family's privacy in the garden. The new suburban kitchen was a much smaller room, with a window usually over the sink to make washing up more interesting. The new kitchen was designed for the convenience of the housewife; although working with no domestic help, she could at least call on an increasing range of new, labour-saving devices.

ESSENTIAL SERVICES

Local authorities were responsible for ensuring an adequate supply of all the mains services to every occupied house. Gas, electricity and water were supplied by either the local authority itself or by private companies. These suppliers had to make them available to any premises within 50 yards of a main supply. Those living further away could buy generators or 'generating plants'. These were not only for electricity: petrol gas plants and acetylene plants could also be found. Acetylene had been in use for some time, for lighting only, but it had become rare by the 1930s.

Nowadays, the ways in which the different services are used in the home are fairly well established; gas is used for cooking and heating, and electricity for cooking and everything else. But this was not the case between the wars. Certainly, heating and cooking were the main uses of gas at the time too, but there were also others. Gas was still widely used for lighting in the late thirties; home maintenance books from the period often included home lighting guides for both electricity and gas. Among other things, gas could power irons and washing machines.

Electricity

Electricity was at the heart of the boom in the number of 'gadgets' which occurred in the 1920s and '30s. During the nineteenth century a great deal of work had gone into developing a powerful and efficient electric generator, and now that effort was paying off. The clock tower of the Palace of Westminster had been lit by an electric arc light in 1873, and in 1880 the first practical incandescent filament light bulb was produced.

This house advert proclaims all the latest mod cons: an 'ultra modern' kitchen and bathroom, cavity walls, power and gas points to all rooms, and the picture shows that it has a garage.

LIVE ONLY ▼ FINCHLEY N.12.
— 6 MILES —
FROM REGENT'S PARK
For 25/8 REPAYMENTS.

Although no expense has been spared to make these detached houses really worthy of the refined neighbourhood in which they are built, prices are exceptionally low. The house illustrated, for instance, costs only £1,195 Freehold, and overlooks an open sports ground. "Tally Ho!" Corner shopping centre, amusements, schools and churches are all within ten minutes of the Estate, while the City and West End are only seven miles away.

OTHER FREEHOLD TYPES From £1,050.   DEPOSIT 10 PER CENT.

THE ESTATE of 70 acres, situated in the most charming position of North London, opposite Woodside Park Station. Entrance in Holden Road.

View our " D " Type House : Front Rooms : 18 ft. 2 in. by 13 ft. 3 in.
Back Rooms : 15 ft. 4 in. by 12 ft. 1¼ in.

Ultra modern kitchen and bathroom. Dual hot water system. Copper cylinder and tubing. Cavity walls. Power and gas points to all rooms. Flush doors and other very attractive features.

LEYLAND CONSTRUCTION CO., LTD.,
THE NEW WOODSIDE PARK ESTATE, N.12

To :—
Leyland Construction Co., Ltd.,
Woodside Park Estate,
Finchley, N.12.

Send Illustrated Brochure

To : ....
....
....

TELEPHONE : HILLSIDE 4441

In that year also, electricity was used to light private houses, although this had to be supplied by a small generator. But it was not only light that could be produced; one of the earliest electric devices for the home was the electric fire, the first Belling model being marketed in 1912.

Despite the obvious benefits of electricity, by 1910 only a tiny proportion of houses – about 2 per cent – were connected to the mains. Even in the years immediately following the First World War, this figure was still under 10 per cent, with electricity almost entirely used for lighting. Over the next few years, rapid developments in wiring systems and the arrival of cheaper and more efficient light bulbs encouraged more widespread use of electricity. With this came new inventions, such as the Goblin upright vacuum cleaner, first introduced in 1921.

One of the biggest drawbacks in using electricity was an inconsistent approach to supply, which involved many different companies and local authorities. The result of this lack of national uniformity meant that prices and even voltages varied greatly from one locality to another, and availability was patchy too. Then, in 1926, the Central Electricity Generating Board was formed, with powers to co-ordinate electricity supply nationally. From this point onwards, new houses were routinely wired up. By 1939 the amount of houses connected to the mains had soared to about 70 per cent.

Electricity was now being used for far more than just lighting. The *Slonetric* catalogue of June 1937 contained the following domestic devices: electric dimmer switches, electric sewing machines (£4), window-mounted extractor fans (£4 14s 6d), electric drills (£6 15s) and screwdrivers (£9 15s), electric hammer drills (£11 15s), 'teasmade' alarms – 'The tea time, light, call and shaving water robot-service while you sleep' – in ivory, pastel green and pastel blue (£4 19s 6d), electric hairdryers (£1 12s 6d) and hair curlers (£1 1s), electric cigarette and cigar lighters (17s 6d and £1), electric floor polishers and electric blankets (£3 3s to £3 10s). Some of these gadgets may seem surprising to us in that most people today would believe them to be products of the 1960s or later.

In 1914

And in 1944

THE quaint looking G.E.C. electric heater of 1914 is linked with its modern stream-lined version by over a quarter of a century of continuous progress in the electrical industry. Science never stands still—not even in wartime—and just as the G.E.C. continued to progress through the last war, so to-day it is keeping abreast of the latest developments and improvements in everything electrical for the home.

Remember

G.E.C.

FOR EVERYTHING ELECTRICAL

This GEC advertisement compares the company's appliances from 1914 and 1941, in order to show how much they had progressed.

ELECTRICAL REPAIRS

The increasing use of electricity meant that householders had to become proficient at minor electrical repairs and that did not just mean the man of the house. Women, too, had to become expert at changing fuses, rewiring plugs and much more. With this in mind, and to promote the use of electricity in the home, in November 1924 the Women's Engineering Society founded the Women's Electrical Association, renamed the Electrical Association for Women (EAW) in 1925. The association produced pamphlets and gave talks on electricity and its uses in the home, so it was natural that, during the war, it would produce similar pamphlets on energy saving and cooking with electricity. These included cards on rationing – 'Cheerful Rationing' – each card giving recipes using non-rationed foods and giving brief advice on electrical equipment. In 1940 the EAW set up its own Mobile Canteen Service, which by 1941 was running twelve canteens, one of which was an electrically driven vehicle. Towards the end of the war, EAW officers gave talks to ATS and other service women on 'The Home of the Future' and other topics that looked towards the post-war world.

A typical multi-purpose 'gadget' from the 1930s – an electric grandfather clock with built-in bookcase and a cocktail-cabinet. These could be bought ready made or, far worse, original clocks could be stripped of their works, and an electric movement added.

One popular group of gadgets might be termed 'combinations': cigarette case and lighter, lighter and watch, loud speaker and table light, gramophone and table light, and the *Slonetric* catalogue contained the 'EAD' fan 'of elegant and novel design, distributing air simultaneously and horizontally in all directions, in consequence all persons sitting round a table with the fan in the centre receive equal benefit'. So far so good, but 'It also serves as an ornamental table centre, or as a receptacle for fruit or floral decoration'!

By the late thirties, therefore, about 80 per cent of homes with an electricity supply had an electric iron; 35 per cent had a vacuum cleaner; 25 per cent had electric fires; about 15 per cent an electric cooker; and a similar amount, electric kettles. As these examples show, people were particular about what they bought and their choices were not primarily determined by price. The cost of a kettle was far less than that of a vacuum cleaner, but the latter seem to be selling at double the rate of the former. It seems that the most important selling point for a gadget was that it should be truly labour saving. Electric kettles had few advantages over their old-fashioned equivalents, which boiled water on the hob, while vacuum cleaners were popular because using a manual sweeper or broom was hard, time-consuming work, not to mention ineffective as it simply moved the dust around rather than sucking it away!

Of course, some devices just didn't work (advertising was far less controlled and far more an exercise in what we now recognise as creative writing). One idea that did not stand the test of time was 'wallpaper heating'. Introduced in the mid-thirties, 'sheets of fibrous asbestos paper, containing heating wires, can be pasted to the ceilings or walls, like wallpaper, and afterwards connected up with the house electricity service'! The whole thing sounds lethal – just imagine driving in a nail to hang a picture!

Electricity had always been sold as modern, clean and up-to-date, but by 1941 GEC was promising that it would also mean fewer accidents and could help to preserve your sight too.

Electric fires and cookers faced competition from appliances powered by other fuels. The first cooker, as distinct from a range, used gas. Gas cookers became popular from about 1875 as a supplement to the solid-fuel range. Their use spread rapidly in the 1890s when gas companies began to rent them out. By 1914, 77 per cent of houses served by the gas companies had a gas-fired cooker. Most of those not using gas cookers were in coal producing areas where solid fuel was supplied cheaply or free to miners.

Electricity was more expensive than coal or gas, but its great selling point was its convenience, especially for the servantless household. Not only was it operated 'at the flick of a switch', as the advertising boasted, but it created no soot or mess to be cleaned up afterwards. However, the attractions of labour-saving gadgets were proclaimed by all the suppliers, not just those using electricity; an advertisement for 'New World' gas cookers depicted a mother reading to her daughter, and declared: 'Free from the kitchen for the rest of the morning – The dinner is cooking itself in the New World with the new "Regulo" control.'

An electric hot water advertisement from the late thirties. As usual, convenience and saving labour are the main selling points.

It was generally the white-collar and professional middle classes in Suburbia who were buying the new labour-saving devices. The old, landed, upper classes might be feeling the pinch on their country estates, but not so much that they had to do without their servants, so they felt little need for gadgets. The inner-city poor had no relief from their Victorian-style slum life, which by its very poverty was devoid of possessions and, especially, gadgets.

Having established electricity as a convenient form of lighting, the electricity boards were keen to promote its use in other ways. A booklet, *The Electric Guide*, produced in the late twenties to show 'How to do electric repairs, alterations or installations yourself', asserted that:

> Everyone using Electricity for lighting will want to know the merits of electric cooking, heating, washing, and other household requirements and accordingly the reader cannot be too strongly recommended to read the companion booklet entitled 'Introducing your convenient servant – electricity' which contains not only a wealth of interesting reading and comparisons between electricity and other methods of heating, cooking, etc. but also quite a few labour-saving and economy hints for electricity users.

The title of the booklet recommended is typical in that electricity was widely advertised as being a servant, or in this case 'your convenient servant', to emphasise its value to the servantless household.

Heating

The inter-war years saw a vast expansion in provision of services to the home. By the 1930s, approximately one-third of the cost of a new house was taken up with providing such things as plumbing, lighting, drainage and heating. Coal or log fires were still popular, especially in winter, and back boilers meant that they could also heat water. Real fires remained the most visually attractive form of heating and their use was especially suited to the traditional-style houses. Yet at the same time coal fires were looked on as a sign that a household could not afford 'up to date' heating; coal was still used by almost every family in poorer areas.

When the house as a whole is warmed in this way, gas or electric fires for occasional use in bedrooms and small rooms used at various times during the day make the heating arrangements highly satisfactory.

Above: A dining-room from *Practical Home Making* with a built-in electric fire. Many electric fires were made to be able to fit into an existing open fireplace.

Above, right: Ease of operating – 'kindled without troublesome laying' – and cleanliness – it burns 'without smoke or soot' – are emphasised in this advert for the Metro Coke Fire, 1930s. The fire was ignited by a gas burner, and coke was available from the Gas Company. (*Good Housekeeping*)

Coal was still very cheap, but it was messy too. This was all right if you could afford a maid to clean out and lay the grate but it was out of place in the labour-saving suburban home, especially in the summer when its erratic use would cause even more work. Electric fire manufacturers had thought of this; many of their fires were designed to fit into an open fire grate, either permanently or for temporary summer use. Some electric fires, introduced in the late thirties, even had a 'real fire effect', including imitation coal and flickering light.

Another option for heating was oil fires and radiators. As these radiators were sealed, they had the added advantage of being portable so were also popular as supplementary heating in houses fully connected to the mains.

Central heating could be powered by gas, electric or oil, with electric being by far the cheapest to install but the most expensive to run; coal cost twice as much, and gas and oil four times as much to install. All involved a boiler, thermostatically controlled, and most involved radiators, although variations included panel heaters.

Water Heating

The Edwardian system whereby water was heated by a boiler attached to the kitchen range had its limitations; if no cooking was being done a fire still had to be kept burning to heat the water, and if a lot of cooking was being done, there was little heat to spare for the water. By the thirties, this system had changed noticeably.

The gas-heated geyser could supply hot water for the kitchen and bathroom. In a flat or bungalow, a single geyser served both rooms – the

instantaneous multi-point. But where the bathroom was upstairs, geysers – instantaneous single-point heaters – were placed in both rooms, with the smaller one over the kitchen sink. Geysers might be electric, oil or gas-fired. On a larger scale, gas-heated thermal storage water heaters, made up of a heating unit and a water storage tank, supplied constant hot water throughout the house. Many new houses were fitted with independent gas or solid fuel boilers. The latter was usually fuelled by coke but kitchen or other flammable waste might also be used. Lastly were the electric immersion heaters that could be fitted into any tank, and the gas-circulating boiler. Each of these could be used by themselves or with a solid fuel boiler, so a fire did not have to be lit in the summer months.

Above, left: A drawing from *The Home of Today* showing the gas cooker and coke boiler combination that was used in many kitchens.

Above: This *Good Housekeeping* advert from the 1920s announces that the Clarkhill gas-fuelled hot water boiler is entirely automatic and offers 'wonderful economy'.

'It's Good to Talk'

A commonly held belief is that telephones of the period were always black. In fact, by the late thirties telephones were also available in ivory, brown, green, red, gold or silver, and the stick telephone, with its separate earpiece, mouthpiece and bell-box, had been largely replaced by the more familiar all-in-one earpiece and microphone unit.

Many of the services provided today – the emergency services, operator service, alarm calls, weather forecasts and the speaking clock – were available then, as well as some that no longer exist, such as the express letter service: 'If it is too late to post for a given overseas mail, a telephone call can be put through to the post office at Tilbury, Southampton, Liverpool, or any other port at which the mail steamer is berthed, and the letter dictated. It will be taken down and delivered on the boat by

As with water and light, so the telephone is a service which should be taken for granted as essential in the home.

Tin-helmeted GPO engineers repairing cables damaged by the bombing. Telephone lines and telegraph poles were often damaged in this way, so that the phone system was often out of order. (HMSO)

messenger' . . . 'With last-minute air-mail letters, the procedure is the same, except that the message is telephoned to Croydon Aerodrome Post Office.'

Charges were well within the means of the average suburban family; connection cost 15*s*, and quarterly rental ranged from £1 6*s* for central London down to £1. Call charges ranged from 1*d* to 4*d* for local calls, 1*s* for three-minute trunk calls at night, 2*s* 6*d* in the daytime, and an evening three-minute call to Germany, for example, 5*s* 6*d*.

Early in the war, homes which had telephones were often used as air raid wardens' posts, or emergency first-aid posts and so on. People were encouraged to keep the lines free for official use, especially during air raid alerts. Raiding caused mayhem with the system, the telephone lines often being among the first victims of the bombs.

THE GARDEN

The garden was an important part of the suburban house. The whole point of a semi-detached home was that it was cut off, if only partially, from other houses, having a front and back garden to isolate it from the rest of the world. This was a reaction to tenement or 'back-to-back' living, where the only gardens that existed were in fact the public parks – for many, a major part of the joy of owning one's own home was to have one's 'own bit of garden'. So the suburban garden was a definite improvement on the yard of many city homes.

The house was usually placed towards the front of the plot, creating a small front garden, and a much larger rear garden. The latter was often screened from the view of neighbours with hedges, shrubs and fences – an expression of the privacy that was so much the desire of the Suburbans.

The style of gardens reflected the style of buildings. As estate agents' advertising slogans suggested, each one was different, being a reflection of their owners' personalities. Yet suburban gardens of the time can be grouped into different types. These include the formal Dutch garden, with a sunken pond and stone paths; the rock or alpine garden; and the rose garden. There was also the grandly titled 'water garden', which usually meant a pond, made, in situ, from concrete. However, as with the houses, the most popular style reflected a traditional approach, often described as the 'English country garden'.

Carter's catalogue, January 1945. The Government encouraged people to grow some flowers, as well as food, realising the morale value of colour and scent. This is a good example of the country cottage style of garden, popular in the thirties.

Many gardens had different sections: a vegetable patch or herb garden; a rock garden; lawn; rose beds; and flower beds with shrubs. If the size of garden allowed, one or more fruit trees, especially apple, were popular. Lawns were the centre-piece of most suburban gardens and, as today, they were often watered with a lawn sprinkler. If space allowed, a greenhouse was common, or a shed, or even both. Ornamental additions were popular, such as wishing wells, summer-houses (often no more than a cupola over a bench), or on a smaller scale, concrete gnomes.

A typical thirties garden was a riot of bright colours. The July 1933 edition of *Home Making Magazine* gave this description: 'You should make sure of having not only the radiant colour and sweet fragrance of flowers in it throughout the day, but also the lovely sweetness of night-scented bloom as well.' Favourite plants in the herbaceous border included sweet peas, lupins, red hot pokers, pansies, snapdragons and Canterbury bells.

Paths were made from a variety of materials, depending on which of the many passing fashions were in favour with the builder or owner; crazy paving, bricks, gravel and grass paths were the most common. Paths were usually edged with low borders of box, forget-me-nots, dwarf campanulas, virginia stock, creeping jenny or saxifrage. Alternatively, paths might be edged with tarred wood, concrete, brick, tile or grass.

Fences were usually of panels made of woven lathe or stakes; Taylor's of Manchester, for instance, advertised the 'Trafford' range of 'Rustic work', which included pergolas, screens, fencings, seats, arches and garden furniture. Galvanised chain link fencing was available but the rustic wooden look was far more popular. When not gardening and

Crazy paving, as shown here in *The Handyman & Home Mechanic*, was all the rage during the inter-war years.

maintaining the house, the family could be found lounging in deck chairs. The most common item of garden furniture, chairs were usually fashioned from wicker, iron or White Madeira, or could be home-made; one magazine showed how to make chairs from old butter tubs.

The tools used in the garden, recommended by a popular book of the period, included: a digging fork, a spade, a border fork, two rakes (one large and one small), a swan-necked hoe, an 'onion' or short handled hoe, a weed fork, a trowel, a dibble, a pair of garden shears, a pair of grass shears, a wheel-barrow and a watering can. If, as was normal, there was a lawn, a mower was required and motor mowers could be acquired for a large garden.

This vast expansion of private gardening was accompanied and encouraged by a host of gardening hints in magazines and books. Books on household management, also very popular at the time, normally included sections on the garden. Weekly magazines carried articles with titles such as 'What to do in your garden in November', 'Things that will make your garden a success' and 'Make old garden furniture as good as new'. There were also many books and magazines devoted entirely to gardening, such as *The Ideal Home Book of Garden Plans*, which contained plans for twenty gardens, and *How to Make a Garden* by Marguerite James.

During the war, many booklets and leaflets were produced offering advice on how to get the most from the garden.

The Wartime Garden

The wartime garden wasn't all 'Dig for Victory' vegetables and fruit. Flowers were still important and the Government encouraged gardeners to keep some. This was firstly to ensure that seed stocks would be available after the war and secondly, because the 'morale value' of flowers – their scent and colour – was needed in a world that was becoming ever more utilitarian and drab. The Women's Voluntary Service (WVS) encouraged this with its windowbox campaigns, especially in bombed areas. In the semi, the answer was usually to keep the front garden for flowers and to use most or all of the back garden for food. This had several advantages. The scheme fitted in terms of the time and area thought appropriate to devote to the two crops, as the back gardens in suburban houses were, on the whole, considerably larger than the front. Secondly, it meant that the house presented a cheery facade to the rest of the world. Last, but certainly not least, there was the question of security. In spite of the propaganda, there were plenty of people who thought that vegetables tasted far better when other people had put the effort into growing them, and who were happy to

A display of produce by the Deptford Allotments & Garden Association, September 1943. Displays by such groups were a common wartime event to encourage others to do the same. Flowers played a big part. Though frowned upon at first, it was soon realised that flower growing could be a great moral booster in a drab wartime Britain. (Lewisham Local Studies Library)

help themselves from other people's gardens. While the back garden was rarely secure from theft, it was far less vulnerable to impulse stealing. The problem also extended to allotments, where holders were forced to set up rotas of plot watchers, like fire watchers, to guard against pilfering.

Like everything else, tools were difficult to come by, and the manuals recommended a much smaller list than their pre-war predecessors. The *Daily Mail*'s *Food from the Garden in Wartime* recommended the following tools: steel spade with riveted strap; steel fork, also with riveted strap; Dutch or push hoe; draw hoe; ten- or twelve-toothed rake; trowel; dibber (this could be made from an old spade or fork handle); hand fork with two or three tines; garden line; 2 gallon watering can with interchangeable roses; and a galvanised or wooden wheelbarrow. Tools were difficult to replace so great emphasis was placed on conserving them, such as having oil and a cloth to wipe down the metal parts regularly to stop rust. An occasional oiling was recommended for wooden handles too, to stop them from becoming splintery.

DIG FOR VICTORY LEAFLET
NUMBER 20 (NEW SERIES)
ISSUED BY THE MINISTRY OF AGRICULTURE

A drawing from *Food from the Wartime Garden*; the subject is 'how to dig'. The Dig for Victory campaign encouraged many to try gardening for the first time, although, presumably, few were so ignorant that they needed quite such fundamental instruction. (*Daily Mail*)

GARAGE SALES

At this time, few new houses were built with a garage, although it was quite common for them to be advertised as having room for one to be added later. Builders would often include 'brick built' garages in the list of optional extras but these were expensive. One typical example from 1925 offered them for £50 extra on a house costing £1,000.

Motoring magazines contained many advertisements for less expensive, sectional garages which could be erected by the homeowner. These came in a variety of materials; weather board and asbestos were the most common. However, one firm's major selling point was that: 'We get our timber from stripping down the huge cases of fine quality seasoned Fir and Pine in which valuable cars are imported from Canada. It is not weather boarding, thick at one edge, thin at the other, but ¾ inch thick throughout and able to stand years of hard wear.'

In reality, garages were usually no more than a type of shed; cheaper timber models, with average dimensions about 7 ft × 14 ft long × 6 ft high (2.1 m × 4.2 m × 1.8 m), could be purchased from £6 in 1930. Larger versions, 16 ft × 8 ft × 8 ft (4.8 m × 2.4 m × 2.4 m), would cost about £10, with asbestos-covered models about £2 extra. Attempts were made to blend some of the more expensive garages in with the houses, with half-timbered gable ends and a few completely half-timbered.

Among other surprising innovations, the August 1936 *Practical Motorist* included an advertisement for 'Roller shutters for the garage'. The doubtless intrigued readers were told these shutters could be further improved by being:

> electrified, which is the acme of convenience since by inserting a Yale key in a lock at the front gate post, the shutter is raised before the car reaches the garage. This also applies to closing when going out. A light can be made to switch on when the shutter is up at night time, allowing the interior to be clearly seen from a distance.

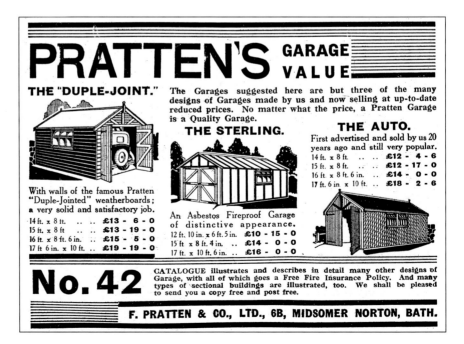

An advertisement for Pratten's garages, 1930. The mock Tudor 'Sterling' in the centre – 'of distinctive appearance' – is, like the other two, a large shed.

THREE

FURNITURE AND FURNISHINGS

FURNITURE

You furnish only once or twice in a lifetime – so give it plenty of thought

This piece of advice gives us an insight into the cost of furniture between the wars. Even cheap furniture was built using real wood panels. The modern practice of using veneered blockboard, even if only plywood or MDF, only really began on any scale after the Second World War. While some flimsy furniture was produced, the vast number of wardrobes,

A typical interior scene from *The Handyman & Home Mechanic*, showing a stepped mirror (far left), standard and table lamps, circular coffee table, and a shaped fabric pelmet with Deco curtains and nets.

sideboards, tables and chairs from the inter-war period still found in junk shops or house clearance shops nearly three-quarters of a century later bears witness to the lasting quality of even quite ordinary pieces. Much of it was hand built (although by the late thirties an increasing amount was made by machine) of hardwood, often oak, mahogany or walnut, with joints dovetailed or morticed, and screws instead of pins or glue.

In the 1920s reproduction styles - of any and every kind – were all the rage in furniture. Mock Chippendale sideboards stood alongside Queen Anne radiograms and Gothic hallstands. These, of course, fitted in well with the Jacobethan style of many new houses, but rarely had the same grace or style as the originals and were often mixed together in a complete mish-mash of periods and designs. The popularity of this 'reproduction-style' furniture did not abate until the late thirties, by which time (1938) many designers expressed relief that it was on the way out: 'Good furniture always looks beautiful and will harmonise with almost

'Functional' – a cartoon by Osbert Lancaster, 1938, featuring tubular-steel and bent ply furniture, Cubist art and a built-in electric fire. (John Murray (Publishers) Ltd)

'Modernistic' – by Osbert Lancaster, 1938, with geometric frieze, rug and cushion, decorative pelmet, and open fire. (John Murray (Publishers) Ltd)

anything, but the craze for pseudo-antiques has done such infinite harm in the last twenty years and has so retarded progress in furniture design, that it is a good thing it has at last subsided.'

As in much else, the 1930s fashion in furniture and furnishing was essentially a reaction to Victorian styles; the Victorian middle class had filled every available piece of space with items of furniture and ornaments in an undisguised display of their wealth. In contrast, high-fashion houses of the thirties were minimalist, their rooms stripped to the bone in terms of decoration and furniture. Even in the less fashionable 'average' semi, the trend was to have fewer pieces of lighter furniture: 'There are now only half a dozen furniture types – say, a bed, table, chair, desk, dress-cupboard, dressing table. There used to be twenty or thirty and only auctioneers were familiar with all of them. At the end of the list (as if the makers despaired of finding any more real names) was the "What-not".'

By the 1930s furniture was lighter, both in colour and wood tone, smaller in size, and simpler; intricate, heavy mouldings were out. This was partly a reaction to Victorian fashions, but it was also a response to the smaller, lower rooms of the semi and the advice was to keep the furniture line below 3 ft 6 in (roughly 1 m).

Modernist furniture designers made use of new materials, especially tubular steel – good examples of this are the Wassily chair by Marcel Breuer (1925) and furniture by Mies van der Rohe. Also in the early twenties, Gerrit Rietveld was producing his Berlin chairs, now commonly known as Rietveld chairs, made of flat rectangular pieces of board, each painted in a different primary colour. Another technique was the use of bent wood frames, used in a similar way to tubular steel, or moulded plywood as used by Alvar Aalto and Marcel Breuer.

Obviously, then as now, designer-built furniture was way beyond the means and interest of the average household, but the methods and materials they pioneered were soon adapted and reproduced for mass markets. Tubular steel in particular lent itself to mass-production and in Britain a range of tables, desks and seats, including stools, dining chairs, armchairs and settees were produced by Practical Equipment Limited (PEL) in the early thirties. For many people, PEL's furniture was too modern to use in the home, where wooden items were preferred as they created a cosy, familiar atmosphere. However, PEL's furniture was popular in cinemas, schools and offices.

Examples of tubular steel furniture, from 1936.

The prices of more traditional furniture varied widely, depending on the quality. The following prices are rough guides for good quality, popular furniture in the mid-thirties. (Like many other 'quality' items of the period, they were priced in guineas; 1 guinea = £1.05.) Three piece suites ranged between 7 and 25 guineas (more with a bed settee); bedroom suites (bed, dressing table, wardrobe and chest of drawers) between 8 and 30 guineas; dining suites (four or six chairs, dining table and sideboard) 10 to 30 guineas.

Utility Furniture

From the very start of the Second World War, timber was in short supply. This was because of shipping restrictions and also because it was a vital war material. Wood was needed for rifles, for ammunition cases, for huts, shelters, military furniture, and for a thousand and one other things. Skilled craftsmen were also at a premium with the increased wartime demand for manpower. In order to prioritise effectively, the Government took over supplies. The first measure was the 'Control of Timber Order', drawn up by the Ministry of Supply on 5 September 1939, which limited the supply of timber to approved manufacturers only.

A room set recreating a kitchen/dining-room of 1945, with items of Utility furniture including a dining-table, kitchen cabinet and Windsor-style chair. (Design Council)

Civilian supplies were a long way down this priority list, yet there was clearly a continuing demand for new furniture for new homes. There were about half a million marriages each year throughout the war, and couples still preferred to set up home with new rather than second-hand furniture. Such scarce resources as there were, both timber and man-hours, could not be wasted on expensive, over-elaborate, hand-carved work, or on cheap, shoddy goods that would soon fall to bits and need replacing. Prices were controlled, but price did not define quality, and standards were hard to enforce.

The logical answer was standardisation of design and materials. This would stop waste of materials and craftsmen's time and would ensure that items were made to a minimum guaranteed standard, producing functional goods that would last. The concept was one that held good not only for furniture, but for many other goods such as cloth for blankets, sheets, curtains, and even clothes. These wartime standard materials began to be known as Utility, and the term became synonymous with quality at a fair price. The Board of Trade was in charge of the project, and worked hard to ensure the co-operation of top designers, so that the public came to associate the term Utility with good design.

By November 1941, just a month after the first official references to Utility clothing, Utility furniture was under discussion too. From this date, only items from a specified list of twenty pieces of furniture could be made, and a maximum amount of timber used in their construction, though there was as yet no attempt to specify designs.

By the beginning of 1942, the timber quota for manufacturers of domestic furniture, already painfully small, was cut by a third. Plywood was withdrawn altogether as it was needed in the production of aircraft such as the Mosquito. Once again, shortages meant that prices began to rise, which in turn meant that profiteering increased – some prices were four times higher than those charged before the war. The Government's Central Price Regulation Committee (the CPRC) was anxious to resolve the problem but found it very difficult to set prices for items that were not built to a standard design. Nevertheless, in May 1942 the Government brought out the 'Furniture (Maximum Prices) Order'. This covered both new and second-hand items; anything built pre-1900 was regarded as antique and was therefore exempt.

Now the Board of Trade, under its new President Hugh Dalton, began to look seriously at the possibility of a Utility scheme for furniture. In July the Board set up an Advisory Committee on Utility Furniture under Charles Tennyson, which included the designer Gordon Russell and two consumer representatives, the Revd Charles Jenkinson, and Mrs E. Winborn, who represented the ordinary housewife. However, the retail trade was unhappy; it wanted representatives on the committee too, arguing that only retailers knew what their customers wanted. But retailers did not understand that the committee was there to set rather than follow fashions in furniture. The Board of Trade's idea was that it should be 'influencing popular taste towards good construction in simple, agreeable designs to the benefit of our after-the-war homes'.

The design parameters set by the Board of Trade were that furniture should be strong and serviceable, of a permanent nature, using only hardwoods (in practice, oak or mahogany). Veneered hardboard had to be used for all panels; all joints were to be morticed or pegged, and screws rather than pins used. The use of plastic for handles and fittings, a practice that had become widespread during the thirties, was banned. Plastic in all its variations had also become a shortage material.

The first Utility furniture range was the work of three designers, Edwin Clinch, H.T. Cutler, and L.J. Barnes. An exhibition was held to show the public the new furniture. On 19 October 1942 the Utility Furniture Exhibition opened at the Building Centre in central London. Reactions were, on the whole, positive; the furniture was a little basic but the use of oak and mahogany gave it a plain and solid look, not unlike that of the turn-of-the-century Arts and Crafts movement. In the three weeks that the exhibition was open, 30,000 people visited. Besides the furniture, Wedgwood's Victory Ware and examples of Utility cooking utensils, including the combined saucepan and kettle, were on show. Only one thing was missing – the prices, which were still being worked out. When the exhibition finished, similar events were arranged throughout the country, beginning with Glasgow.

To arrive at a fair price, the Board of Trade's accountants looked at a report made by the Council for Art and Industry in 1937; at that time, the average cost of furnishing a working-class home had been calculated at £39 14s 5d. This covered the cost of a double bed, wardrobe, tallboy, dressing chest, dining table, sideboard, easy chair, three dining chairs, kitchen table and one kitchen chair. The price of equivalent Utility furniture in oak was put at £54 9s 9d, and this was set as the maximum cost. The maximum price for the same furniture in mahogany was set at £72 19s 6d. These prices included a one-third profit margin for the trade. They were unhappy at the proposal, wanting 50 per cent; they also wanted the prices to be set, rather than to be the maximum of a range. In both cases, the Board of Trade overruled them. The cost was kept low when, in November 1942, the Chancellor of the Exchequer agreed to exempt Utility furniture from Purchase Tax.

Another order was issued in November announcing that the Utility furniture scheme would be introduced in January 1943. Utility furniture could only be manufactured under license. When the scheme started in January, seventy-two firms had received such licenses; within a couple of months this had risen to 150. The order also stated that any non-Utility furniture under construction had to be completed by the end of January and that any non-Utility furniture still in the shops had to be sold before the end of February.

A Utility furniture advertisement from January 1945. Utility furniture could only be purchased with coupons, available exclusively to those who had been bombed out or who were setting up home for the first time.

A bedroom showing a Morrison shelter and items of Utility furniture including a tubular-steel bedstead (*c.* April 1945), a 'Chiltern' dressing table, woven fibre chair, and tallboy in light oak. (Design Council)

And so it was that the first Utility furniture catalogue was issued on 1 January 1943. It was divided into five sections: the living-room, bedroom, kitchen, nursery and miscellaneous. All the items, with the exception of nursery furniture, were only available by permit, and these were normally issued only to newly-weds and those whose homes had suffered bomb damage. The permit carried sixty coupons, which could be used like points or clothing coupons; a chair was one point, a wardrobe eight. An exception was the bed settee (fifteen coupons), which needed a special permit issued only to people who lived in bed-sits. The coupons were valid for three months. In the first two months of 1943, 18,500 permits were issued.

The catalogue was necessary for ordering your furniture; retailers were only supplied with furniture that had been ordered and for which they had been given the coupons by the customer, although they could display pieces that were awaiting delivery. It was not unknown for retailers to beg, or even bribe, a customer to leave furniture with them for a while so that they had something to display.

Demand continued to outstrip supply and in September the amount of coupons was cut by half to thirty. To make up for this (in a small way), people buying Utility furniture were able to buy 15 square yards of curtain material without coupons. This was far from satisfactory and eventually the rules were relaxed. A year later, in August 1944, all those who had received only thirty coupons were given another thirty. Those receiving permits after that date once again got sixty, but thirty of them were 'deferred', that is, post dated. In the same month the Utility furniture scheme was extended to Northern Ireland.

The end of the war was obviously approaching but it was equally obvious to the Government, as well as to the general public, that shortages and rationing would have to continue for some time after the cessation of hostilities. The design panel therefore, continued to meet to produce designs for post-war reconstruction. In April 1945, with the Russians fighting on the streets of Berlin, all-steel bedsteads in a variety of colours were added to the Utility range.

At the time of the VE-Day celebrations another exhibition was organised. 'Design for the Home', staged at the National Gallery, included some of the prototype furniture upon which the design panel had been working. The pieces were of a style that had become recognisable as Utility – simple, well built, functional and reasonably priced, without being 'cheap'.

BLITZ

The shortages of furniture at the beginning of the war were compounded by the onset of the Blitz in September 1940. During that autumn, many thousands of homes were destroyed or damaged. In February 1941 the Government announced the introduction of 'Standard Emergency Furniture'. Very plain and simple, made mostly from plywood, it was an attempt to provide temporary replacements for those whose homes had been bomb damaged. The work was carried out by firms on a Government list, most of whom had been building furniture for Government or service use. It was therefore no coincidence that the emergency furniture was very similar to that found in army camps or Government canteens. At this time, it was still possible to get non-standard furniture although the number of firms producing it was dwindling and they were finding it more and more difficult to get hold of the timber. By contrast, most furniture manufacturers were able to get large Government contracts quite easily; a typical order might be for thousands of bunks to be used in air raid shelters.

During 1941 the Government took increasing control of private industry, co-ordinating who could make what, and where. From April only women, and men over forty, could work in the furniture industry; younger men were called up or moved to reserved occupations.

FURNISHINGS

Textiles

There were three main types of textiles used in furnishing the house – carpets, curtains and upholstery material – and even these items did not escape the effects of the war. The Advisory Committee on Utility Furniture continued to meet after the initial range of furniture was available, with the aim of creating new designs. To this end, the designer Gordon Russell prepared a report suggesting that a small group be formed. The Design Panel, as it was called, was constituted in June 1943, with Russell himself chairing it. The panel was made up of designers including Clinch and Cutler, who had done most of the work on the first Utility range. They were joined by architects and later the textile designer, Enid Marx.

Marx was soon creating textiles for Utility furniture upholstery, starting with two designs called 'Skelda' and 'Flora', which were introduced in 1944. Utility fabrics had to have small patterns, with a repeat of no more than 3 or 4 inches, so that matching adjoining pieces would create as little wastage as possible. The weight of the fabric was kept low, as was the choice of colours, which were limited to rust, green, blue and natural (cream).

In the last few years there has been a great vogue for the coarse tweeds as furniture coverings.

Carpets

Art Deco designs could be very effective in carpets, although more traditional designs were still popular. While geometric designs were generally used throughout the thirties, by the last few years of the decade plain carpets became more fashionable in colours such as green, fawn, blue and brown, sometimes with a darker border. Fitted carpets were introduced before the Second World War, but were popular only with a minority of people.

A bedroom from *Practical Home Making*. The curtains have been hung inside the window opening. Also typical are the geometric rug, wall-light and wallpaper scheme.

Curtains

Artificial silk, cotton, folk weave, slub damask and, most exotically named of all, slub repp were among the large range of curtain materials on offer. 'Perhaps the most attractive are those designed for the nursery, of which giraffes, bears, funny little men and women disport themselves among Noah's Ark trees in gay pretty colour on a cream ground', a typical magazine commented. Stripes and checks were fashionable in the mid-thirties, and in 1939, another magazine article advised: 'At present there is a movement away from the angular abstract designs of recent years. Large formalised floral patterns, gayer colourings and richer materials – silks, satins and velvets – reflect the return of prosperity and a general swing of the pendulum.'

Upholstery Materials

Leather, or cowhide as it was often called in furniture catalogues, was prized. For those who could not afford it there were cheaper imitations; 'rexine' was the most common, and some chairs were advertised as being in 'antique rexine'. Tapestry, in stripes or checks, was common in the middle of the decade, although florals and zigzags were also available.

Wallpaper and Paint

By the 1930s wallpaper was increasingly popular and the range of papers available was becoming more varied. There were plain papers, washable papers (sometimes called sanitary paper), flock papers, textured papers, embossed papers, and other variations, such as 'Realwood panelling'. This last example was applied like wallpaper, had a wood veneer mounted on a flexible base (normally thick canvas), and could also be used to cover doors

A room decorated with wood-grain wallpaper designs, from 1936. The panel over the fireplace is 'walnut', with a 'maple' border, while 'gumwood' has been used for the rest of the room, with a 'walnut' border.

and furniture. In 1936 in oak, walnut and mahogany versions were advertised. There were even real wood veneer wallpapers 'which are very lovely. These consist of the thinnest imaginable layer of actual wood with a paper backing.' Other wall coverings included Vitrolite glass, real wood panelling, leather preparations, fabrics and different paint effects.

The range of wallpaper patterns was very wide, from traditional florals to geometric Art Deco patterns, but like the houses themselves, the norm was often a combination of the two. Most rooms had a picture rail, or dado rail, and paper would usually only extend to this, with the wall above painted with distemper or whitewash. It was not uncommon to have a border, either bought separately or painted using a stencil. It was also common to have one wall, or part of one wall such as the chimney breast, picked out in a contrasting paper. Striped papers were often used, hung horizontally, and sometimes different yet complementary papers might be hung alternately, either vertically or horizontally.

If walls were not papered they would in all probability be painted. By the late thirties there were many good pre-mixed paints on the market.

The most commonly used paint for walls was distemper, although there were many others, including enamels, enamel paints (they were different), oil paints, interior varnish (sometimes called church varnish), cellulose paints, even metallic paints that could be used on walls that had been sized properly first. Oil paints and varnishes were often used in bathrooms and kitchens where the walls would become damp, or in rooms such as nurseries where they would need frequent washing.

Painted walls could be patterned by stippling – dabbing the paint with a stiff brush to make a mottled finish – or by rag-rolling – rolling a loosely rolled wad of cloth over the paint while still wet.

For those who could afford professional help or, more likely, had the skills to do it themselves, murals were popular, especially in the bathroom or the nursery. Often these took the form of friezes at dado or picture rail level, such as a carnival of animals:

> Nursery friezes, particularly those illustrating well-known nursery rhymes or fairy stories, afford sufficient decoration when used on a plain wall. They should, however, be fixed at a height which would allow the small occupants to enjoy them in comfort. I have seen at least one nursery used by toddlers with the frieze at picture rail height, which is the equivalent to asking an adult to strain his head back every time he wishes to look at the frieze.

In purchasing ready made paint, always buy the best, as it is a great mistake to buy a very cheap one of unknown origin. Such paint very often contains as a base a large proportion of whiting [ground chalk] which is useless as a protective medium, while the other ingredients are usually of the poorest quality.

Nursery wallpaper friezes, from 1936.

Lighting

In the inter-war period gas and electricity fought for dominance in the field of domestic lighting. Gas had proved to be a wonderful replacement for oil and candles in the nineteenth century; initially the electric companies concentrated on the convenience of electric lighting. It was only in the 1920s, when electricity had all but claimed victory, that electric lights became more than modified versions of gas burners as designers started to appreciate the possibilities of electricity.

By the 1930s there were four recognised types of electric lighting: direct, semi-direct, indirect and semi-indirect. Direct lighting throws light directly on the object to be illuminated; semi-direct is where a direct light is diffused by passing through a shade or some other screen; indirect throws light away from the object, where it is reflected off a wall or ceiling back on to the object, giving a softer, more diffused light; while semi-indirect lights have part of their light reflected, and part thrown directly on the object.

Electric lights were easily portable so the table lamp and the standard lamp became popular. These made up a great deal of the semi-direct lighting in the home; very few sitting-rooms did not have one or, more likely, both. One of the new inventions was the angle-poise lamp, at first found almost exclusively in offices. It soon began to infiltrate the home, especially in the lounge for reading or sewing.

Indirect light often came from 'uplighting' – standard, table or wall lights with solid shades, often in the form of brass or chrome 'fruit bowls', which directed the light upwards onto the ceiling. Many semi-direct lights had glass shades of either white glass or opaque glass formed by acid-etching or sand-blasting, which had a similar effect of diffusing the light; the white glass globe was widely used.

By now a bewildering array of electric bulbs was available – far more than today – including the long candle, a tube about a foot long, which was often used in chrome fittings to create Modernist wall and table lamps. Fabric-covered shades were still popular, some with fringes of fabric or glass beading.

Now lighting was artistic as well as functional:

If you have a specially lovely piece of china which stands in an alcove in your drawing-room there are attractive possibilities in illuminating it with a soft light and keeping the rest of the room in a subdued light except for direct illumination on what you are doing.

A Mazda advertisement illustrating the wide range of light bulbs available for home use in the late thirties.

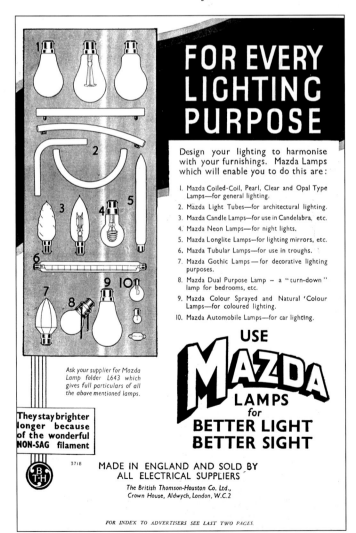

FOR EVERY LIGHTING PURPOSE

Design your lighting to harmonise with your furnishings. Mazda Lamps which will enable you to do this are:

1. Mazda Coiled-Coil, Pearl, Clear and Opal Type Lamps—for general lighting.
2. Mazda Light Tubes—for architectural lighting.
3. Mazda Candle Lamps—for use in Candelabra, etc.
4. Mazda Neon Lamps—for night lights.
5. Mazda Longlite Lamps—for lighting mirrors, etc.
6. Mazda Tubular Lamps—for use in troughs.
7. Mazda Gothic Lamps—for decorative lighting purposes.
8. Mazda Dual Purpose Lamp – a "turn-down" lamp for bedrooms, etc.
9. Mazda Colour Sprayed and Natural 'Colour Lamps—for coloured lighting.
10. Mazda Automobile Lamps—for car lighting.

Ask your supplier for Mazda Lamp folder L643 which gives full particulars of all the above mentioned lamps.

They stay brighter longer because of the wonderful NON-SAG filament

USE MAZDA LAMPS for BETTER LIGHT BETTER SIGHT

MADE IN ENGLAND AND SOLD BY ALL ELECTRICAL SUPPLIERS
The British Thomson-Houston Co. Ltd., Crown House, Aldwych, London, W.C.2

FOR INDEX TO ADVERTISERS SEE LAST TWO PAGES.

Flood-lighting your curtains from inside the pelmet or behind a piece of furniture is another idea and some very lovely effects can be achieved by using coloured lights in this way.

The war brought the blackout but this did not mean switching off all the lights and sitting in the dark. The blackout required that no lights be seen from the outside, so windows had to be covered by thick curtains. Light fittings could be bought with a bayonet fixture at one end so they could be plugged in to a normal light fitting and, with an unreflected torch bulb at the other end, halls, porches and the like could be lit without showing so much light that a blackout was necessary.

> *Lighted mirrors, set in a niche accommodating a vase of flowers or piece of statuary, provide a centre of attraction which can be emphasised or not as preferred.*

Floors

Hardwood flooring was very popular. One company offered oak parquet blocks at 5s 6d a square yard, or 13s laid and polished. Other alternatives included lino of widely varying quality. Most books warned against the cheapest, which was thin with a printed pattern. It was something of a race between the lino and the pattern as to which would wear out first. Better quality cork lino (costing about 2s 6d a square yard) lasted much longer and had an integral pattern, frequently the geometric, Art Deco type. Popular lino patterns were imitation parquet, and the ubiquitous black and white check. Also popular were cork tiles (12s to 14s a square yard), rubber floors (most suitable for kitchens, bathrooms and nurseries – 9s to 23s) and asbestos cement composition floors (usually for halls and kitchens – 7s 6d).

Ornaments

As we have already said, the fashion was to cut back on 'frills', but even the most austerely functional house would have one or two wall-masks or statuettes. Wall-masks, especially of women, were produced in plaster or ceramic by a host of manufacturers including Clarice Cliff, Goldscheider and

Ornaments came in a wide range of styles and materials. This selection includes a ceramic hare, a plaster figurine, an Egyptian-style wooden cigarette box, a photo-frame and a geometric vase.

Plaster and ceramic wallmasks.

Lenci. Clarice Cliff produced one mask, 'Flora', in a range of sizes from 4½ in to 15 in. They could be realistic or stylised, painted in flesh tones or monotones, small or large. Wallpockets, basically a cross between a vase and a wall-mask, were another way of adding a third dimension to a flat wall.

For many, the stylised statuette of the naked or semi-naked young woman epitomises ornaments of the thirties; these were a continuation of the work of Dimitri Chiparus in the years immediately after the First World War, and came in a range of materials including plaster, ceramic, spelter, chrome and glass. Some of the best known were designed by Leslie Harradine, Preiss and Lorenzl. One popular figure was that of Diana the huntress, complete with bow, often accompanied by that most Art Deco of dogs, the greyhound. They might be straight figurines, match holders, mirror holders, candlesticks, lamps, clocks, bookends or a thousand and one other gadgets.

Vases or ornamental bowls could be found in most homes and leading designers of the time included Keith Murray for Wedgwood, Sylvac, or Shelley.

Smoking was fashionable for men and women so smoking paraphernalia such as ashtrays, pipe racks, cigarette boxes and table lighters were popular in a vast range of materials ranging from Jacobethan pewter or wood to Bakelite, Perspex, chrome, and ceramic.

A GUIDED TOUR

Now we will take a room-by-room look at the furniture and furnishings popular in the semis of the time, with comments and advice taken from just a few of the many homemaker books and manuals produced in the 1930s.

The Hall

The use of flame-sprayed lamps will add to the feeling of warm welcome which a well-lit hall should convey.

One of the few pieces of furniture found in the average hall was the hallstand. This was a multi-purpose object designed to take the hats, coats and so on of the family and guests. Most commonly it was about the size of a small door, usually of wood, bearing several coat hooks, a mirror and, at the bottom, a rack or racks for umbrellas and walking sticks. Sometimes they had a small chest built in which doubled as a seat. Smaller halls might have only a separate umbrella stand, with the family coats going into the cupboard under the stairs. If you had a grander hall you might boast a hall wardrobe – quite simply, a small wardrobe for the hall.

The Lounge or Drawing-room

The centre-piece of the lounge or drawing-room was usually the fireplace. In Tudor-style houses this was often in red brick, but in most houses it had a tiled surround. Some had a built-in fender, or kerb as they were called, but most rooms would have a separate fender of wood, chrome, brass or Bakelite. There was a vast range of styles to match the decor, from repro-medieval, incorporating seats on either side, through 'Cosy Cottage' to Art Deco. Most had an accompanying coal scuttle, fire screen

DRAWING ROOM FURNITURE

No, 151— FIRESIDE EASY CHAIR with spring seat and high back. Finished Walnut or Mahogany and covered in Tapestry.
USUAL PRICE 42/-
SALE PRICE 29/6 CASH SALE PRICE 27/6

No. 152—FIRESIDE CHAIR finished Walnut shade, with cushion seat covered in Damask.
USUAL PRICE 55/-
SALE PRICE 36/- CASH SALE PRICE 33/6

No. 153 — OAK FIRESIDE ARMCHAIR, covered in Damask. *USUAL PRICE 25/-*
SALE PRICE 16/6 CASH SALE PRICE15/6

No. 154—FIRESIDE ARM CHAIR, finished Jacobean Oak, Mahogany or Walnut shade. With cushion seat covered in Tapestry.
USUAL PRICE 52/6
SALE PRICE 37/6 CASH SALE PRICE 35/-

No. 155—FIRESIDE ARM CHAIR, finished Walnut. With Damask cushion and polished Brown Hide back. *USUAL PRICE 65/-*
SALE PRICE 42/6 CASH SALE PRICE 39/6

No. 156—FIRESIDE CHAIR, finished Walnut shade, with cushion seat covered in Damask.
USUAL PRICE 3 GNS.
SALE PRICE 39/6 CASH SALE PRICE 37/6

No. 157—FIRESIDE ARM CHAIR, finished Walnut. With cushion seat covered in Tapestry.
USUAL PRICE 55/-
SALE PRICE 36/- CASH SALE PRICE 33/6

No. 158—FIRESIDE ARM CHAIR with high cane back. Finished Jacobean Oak, Mahogany or Walnut shade. With cushion seat covered in Tapestry. *USUAL PRICE 69/6*
SALE PRICE 48/6 CASH SALE PRICE 45/-

No. 159—FIRESIDE EASY CHAIR with high cane back and seat covered in Tapestry. Finished Walnut.
USUAL PRICE 5 GNS.
SALE PRICE 70/- CASH SALE PRICE 65/-

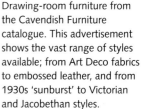

Drawing-room furniture from the Cavendish Furniture catalogue. This advertisement shows the vast range of styles available; from Art Deco fabrics to embossed leather, and from 1930s 'sunburst' to Victorian and Jacobethan styles.

and companion set (poker, brush, coal tongs and shovel), although these might be bought separately.

Lounge furniture would include easy chairs and/or a three piece suite, bookcase, bureau or desk, and of course the wireless set, which increasingly became the focus of the room until television took over in the fifties. Additionally, there might be a tea wagon (trolley), cocktail cabinet, china cabinet, and an upright piano.

The Dining-room

The principal items of furniture here would be a suite of dining table (usually draw-leaf, which could double as a card table), chairs and sideboard, containing the canteen of (often silver or plate) cutlery.

Above: An illustration from the Cavendish Furniture catalogue showing an Art Deco mahogany dining-room suite.

Above, right: The 'Challenge' traditional-style oak dining-room suite from the Cavendish Furniture catalogue.

Scarlet American cloth curtains against a black background of black tiled walls and a black bath, with a red tiled floor, give a very striking effect.

Additionally, there might be a bureau or desk, gramophone, sideboard-dresser or cocktail cabinet.

The Bathroom

White was still a popular choice for bathroom suites but during the thirties, a wide range of colours became available. A Baxendale's sanitary ware catalogue from the late 1930s is illustrated with tinted plates showing toilets, baths, washbasins and bidets in jade green, primrose, blue, lavender blue, lilac, coral pink, old ivory, black as well as white.

> Delightful colour schemes are the chief features of the modern bathroom now that walls, floor, baths and general equipment are obtainable in such wonderful ranges of colour. Indeed, the introduction of glass, coloured tiles, cellulose enamel, and other modern accessories, has made the bathroom the most colourful room in the house.

One major difference from today was the use of the word lavatory; at that time, a lavatory was a bathroom washbasin, the word coming from the French 'laver', meaning 'to wash'. Like most sanitary ware manufacturers, Baxendale sold the 'combination bath and lavatory', a washbasin that fitted over the bath, for use in small bathrooms.

Toilet seats were still predominantly made of hardwood, with more expensive versions in teak, mahogany and walnut, but Bakelite versions, available in black, white or mahogany, became more popular. So, too, did another version, of wood covered with plastic in a mottled, opalescent finish, which was available in a wide range of colours. Bidets were optional extras in many bathroom suites. The WC suites available included low-level, high-pressure and noiseless syphonic versions.

Fittings were usually chrome and including heated towel rails and spectacular Art Deco-style taps, overflows and shower fittings. Chrome was used not just because it looked good; it was stressed at the time that, unlike brass, it did not need polishing and was therefore labour saving.

Bathroom floors were usually covered with linoleum, rubber or cork. Walls were normally tiled – often a flush dado rail, the most common of which was a thin strip of black and white chequered tiles, although there were many variations available, including chevrons. A more expensive wall cladding was Vitrolite glass panels, which came in plain or marbled finishes and in various colours. Walls might be covered completely, as well as the bath surround; alternatively, smaller pieces might be used as shelving, or as a panel behind the sink. Vitrolite splashbacks (often in black), with a built-in mirror, shelf, toothbrush and glass holders, were common additions to many bathrooms.

A popular material for bathroom curtains was American cloth, also known as Lancaster cloth or oil-baize. This was a cloth backing on which resin, gums and paint were applied and subjected to great pressure. Being waterproof and washable, it made excellent curtains for the bathroom.

The bathroom did not miss out on the electric gadget boom. Bathroom gadgets included electric bathroom radiators in chrome and enamel finish (£4 19s 6d to £5 19s 6d), electric towel rails (£2 12s 6d to £8 12s 6d) and towel dryers (£6 6s to £10 10s 6d), electric safety razors (£1 5s), and bathroom cabinets with built-in lights – some even had a built-in electric clock as well.

An August 1939 advertisement for Shanks china, showing a very modern bathroom, which might surprise those who would expect a white bathroom with a high-level cistern. The circular mirror, wall-lights and tubular-steel stool are especially Modernist.

The Bedroom

The central feature of most adult bedrooms was the dressing table, often by far the most stylised piece of furniture in the room. More expensive versions often had built-in lights. Circular mirrors were common, although it is difficult to be too specific about an item of furniture that was probably unequalled in the house for the huge range of styles and

A drawing from *The Home of Today*, with tubular-steel bedroom furniture, a material that was widely used for furniture, especially chairs.

shapes available. Beds commonly had integral or accompanying bedside cabinets; and following the trend towards reduction, the better wardrobes incorporated the tallboy, which had drawers on one side, sometimes with glass fronts.

Bedrooms for younger children were called 'the nursery' by people intent on a bit of social climbing. These were usually very light rooms – colour schemes were predominantly pastels or primary colours, cream or white – and a wide range of scaled-down furniture, beds, bunks, cupboards and bookcases was available.

FOUR

HOUSEWORK AND DIY

WOMEN AT HOME

While many regarded it as quite respectable for single middle-class women to be engaged in 'suitable' employment, such as clerical work, or as a governess, teacher or nurse, the situation was completely different for married middle-class women. A suburban wife who worked could be a source of shame to her husband as it implied that he did not earn enough to keep her. This applied also to better paid manual workers for whom a wife who stayed at home was a symbol of their status as skilled craftsmen. Upon marriage, a 'respectable' woman was expected to give up working and devote her time to the care of her husband, her home and, in due course, her children. Many employers, for example, the Civil Service and most local authorities, offered women employees contracts that automatically ended upon marriage. However, the availability of work in the thirties varied according to the effects of the Depression and increasing numbers of married women had started going to work, often because their husbands could find none. When war broke out, women began to take on all kinds of jobs – including those seen previously as entirely male preserves – as the menfolk were called up.

However, between the wars it was unusual for suburban wives to be in employment. Add to this the falling birth rate, especially marked among the middle classes – by the 1930s the average number of children in the suburban house was a little under two – and the result is that the suburban housewife had a great deal of time on her hands. The lack of servants meant that much of this time was taken up with housework, shopping and cooking, and despite the plethora of labour-saving devices, there was still much to be done around the house.

A series of photographs showing the vacuum cleaner in use.

On left
TWO CLEANERS OF HANDLE TYPE WITH SUSPENDED DUST-BAGS

ILLUSTRATES THE CORRECT METHOD OF EMPTYING THE DUST-BAG

THE ATTACHMENTS OF A VACUUM CLEANER ENABLE THE DUST TO BE REMOVED FROM LEDGES, HANGINGS, ETC., DUSTLESSLY

THIS VACUUM CLEANER IS PROVIDED WITH ITS OWN ELECTRIC LIGHT, WHICH SIMPLIFIES THE CLEANING OF DARK PLACES

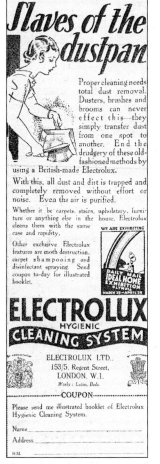

The vacuum cleaner was one of a host of labour-saving devices produced to help the suburban housewife. They were marketed as such, as in this example where those without a vacuum cleaner are destined to be 'slaves of the dustpan'.

HOUSEWORK

Polishing and Cleaning

The type of housework that had to be done will be all too familiar; apart from Hoovering, it was mainly dusting, polishing and cleaning.

One of the quickest ways of polishing the surface (of paint and woodwork) is to rub it with a soft, lintless duster, upon which a few drops of paraffin have been sprinkled. Paraffin is, indeed, a very great help at cleaning time, and it is an excellent plan to put some in a sprinkler-top bottle and carry it about from room to room. This will clean and polish paint, brass, floors, windows, and most of the oddments, and at the same time disinfect and keep away flies and other insect pests.

Flies and other insect pests may well have had more sense than to stay in a house that had been liberally sprinkled with paraffin. Considering the rudimentary state of some of the electrical wiring and fittings, and the home dry-cleaning described a little further on, it is a wonder anyone, never mind the flies, survived the thirties.

Not all home-made preparations were lethal. One polish for old oak was a mixture of beer, beeswax and coarse sugar, mixed in the ratio of a quart of hot beer with one-quarter ounce of beeswax and a spoonful of sugar stirred in. Brushed on to the cleaned wood, it had to be rigorously polished to achieve a deep, lasting shine. For light oak, salad oil was recommended (definitely not to be confused with salad cream).

For the majority who had open fires, cleaning out and re-laying the fire was a daily job in the winter, and perhaps once a week the grate would

---

TOOLS OF THE TRADE

Many of the tools recommended for housework were the same as those that had been used before the arrival of the many new gadgets and devices for the home – the *Home Owner's Handbook* of 1938 suggested the following:

Vacuum cleaner; a small electrically-operated duster for stairs and difficult places
Floor polisher; either electrically- or hand-operated
Carpet sweeper
Long-handled dusting mop for floors. (A cheaper alternative was to tie a duster round a broom.)
Long-handled soft broom for kitchen and other floors
Scrubbing brush of ordinary type, together with long-handled one if there are extensive areas to be scrubbed
Grate-brushes, if there should be any grates to be blackleaded
Boot and shoe brushes
Silver brushes
Leathers for silver and windows
Dusters of soft absorbent quality, those of machine-knitted stockinette fabric being excellent
A few cloths of the type impregnated with polish for rubbing up metalware
Washing-up mop
Floor cloths

In addition to the above, a full complement of cleaning accessories includes soap, abrasive cleaner, silver and brass polishes, wax polish, furniture cream, turpentine or cheaper substitute, steel-wool – for cleaning hard-wood floors and similar surfaces.

be blackleaded. This meant cleaning the grate with a stiff brush, and applying blacklead, usually bought in a tube – the most common make was Zebo or Zebrite. The grate would then be polished, rather like a pair of shoes.

Washing Up

For the fortunate few, electric dishwashers were available in the thirties. The *Slonetric* catalogue listed 'Little friend' electric dishwashers that 'have solved a problem by enabling the housewife to avoid soaking her hands in hot greasy dishwater'. Our particular favourite is the 'portable' model P1, which fitted into a butler sink, 'converting an ordinary sink temporarily into an electric dish washer', and all for 12 guineas. There were also self-standing models that went up to 38 guineas, depending on size. Best of these was the model D2 (18 guineas). It had an optional clothes drying attachment (for 2 guineas), which was 'collapsible, folds flat and is designed to make use of the mechanism of the dishwasher for drying clothes in small kitchenettes and flats where space is at a premium'. Finally, a range of electric water softeners was available, which could be connected directly to the household water supply.

The majority of people did their washing up in the sink, by hand, often using a washing-up mop. This was a miniature mop, about a foot long, which nowadays has been largely replaced by the nylon brush.

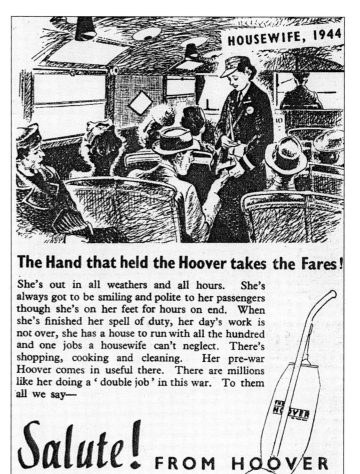

HOUSEWIFE, 1944

The Hand that held the Hoover takes the Fares!

She's out in all weathers and all hours. She's always got to be smiling and polite to her passengers though she's on her feet for hours on end. When she's finished her spell of duty, her day's work is not over, she has a house to run with all the hundred and one jobs a housewife can't neglect. There's shopping, cooking and cleaning. Her pre-war Hoover comes in useful there. There are millions like her doing a 'double job' in this war. To them all we say—

Salute! FROM HOOVER

A wartime Hoover advert. With the added demands on their time that came with the war, labour-saving devices were all the more necessary. As the advert makes clear, they were no longer available during the war, but it was common for firms to advertise products that would be in supply afterwards.

HELPING HANDS

Rubber gloves – for nothing is so cruel to the hands as housework, so don't use your gloves only for washing up. Cleaning the flues and blacking the grates – even dusting, for dusting is the most engriming job. Doing the flowers asks for this aid, for dirty stalks and sloughing stain the hands badly, and such marks are hard to eradicate. The hands betray an individual. I have heard people say they cannot work in gloves, but today they fit so well that one hardly knows one has them on, and I typewrite in them because I find that carbons mark the fingers.

Have you thought of the dozens of other kitchen aids that this product has brought into the home? Anti-drip spouts for that maddening tap? Window wedges that stop the rattling in irritable windows? Soap dishes with suction pads, soap savers, rubber plates and saucepan scrapers, and rubber trays and sections for ice cubes in the refrigerator.

PLAN OF WORK FOR A SMALL SERVANTLESS HOUSE
(3 or 4 in family)

	7.0.	Get up ; dress.	2.0.	Wash up, tidy kitchen and scullery.	
	10.	Strip the bed and air the rooms.	10.		
	20.	Unlock the house.	20.		
	30.	Stoke the boiler.	30.		
	40.	Light living-room fire if necessary.	40.		
	50.	Prepare breakfast.	50.	Change.	
	8.0.	Have breakfast.	3.0.		
	10.		10.		
	20.	Clear away, wash up breakfast things. (Accompany child to school when required.)	20.		
	30.		30.	Recreation, resting, visiting or special duties such as ironing, gardening, needlework according to weather and season. Minding young children if necessary.	
	40.		40.		
	50.		50.		
	9.0.	Sweep porch and steps.	4.0.		
	10.	Lay sitting-room fire if needed.	10.		
	20.	Do dining-room and sitting-room carpets with vacuum cleaner. Mop the surrounds and dust.	20.		
	30.		30.		
	40.		40.	Prepare and serve tea.	
	50.		50.		
	10.0.	Make beds.	5.0.		
	10.	Mop and dust upstair rooms and W.C.	10.	Wash up tea things.	
	20.	Attend to bathroom. Wash out bath and lavatory basin. Sweep and mop bathroom floor and landing. Sweep stairs.	20.		
	30.		30.		
	40.		40.		
	50.		50.		
	11.0.	Look over larder.	6.0.	Prepare food for supper or dinner, and cook the meal.	
	10.	Prepare vegetables or pastry for midday or evening meal.	10.		
	20.		20.		
	30.		30.		
	40.		40.		
	50.		50.		
	12.0.	Shopping when required and special weekly duties.	7.0.	Put children to bed.	
	10.		10.		
	20.		20.		
	30.		30.		
	40.	Finish off cooking, and prepare lunch.	40.	Serve and have dinner.	
	50.		50.		
	1.0.	Serve lunch or dinner.	8.0.	Clear away meal. Wash up if liked, but this can be deferred until the morning.	
	10.		10.		
	20.	Have lunch, and clear away.	20.		
	30.		30.		
	40.		40.	Reading, recreation, letter writing, accounts.	
	50.		50.		

As meal-times vary considerably in different families and in different parts of the country, according to the nature of the husband's work the principal meal is sometimes taken in the middle and sometimes at the end of the day. As a general rule, when the husband's work is near at hand and he can take all meals at home, the principal meal is taken at midday, and the housewife's morning will be necessarily busier, but she should have more leisure between tea and supper.

HOUSEWIFE'S WEEKLY DUTIES
From 11.30 to 12.30.

MONDAY. Brush all clothes used over the week-end and put away. Collect large articles and send to laundry or do laundrywork at home. If all family laundry is done at home, help may be necessary.
Wash silk and woollens first, followed by white things. These can be done in alternate weeks if preferred.
TUESDAY. Turn out dining-room. Clean silver.
WEDNESDAY. Special turning out of two bedrooms each week.
THURSDAY. Special turning out of sitting-room.
FRIDAY. Thorough weekly clean of bathroom, W.C., landing and stairs. Baking.
SATURDAY. Special cleaning of hall, kitchen and scullery. Extra cooking for week-end.

Plan of daily and weekly work for a small servantless house from *The Housewife's Book*.

LAUNDRY

Washing clothes at the turn of the century had been a labour-intensive, unpleasant job – hot, back-breaking and steamy. It was certainly not a job for the middle-class housewife, and was left to the domestic servants. With their demise, it became a job for the commercial laundries, whose vans were a common sight and whose presence was certainly far more widespread then than today. (Every second murder film of the time has the unknown victim identified by laundry marks on their clothes.)

LAUNDRY WORK

The amount of washing done at home naturally depends on circumstances. It is, for instance, difficult or almost impossible to do much washing if you live in a flat, or a small country house with no place to use for drying. In the country, where there is more room, more is done. Every woman, nowadays, however, does some laundry work, if it is only the washing of stockings or light silk underclothes. Possibly most of the clothes are washed at home, and only the larger, more difficult things, like sheets, are sent to a laundry.

In many houses there is a small scullery, where there is usually a good copper installed, and a table, sink and zinc bath which can be used for the laundry operations. If you have room and time to wash at home then it is well worthwhile going into the matter of special labour-saving equipment for this purpose. Everything helpful can be bought, from washing machines and wringers to improved ironing boards and irons.

However, like so much else, this was changing. By 1934 (when the extract quoted above was written), clothes washing had caught the attentions of the labour-savers, and the 1930s saw the development of the washing machine.

The onset of war brought changes too. Many commercial laundries were taken over and converted ready for use as cleansing stations for clothing and other material contaminated in poison gas raids. Those that remained were hardly seen as an essential use of labour at a time of great shortage and even greater Government control. The *Housewife* magazine of August 1943 carried an article about home laundry. It begins by bemoaning the disappearance of the commercial service:

Laundries haven't actually ceased to exist, but they are having a hard struggle to carry on, and in many districts the housewife is fortunate who sees the laundry van at her gate more often than once a month. Few wardrobes or linen cupboards are so amply stocked that they can stand this time lag, and so inevitably more washing has to be done at home.

The article predicts that this situation will probably not improve for some time after peace is established. It is interesting that as early as 1943 the general public was being warned that victory would not be the end of shortages.

Better washing equipment in the home was needed, and this was provided by the 'combined tub-and-sink unit', consisting of a fireclay fitting, 48 inches by 20 inches, containing two sinks, each with taps, with a fixture for a wringer between the sinks. These were 'designed to cope quickly and simply with the three stages of laundering – soaking, washing and rinsing', and cost between £16 to £18.

By the mid-thirties, increasingly, middle-class housewives were doing more of the washing at home. Although markedly old-fashioned by then, the dolly tub and peg were nevertheless still in use in some households. The dolly peg was a wooden stick, about half a metre long, with a bar across the top, forming a T shape, and an arrangement like a small three-legged milking stool at the bottom. It was used by holding the handle with the stool end in the tub, among the washing, and turning it to propel the clothes backwards and forwards in a rotary movement. This was adapted in the various

Advice from *Good Housekeeping* for the busy housewife, 1930s. Parozone would, apparently, give a 'snowy whiteness with a minimum of effort' while bringing 'the secret of sunshine and brightness' to every corner of the home.

SUGGESTIONS FOR MONTHLY WORK THROUGHOUT THE YEAR

JANUARY Complete the yearly Accounts. Spare time for sales, and extra entertaining, parties for children and adults. Cleaning the house after Christmas Festivities. Marmalade making.	**JULY** Jam making. Fruit and vegetable bottling. Holidays.
FEBRUARY Thorough turning out of all cupboards, shelves, bookcases, chests, in readiness for Spring Cleaning.	**AUGUST** Preserving. Sewing. Buy winter coal. Holidays.
MARCH Early Spring Cleaning, interior decorating, upholstery, making curtains, chair covers.	**SEPTEMBER** Making pickles and sauces. Plum and Damson jam. Getting in winter stores when needed.
APRIL Spring Cleaning, washing curtains, preparing for Easter. Spring gardening.	**OCTOBER** Harvesting of Vegetables. Packing away summer clothes. Launder or send away to be cleaned. Renovate the wardrobe. Unpack winter clothes and furs. Inspect the outside of the house and carry out any small repairs.
MAY Late Spring Cleaning. Attend to outhouses. Spring Clean the garage, tool-sheds. Clean and put away winter clothes. Protect from moth. Gardening. Bedding out. Window boxes.	**NOVEMBER** Preparing Christmas Puddings, Mincemeat, Cakes. Christmas Shopping.
JUNE Preparation and sewing for the holidays. Fruit bottling.	**DECEMBER** Making and buying Christmas Presents. Christmas Cooking and Letter Writing. Overhauling children's wardrobe when they come home for holidays.

Suggestions for monthly work throughout the year from *The Housewife's Book*.

'clothes washers' or washing machines, which began to appear throughout the decade, many of which featured an 'agitator' that did the same job as the dolly peg.

Another washing device was the boiler, or copper, as it was commonly known. Originally this was built in to a brick furnace, heated by a mixture of coke and cinders, or wood, or any sort of combustible household rubbish. By the thirties, most of these, except in rural districts, had been superseded by portable types, fuelled by gas, electricity or oil. These had to be filled with water fed through a short length of hose connected to the tap and heated to the appropriate temperature. At this point, the washing would be put in and agitated with a dolly or simply a piece of wood such as a broken broom handle. After washing, items were removed, often with a pair of long wooden tongs, and the water drained off via a tap at the bottom of the boiler. The process might be repeated for extra dirty clothes, and then the washing would be rinsed, usually in the sink. Generally, a tub or zinc bath was regarded as a necessary accessory to the copper. Clothes were kept in it while the water in the copper was changed. A corrugated washing board was used to get the dirt out of really dirty clothes, the fabric being rubbed vigorously up and down the board. Once cleaned and rinsed, clothes would then be wrung out using a wringer or mangle – another back-breaking job. Some boilers had a built-in wringer, but most people had either the old-fashioned mangle with wooden rollers standing on legs, or the more modern small wringer with rubber rollers which could be clamped to a table or on to the edge of the sink. The *Slonetric* catalogue of 1937 included electric clothes boilers (£2 15s 2d to £13 13s), some of which doubled as bath water heaters, and one as a kitchen heater.

There were also hand washers – washing machines operated by hand. Some of the most efficient were a closed wooden or metal box or cylinder, fitted on spindles in a frame so that it could be easily revolved by hand. The clothes were loaded in with hot soapy water and the washing done by constant revolution. Hand washers were recommended where only a small amount of the washing was done at home. The manufacturers of one type of gas-heated hand-washing machine also boasted that it doubled as a dish washer. When washing clothes, the handle was turned slowly, and the rinsing done by another movement. When washing up, the crockery and cutlery were put into specially made wire baskets, and hot soda water added:

> The handle is worked up and down to get plates clean; the water is run off and clean water put in; the same movement is used and the plates are rinsed; again the water is run off, the lid is removed, and the same movement of the handle fans the crockery with hot air and dries it. Only the silver and glass need to be polished afterwards.

This amazing NEW **Apex-Vactric** "Popular" ELECTRIC washer takes the washing off your hands!

No more wash-worn hands ; no more clothes worn and strained by rubbing, scrubbing and boiling ! Just soak the tubful for 15 minutes (22 small pieces or 15 medium pieces), then let the gentle action agitator do the rest of the work for you, coaxing out every vestige of dirt, bringing your clothes to snowy whiteness. Think how much time you save and how much money, too, in laundry bills saved and clothes that last longer.

GREAT INTRODUCTORY FREE OFFER!

The Roll-A-Way Stand can be folded round the tub and rolled under the sink or draining-board. Light, strong and steady.

WRINGER free!

FULL SIZE PACKAGE OF RINSO free!

BOOK-HOW TO WASH CLOTHES THE MODERN WAY free!

AUTOMATIC ADJUSTABLE STAND free!

10 GNS or ONLY 2/- WEEKLY

The pre-war washing machine was very different to a modern version. This one clearly shows its evolution from the household boiler.

"And it's all ready for work in no time" says Mrs. Twenty Five

"So I see, and I do like the colour scheme" says Mrs. Fifty Five

The world's finest wringer-mangle combined with the ideal kitchen cabinet table.

Patented pressed steel construction with rust-proofed non-chipping enamel — all working parts cased in steel.

Super-reinforced solid rubber rollers will not break buttons or fasteners.

Unique cantilever pressure system — will take blankets as easily as bibs.

This 'Cabinet' will take any size or shape of dolly tub, zinc, or enamel bath, or 'Nesta' Tubs.

Every machine is fully covered by a generous 10 years free replacement guarantee.

Obtainable of all the best ironmongers, hardware and furnishing stores.

Here, in one compact 'Cabinet' are four things without which no kitchen can be really efficient. First, the ACME Wringer—it takes the toil out of wringing and mangling. Second, complete facilities to centralise all your washday duties. Third, a steady mangling and ironing table standing firm on any floor. Finally—a most modern touch—a sparkling white enamelled kitchen table. And now you have a choice of four finishes at no extra cost—blue mottle, green mottle, grey mottle and oak finish—to suit your colour scheme.

ACME
CABINET
WRINGER-MANGLE

IF YOU ARE SHORT OF SPACE choose either the ACME 'Folding' model at 69/6 or the ACME 'Portable' model at 43/- for the 16" size or 39/- for the 14" size. For literature giving details of all three ACMES write for booklet W.M.11, to ACME Wringers Ltd., David St., Glasgow, S.E.

The Acme Cabinet Wringer-Mangle offered not only a wringer and mangle, but also an ideal kitchen cabinet table and an ironing table. It came in four finishes, to fit in with any colour scheme. (*Good Housekeeping*)

The *Slonetric* catalogue also featured electric clothes washers. There were basically boilers that had an integral agitator and a built-in wringer over the tub, so that the heating and agitation were done automatically. Unlike modern machines, they did not automatically rinse and spin the washing as well, although in the electric models the wringer was electrically operated – 'this in itself is often worth the price paid for the machine', one book claimed. Various models had special features, such as the Locomotive model DH 25 (£25), which boasted that 'the ridged formation of tub materially increases the water agitation', or model SDH30 (£30), which claimed to have a 'new exclusively designed agitator fitted which increases the suds on the top of the water'. Others had a second tank in which clothes were rinsed. When this was done you could use an electric clothes drying cabinet (22 or 32 guineas), and finish the job with your electric iron (7s 9d to £1 11s). There were even electric flat irons (the irons were heated on a special electric hot plate) and a table-top rotary model (£21).

Electricity was not completely dominant as a fuel for washing machines. There were several gas-powered washing machines on the market, most of which were cheaper than their electric equivalents. Some of the advertising for these machines makes interesting, if mystifying reading:

One little washer occupies a space only 2 feet square, and will wash anything, from engineers' overalls to the most delicate of silk underclothing. Its makers claim that in from three to five minutes it will wash two blankets, three sheets, or twenty towels; and that it even cleans collar bands and cuff bands of shirts. It employs four methods to achieve these ends, namely; rubbing and squeezing, in which the clothes are kneaded and pressed against specially constructed boards at the sides of the container; stirring, which is effected by half-circle turns in the water, and suction by means of inverted cups. There is no complicated mechanism to get out of order.

Electric washers tended to be more simply explained by their manufacturers:

The clothes are put into the already prepared soapy water, the switch is turned on, and at the end of fifteen or twenty minutes the first batch of clothes is removed and another put into the boiler. The same water will wash four lots of clothes, and one to one and a half hours' work will see the whole of the washing carried out. Rinsing can be done in the same machine, using very hot water. No boiling is necessary.

The wringer which is usually attached to most electrical washing machines is operated from the same switch, so that the clothes can be wrung out directly they leave the washing machine, and deposited in a bowl or basket.

This photograph from *The Housewife's Book* shows the wringer on a washing machine in use.

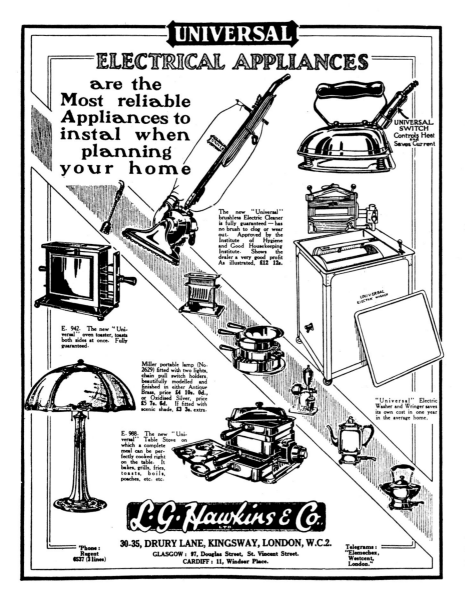

An advertisement for Universal electric appliances showing some of the company's vast range of domestic devices.

Rinsing had to be done several times, first in tepid water – cold water hardens the soap and makes it more difficult to remove – then in cold water. If bed linen faded and began to go dingy, it was bleached, preferably not with a chemical bleach. Best, if you had one, was a garden with lawn and bushes on to which the offending articles could be spread or hung in the sunshine after washing but before rinsing, while the soap was still present. It was pointed out that the washing should be allowed to cool down first, as sheets soaked in boiling water tended to kill lawns and plants. Sheets would be left for some time and then rinsed and dried as normal.

Of course, the clothes line and wooden pegs were by far the most common method for drying washing, but for flats generally, and for other houses in bad weather, other solutions were needed. Traditionally, the clothes horse had been the answer, and so it remained for most people, although it was being replaced by more modern alternatives. A very popular idea in the mid-thirties was the ceiling dryer and airer, an arrangement of half a dozen or so slats of wood, usually about 5 to 6 feet

long, on which the washing could be hung, and which, by means of pulleys, could be hoisted up to the ceiling. The airer had the dual advantage of being out of the way, and also of hanging in the warmest part of the room, thus speeding up the drying process. There were also the tree clothes horse, and the similar radial dryer, which were like smaller indoor versions of the modern rotary clothes line. Other variations to the classic clothes horse included the sliding horse, basically a horse with adjustable sides which could be fitted round a small stove or fire, and an airer that could be attached to the mantelpiece and swung out as a canopy from which the clothes hung over the fire to dry. If you could afford it, there were gas-heated drying and airing cabinets made from white enamelled sheets with an asbestos lining. The clothes were put on to rails which slid in and out for the purpose, and a current of warm air passed through: 'A cabinet like this will dry a heavy week's washing for seven people in three hours. The cupboard can be reloaded with clothes four times during this period and the gas used costs about 4½d.'

Government campaigns often made use of cartoon characters. Mrs Sew-and-Sew fronted the 'Sew and Save' campaign. Here she is with hints for saving linen.

Scrubb's cloudy ammonia saved soap, fuel and labour, and came with a royal seal of approval.

Cleaning Products

Besides soap flakes for laundry, solid bars of soap were used, usually rubbed directly into dirty areas such as collars and cuffs. Soda was used as a softener, and also for dealing with coarse and very greasy articles, such as floor cloths. Salt was used to harden the water and to prevent colours from running; it was usually added to the rinsing water, at about the ratio of one tablespoonful to each quart of water. Vinegar was also used for this, mixed in the same ratio; it was also recommended for restoring faded colours. Ammonia was used for washing wool or flannel articles as it did not need rubbing in and therefore avoiding damage to the clothes. However, it was stressed that only a small amount was needed.

Blue, or dolly blue, was used to make whites whiter. This was a substance made from indigo or ultramarine, and was put into the water in which articles were rinsed, giving them a slight blue tint which countered yellowing. Some manufacturers produced it in small blue bags, one of which was put in with the rinsing water. The best quality was block blue, which came in a larger bag that was swished about in the water until the right shade of blue was achieved. Different items needed different amounts of blue; table linen needed very little, towels far more.

GETTING INTO A LATHER

During the war soap, including granulated soap, and soap powder was rationed, and people were encouraged to save fuel. In 1943 women's magazines carried ads for 'Mazo – the new wonder washing tablets – puts extra pep in your soap – gives extra suds – heaps more lather. What's more, it adds more lather to your favourite soap.' By 1944, Mrs Sew-and-Sew, the character used to front the Government's 'Make Do and Mend' campaign, was advising: 'If you wash at home, never boil dirt in. Soak it out in cold suds first.' Rinso soap powder carried on with the theme, their ads showing harassed housewives trying to keep the washing clean while working in the factory or as a warden, with no time to boil the copper:

'Surely you don't boil?'

'Of course! You can't get things clean otherwise.'

'But you can! Soak them in Rinso suds for 12 minutes. Then wash through and rinse. Try it – you'll be through in no time!'

An advert for Rinso, from *Picture Post*, August 1944.

Each item had to be dipped into the water individually to ensure a consistent 'blueing' and to avoid patchiness.

The last laundering agent was starch, used for stiffening sheets, shirts, collars, table linen and antimacassars. Starch could be purchased in packets ready for mixing, the best quality being rice starch. It was mixed according to the effect required. For heavy stiffening a hot water starch was used, made up of one tablespoonful of white starch and one teaspoonful of borax: 'Mix to a thin paste with two or three teaspoonfuls of cold water. Add a few shreds of paraffin wax or white candle, dissolve the borax in a little boiling water, and stir it into the paste until it thickens.' The borax gave the glossy finish you see in the old shirt collars and cuffs, and the wax stopped the iron sticking. As an alternative to adding wax, the mixture might be stirred with a white candle while it was still hot.

Cold water starch was made from two tablespoonfuls of starch mixed up with a tablespoonful of boiling water in which a little borax had been dissolved. Two pints of cold water, to which a few drops of turpentine might be added, were mixed in. This had to be made up about half an hour before use. Of course, the starch powder could be used on its own, where a high finish to the ironing was not necessary. In these cases, the starch could be added to the blue water, or a blue starch could be used, which did both tasks together.

Dry Cleaning

It was quite common at this time to do dry cleaning at home. Fabrics recommended for home dry cleaning included artificial silk, satin, velours and velvets, as well as felt or velour hats, woollen and knitted sports suits and costumes. Small articles could be put in a screw-topped jar filled with petrol and gently shaken up and down until clean. 'Larger articles should be placed in a pail of petrol covered by a wooden box lid with a hole in the centre, through which the handle of a small vacuum washer, or a rubber suction cap is inserted. This handle should be worked up and down for five to six minutes until all the dirt has been pressed out.' Once war was declared, petrol was the first thing to be rationed so this form of cleaning disappeared, which is probably just as well.

Dry agents for the home included Fuller's earth powder and bran, which was used for all types of fur, cretonnes, repps and furnishing fabrics. Bran was especially recommended for furs and other coats. It was heated thoroughly, rubbed vigorously into the material to be cleaned, then brushed and shaken out, taking the dirt with it. Suede could be cleaned with a 'cloth ball', which came in a wide range of colours.

Many home remedies were used to remove stains, including lemon juice and salt for rust or fruit stains, ammonia for blood or grass stains, turpentine for paint or tar, borax for tea, and even hydrochloric or oxalic acid for some stubborn stains. All of them needed to be diluted with water, and could not be used without great care, trying a test patch first.

SHOPPING

As well as keeping the house spick and span, the woman of the 1940s would probably be solely responsible for the shopping, and this part of everyday life is one in which some of the greatest changes have taken place over the last fifty years. In wartime, there were no supermarkets or out-of-town shopping complexes. Instead, people went to small, specialist shops – the greengrocer, fishmonger, ironmonger, and so on – in the local High Street.

While the lucky few might own a refrigerator, there were certainly no freezers. Food, then, would be bought in smaller amounts so as to keep fresh, which in turn meant that shopping was done more often. Home deliveries were commonplace; the butcher's or baker's boys using their trade bikes, with large baskets on the front, were an everyday sight, taking the weekly deliveries to the suburban housewife, who had often ordered over the telephone.

There were some larger shops, such as Woolworth's and Sainsbury's, and large department stores like Harrods or John Lewis. But these were in town or city centres and were used on special occasions, when the whole family might make a day of it. Everyday shopping was done at the local parade of shops or the market, where not only goods but also the latest gossip and news of the war changed hands.

It was this regular shopping that was the basis of the food rationing system, which arrived in 1940 (see Chapter Five). Consumers had to register with their local supplier – you could not buy rationed food wherever you chose. Having regular customers meant that shops would know very accurately how much of these shortage foods they would need each week, and could themselves be supplied with the correct amount, meaning that wastage was extremely small, and that everyone was able to get their fair share.

Some electric gadgets continued to be available during the war, but were difficult to get. This advert for fridges and washers dates from March 1942.

TAKING A BREAK

A busy grocery department in a wartime store. (Imperial War Museum)

By the mid-thirties fashion emphasised health, sun-bathing and even naturism, and exercise was considered important for health and beauty. However, rather than taking a break from the housework in order to participate in an enjoyable sporting pastime, housework, somewhat depressingly, was itself presented as an opportunity for healthy activity:

> Properly done, housework can become an important health factor. Most house-workers are muscle-lazy, and therefore do not experience the joy of feeling muscles working as smoothly and harmoniously as when playing tennis or golf.
>
> Scrubbing is a good example, as it gives an opportunity for the worker to exercise the deep muscles of the back, waist and abdomen – muscles which directly affect health and vitality, and are, as a rule, sadly neglected.

There were limits as to how much one could treat housework as leisure. For example, every magazine or house-management book spoke of the vacuum cleaner as an absolute necessity. By this time, cleaners came with an array of attachments: soft and hard brushes, flattened tubes, and 'The blower attachment . . . [which] . . . can also be used in an emergency to dry clothes or hair'!

The suburban woman of the thirties was often involved in voluntary or charity work. She might also take up activities at home such as rug-

The natural rhythmic use of the body will – if practised – turn housework from jerky, wearing activity into health-giving exercise.

The woman of today is not a slave to her house, the care of it takes its proper place in her day; she has time for other and perhaps more congenial work, pleasures, and hobbies.

The Carnell Girl shows you how simple it is to make a rug. Just a needle, rug design and ball of wool.

'The simple and homely art of rug-making' from *The Woolworker*, 1935. Making your own rugs was a very popular hobby between the wars, but wartime wool shortages meant it became much less common.

WOMEN'S MAGAZINES

Besides specific craft magazines, there were many other magazines aimed specifically at women. Women's magazines had been popular since Victorian times, but these ones were different. They included fiction but also carried articles covering the whole range of home finding, furnishing and decorating, plus gardening, crafts, fashion and health. New women's magazines included *Good Housekeeping* (first edition 1922), *Woman and Home* (1926), *Wife and Home* (1929), *Harpers Bazaar* (1929), *Woman's Own* (1932), *Woman's Illustrated* (1936) and *Woman* (1937).

making or embroidery. Once again, an increasing number of books and magazines catered for these interests. The *Woolworker* included instructions and plans for making blankets, rugs, cushion covers, beadwork, and for embroidery and knitting.

DIY AND REPAIRS

Home ownership meant that people were far more likely, through interest or financial necessity, to do repairs and redecoration themselves. The vast increase in owner-occupiers added to the British scene a new set of pastimes which had once been the domain of a privileged few – gardening, furnishing, decorating, and maintaining the fabric of their property. But those who had previously been able to afford these things had also been able to afford the staff to do them. Now the fashion was towards 'Do It Yourself' and a plethora of books and new magazines were published to help the householder.

Work, a 'weekly journal for amateur mechanics' was advertised with the words: 'Knowing how to do "odd jobs" and repairs, and how to make things for the home, means the saving of expense in many directions. Most men could be handymen but lack the necessary knowledge.' Part works, such as the *Home Mechanic* were popular as were books such as the *Home Workshop* and the *Handy Man and Home Mechanic*. Manufacturers did not

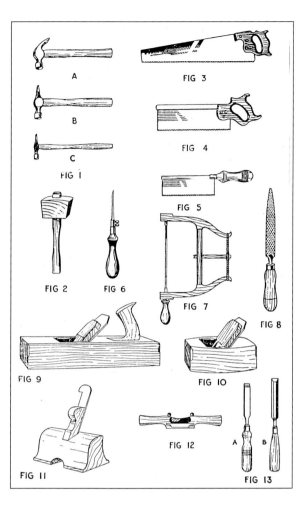

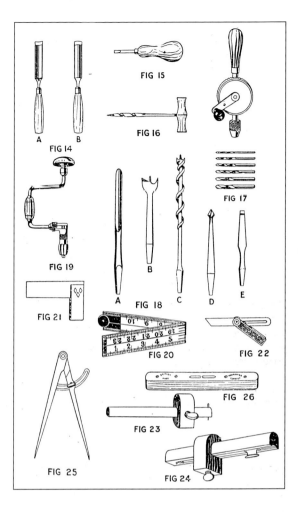

fail to see the potential market, so many tools and materials became far more 'user friendly', and the range of goods available grew.

Illustrations from *The Handyman & Home Mechanic* showing some of the tools required by the DIY practitioner.

Painting

One of the big drawbacks was that many of the tasks that a lot of us do today almost as a matter of course, such as painting and paper-hanging, were far more complicated then because materials and tools were more rudimentary. Nowadays, the most difficult thing about repainting is choosing from the colours available. This extract from a 1922 handbook – *House Painting and Decorating* – makes clear some of the problems facing the twenties DIY enthusiast:

A paint must have a 'base'. There is no base or pigment easier to use than white lead, and allowing all the virtues claimed for zinc oxide, it is an open question whether the latter surpasses white lead for undercoats. Only the best white lead should always be bought, and the easiest way to ensure getting the proper article is to purchase from a firm of repute. There are several methods of testing white lead to see if it contains adulteration or reduction; but for practical purposes there is nothing better than rubbing a little of the lead in equal parts of linseed oil and turpentine, and coating a piece of glass and a piece of black-painted board. Hold the

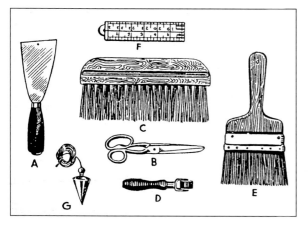

Illustrations from *The Handyman & Home Mechanic* showing some of the tools required by the home decorator.

glass up to the light to test the fineness of the particles, remembering that a finely ground paint is usually a good covering paint. Test on the black board for hiding qualities. If these tests are made side by side with a sample of white lead of known quality, the worker will be fairly well able to judge the quality of his purchase. Of course, for ordinary painting, paste white and not dry white lead is used.

The base needs to be mixed with a 'vehicle' – raw linseed oil – and thinned with turpentine, or a turpentine substitute. It may be tinted with a second pigment, and a further addition is a 'drier' to assist drying. The drying of a paint is not a simple evaporation ; it is actually an oxidisation. The driers may be paste, known as patent driers, or terebine frequently called liquid driers. The same thing applies to these as to the lead; they should be bought from a reliable source.

With such complicated rules and regulations, we would not be surprised if most people gave up!

Wallpapering

Cotterell Brothers Ltd, Bristol, produced wallpapers and paints. Their catalogues contained examples of their designs along with the prices for each wallpaper.

The main differences in the art of wallpapering were that cracks in the wall were normally filled with plaster of Paris, or a slow-setting mixture called Keene's cement, and that paper normally came with a border that was either used for an overlap, or was cut off for butt fixing. The basic tools were the same as we would use today; scissors, brushes and seam-rollers. Another example of how things were made easier for the do-it-yourselfer was the introduction of improved wallpaper paste: 'Making the paste used to be quite a work of art in itself, for you mixed flour and cold water to make a cream and then added boiling water which invariably turned it lumpy. After that you strained out the lumps and used what was left. But now [1940] you can buy specially prepared packets to make what is called cold-water paste.'

Wartime DIY

In December 1940 the Ministry of Home Security issued a leaflet 'After the Raid', with advice for those whose homes had been hit:

Compensation for Damage to Houses. If you own your own house or hold it on a long lease and it is damaged or destroyed, whatever your income, you should, as soon as possible, make a claim on form VOW1. The amount of your compensation and the time of paying it will depend on the passing of the War Damage Bill now before Parliament.

Repairs. If your house can be made fit to live in with a few simple repairs the local authority will put it right if the landlord is not able to do it. But how quickly the local authority can do this depends on local conditions.

The *Daily Express* book *War Time Household Repairs* said, 'Unless you are in financial difficulties no payment will be made until after the war has ceased.' It pointed out that 'Most of the houses which suffer as a result of raids are made uncomfortable rather than dangerous and, if you are by nature a handy person, you will want to set about making the place once more habitable. Temporary or urgent repairs may be done immediately, but others of a permanent nature should be started on only with the permission of the surveyor's department.'

Estimates of the numbers of houses damaged by raids during the war ranged between one-third and one-fifth of all the houses in the country, although many of these suffered only from broken glass or missing roof tiles. Materials were scarce, but even more scarce were the skilled craftsmen, so there could be a long wait for work to be done. The Government therefore encouraged people to do their own repairs whenever possible.

In some of the worst hit boroughs, emergency materials could be obtained at air raid wardens' posts. *War Time Household Repairs* suggested one solution: 'In any kind of temporary repair the great thing is to use makeshift materials that already exist in the home and to buy as little new material as possible.'

One material in short supply was glass; millions of panes were damaged by enemy action and there was a real famine of sheet glass. The recommended temporary repair was to use an old bed sheet cut

---

DEVASTATION

The devastation of the war continued for years, although the source of that destruction changed as the conflict progressed. By September 1944 a new threat had arrived – the V weapons. V1 flying bombs and V2 rockets each carried about a ton of explosives and could completely flatten several houses, shatter windows and damage roofs over a large area. The destruction they caused was significant; of 84,000 houses destroyed in London throughout the war, 23,000 were destroyed by V weapons.

The suburbs were not always places of safety – this 'bungalow' is all that remains of a detached house in Bromley after a German raid in November 1940. (Bromley Local Studies Library)

AVOID WINDOWS IN A RAID
Wall space between windows offers good protection,
for here one is out of range of broken glass and
splinters.

In an air raid, flying glass could be lethal. This diagram was part of early advice on the subject; like many of the early directions, it was not particularly practical.

Emergency repair materials were available from suppliers such as this one, advertised in the *Bath Chronicle and Herald*, May 1942.

slightly larger than the broken panes (if a window included several broken panes there was no need to mend each one individually). The piece of sheet should then be spread out on a table and painted on one side with any vegetable oil, as with paint. When it was dry and the last of the broken glass removed, the sheet was to be tacked on to the window frame, oiled side out. One-inch wide strips of cardboard were then to be tacked round the edge of each pane or gap to give strength to the repair. Although rather makeshift, this did at least keep the wind out, while allowing quite a lot of light in. It was not, however, very secure, and if the hole was large enough, or in such a position that a burglar might use it – a common problem with houses left unoccupied during raids – then the gap should be filled with plywood or, failing this, with a piece of linoleum.

'Make Do and Mend'

As do-it-yourself had become popular in many suburban homes during the inter-war years, so the wartime concept of 'Make Do and Mend' was almost a natural progression. This popular wartime phrase is actually only a variation of a pre-war phrase, 'Make and Mend', used in the 1939 *News Chronicle* do-it-yourself book, *Modern Make and Mend*.

Many today think of the phrase purely in terms of clothing, but in fact its scope was much broader, covering almost every aspect of everyday life, repairing or making things yourself, and thereby saving the scarce resources of materials and manpower. Like several other household books of the time, *Modern Make and Mend* dealt with most of the standard wartime themes in terms of minor house repairs – for example, faulty ball-cocks and cracks in ceilings – as well as household repairs such as fixing vacuum cleaners and electric irons. It also covered building new items, such as a cooker hood (another surprisingly old idea), plate racks and airing cupboards, and contained sections on mending shoes, 'how to press a suit', and Air Raid Precautions in the home.

One feature of 'Make Do and Mend' was handmade gifts for Christmas and birthdays. Many magazines had ideas such as knitting patterns for dolls' clothes and instructions for making babies' rattles out of old coffee tins. Inevitably, books were produced on the subject, two of which were *Gifts You Can Make Yourself* and *Rag-Bag Toys*. Among other things, these books described how to make toys from scrap; a teddy bear from a 'moth-eaten motor rug', and dolls from 'your old hat', or even an old swimsuit or stockinette undies. Other ideas included crocheted dolls' house furniture (weird but true), necklaces made from old buttons, knitted slippers, and a handbag made from knotted string.

'Sew and Save'

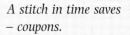

The 'Make Do and Mend' scheme included the 'Sew and Save' campaign. Like the 'Food Front' campaign, it was supported in newspaper articles, and these regularly featured Mrs Sew-and-Sew, a rag doll. She would demonstrate how to turn old clothes into new clothes, a lady's dress into two children's frocks, last year's cocktail dress into a new summer outfit and so on. A fair amount of skill was often needed and many families dreaded receiving the latest efforts from a well-meaning relative.

As with 'Make Do and Mend', the 'Sew and Save' campaign consisted of far more than merely encouraging the re-use of old clothes. The *Daily Mail*'s book *Sew and Save* advised on how to repair ladders in stockings (very hard to replace), looked at taking care of your existing clothes and making the most of your coupons by planning your wardrobe, and had handy hints for its readers such as what to do with your shoes if caught in the rain: 'Never dry them in front of a fire. Stuff them immediately with newspaper and leave them in a dry atmosphere.'

If making new clothes, advice was freely available on how to choose the best materials, which tools were needed, and how to get the best ones. One tip described how to sharpen scissors 'by opening the blades against the neck of a strong glass bottle, and then closing them slowly as if trying to cut the neck off the bottle'.

The range of items that could be made by hand was huge. For example, one magazine article gave instructions on how to make 'An extra pair of coupon-free sandals, tough enough for garden wear'. These were made with rope soles, and required about 5 yards of clothes line or thin rope, 2 oz of dishcloth cotton, half a yard of cotton fabric, (which could be in odd pieces), a bodkin and some wadding.

Below, left: Women's magazines carried articles on making clothes last longer. This advice is from the May 1943 issue of *Housewife*, and explains invisible mending for laddered stockings, which were very difficult to replace.

Below: A Singer sewing machine advertisement. The wartime activities suggested by the 'Sew and Save' and 'Make Do and Mend' campaigns were certainly not new to many working-class and lower middle-class housewives who had always made their own clothes and furnishings.

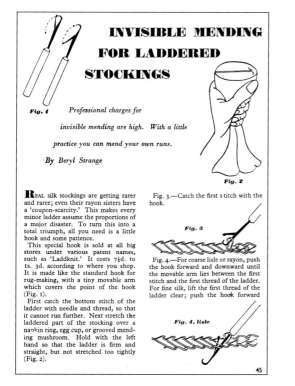

Some companies got in on the act too. To make men's trousers last, one company produced the 'Trouser bottom protectors'. These did not, as you might think, protect the seat, but the bottom of the legs – what the Americans call the trouser cuff. These protectors consisted of four leather strips, each about 3 inches long by a half an inch wide, punched with pairs of holes about every three-quarters of an inch. These were then stapled to either side of the inside of the end of each leg, to stop them wearing against the shoes. They were also sewn on to Utility trousers, which had no turn-ups.

Running Repairs

During the war the paper shortage affected the supply of wallpaper, and, like clothes, the operative phrase became 'Make Do and Mend'. People were reminded that many papers were washable but it was advisable to test first using a small area normally covered by a picture, or behind a piece of furniture that rested against the wall. Even if the paper was washable, people were cautioned not to use soap, just a small amount of water (too much could cause the paper to bubble or lift) and to dab rather than scrub. Papers unsuitable for washing could be cleaned with bread, neither so fresh as to be crumbly nor so stale as to break up. Alternatively, an India rubber could be used or, in the case of a grease mark, benzine, painted on and the excess removed with blotting paper.

Scratches could be painted over with carefully mixed water paint. Any holes in the plaster could be filled in with Keene's cement, having first carefully peeled back the paper, and the paper pasted back over once the cement was dry. Large areas of damaged paper could be patched with off-cuts of the paper (if the owners were wise enough to keep them at the time of decoration – manuals from the period always advised you to do so). If you had no spare paper, a patch could be cut out from behind a piece of furniture. Should the paper be patterned, the cuts should be made around the pattern; if there were no pattern, the piece should be cut irregularly, as it would then be far less visible: 'When the patch has dried the thickness of the paper may show as a white edging. You can tone this down by running a pencil along it.'

For distempering a wall, *War Time Household Repairs* recommended stippling. It points out that most amateur attempts at using distemper finish up patchy, and stippling is the best way to cover this up. Stippling brushes were expensive, but it suggested that 'a very reasonable substitute is one of the flat brushes with an arched handle that housewives use for polishing fire grates'. It continues: 'Stippling is really a job for two people. While one applies the distemper the other almost immediately dabs it with his short-haired brush. He holds the brush parallel with the wall and brings the hairs up to it squarely.'

FIVE

RATIONING

ONCE BITTEN, TWICE SHY?

During the First World War, Britain and Germany had tried to starve each other out, like two medieval armies. Britain used her superior fleet to blockade the German ports, and Germany with her U-Boat fleet (*Untersee-Boot*; submarine) attacked supply vessels. It had been a close-run thing and the lessons were not forgotten. Rationing was introduced in 1916, but with hindsight it was seen that this was a mistake – it should have been introduced before then. Food prices had risen by 60 per cent, and those less well-off had complained of shortages and hoarding by the rich. It was precisely these conditions and complaints that had led to civil unrest and Communist uprisings in Russia and Germany. The British Government was determined that another war should not mean that this country would suffer the same fate. But during the twenties and early thirties the momentum for action was lost as Britain slipped into complacency. After all, 'the war to end all wars' had surely convinced everyone that another European war was unthinkable. People were jolted out of their complacency by the Munich Crisis in 1938, and they began, somewhat belatedly, to prepare themselves and their houses for war.

Food rationing was to have the greatest impact on the population, and rationing and restrictions were not just about shortages of foodstuffs and raw materials. More and more men were needed for the services, while at the same time industrial output had to increase to meet wartime needs. So, from the very beginning of the war, the production of non-essential consumer goods began to be restricted.

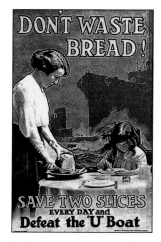

Rationing was not a new idea. This poster from the First World War encourages people to save bread to help defeat the U-boats.

A HEAVY PRICE

As expected, from the very beginning Germany set out to starve Britain into submission. Within hours of the declaration of war, the liner *Athena* was sunk by a U-boat. Even through the Phoney War, during the winter of 1939, while so little was happening elsewhere, Britain's Merchant Navy was battered by U-Boats and surface raiders. Losses were so heavy that the Government suppressed the figures. Almost 200,000 tons of shipping went down each month in September, October and December 1939, with a slight decrease to about 160,000 tons in November. January and February 1940 stayed at about 200,000 tons again, dropping back to about 100,000 in March and April. Then in May there was a steep increase, followed by another in June to over a half a million tons. For the next year, the average losses in these Merchant Navy convoys were about 400,000 tons a month, peaking at almost 600,000 tons in April 1941. Worse, the fall of so many European countries and Italy's entry into the war robbed Britain of several of our largest food suppliers.

Consequently, the home front moved into a long period of shortages which, in a good many instances, lasted long after the war. Compared with September 1939, supplies of consumer goods were down one-third by May 1940, two-thirds by May 1941 and three-quarters by November that year. Some supplies were even worse, such as newsprint, the supply of which was down 81 per cent over this period.

FOOD RATIONING

In November 1939, it was announced that food rationing was to commence in January. People had to register with a supplier. This Co-operative Society leaflet is advising people of the importance of registering (at one of their stores, of course!).

Showing unusual foresight, the Government had actually begun to make plans several years before the outbreak of the Second World War. In 1936 the Board of Trade had set up a Food (Defence Plans) Department, which had made preparations for a coming war, laying in national stocks of non-perishable foodstuffs such as sugar and wheat, and splitting up the country into fifteen administrative divisions. Every local council had to appoint a food executive officer. The department drew up the outlines of a national rationing scheme, and blank ration books were prepared as early as 1938.

The following sections describe how food rationing was controlled and what effects it had on the public between 1939 and 1943.

1939

As world peace began to look more and more fragile, one of the questions that arose was whether it was a wise precaution to lay in a store, or was it hoarding, which was selfish and unpatriotic? On 2 February 1939 the President of the Board of Trade told Parliament, 'I see no objection to the accumulation by householders in peace time of small reserves of suitable foodstuffs equivalent to about one week's normal requirements.' He went even further, 'Household reserves of this kind would constitute a useful addition to the total stocks of the country.' So it was not only all right, it was the act of responsible citizens.

Several publications and articles followed, full of suggestions as to the best foods to store. The Canned Foods Advisory Bureau issued a booklet, *ARP home storage of food*, which was produced for public distribution early in 1939. It was therefore no secret that rationing was to be introduced. When it eventually came, in January 1940, it was far less stringent than everyone had expected.

One of the innumerable booklets and leaflets produced during the war to advise people on making the best of food rationing.

The booklet suggested several lists, mostly of canned foods, with menus and recipes for their use. Non-canned foods included flour, tea, cocoa, coffee, sugar, cereals, baby and invalid foods and dried fruit. These were to be stored in metal containers with tightly fitting lids. The lists of food were differentiated by cost, with suggested lists costing 5s, 10s and £1. It also gave a recommended list for feeding a family of four, three meals a day, for a week. It worked on the basis that 'the Nation would be immediately rationed with a limited supply of meat, butter, cheese, milk, flour, tea, sugar, potatoes and cereals'. This was an overly pessimistic supposition; some of these items were never rationed. The list continued:

four large cans of thick soup, one large can of herrings or kippers, one small can of sardines or Brisling, a one-pound can of salmon, one can of herrings or cod roe or one pound of sausages, one sixteen-ounce can of meat roll or galantine, one twelve-ounce can of corned beef, two large cans of baked beans in sauce, two medium cans of peas, one medium can of spinach, one medium can of carrots, one medium can of tomatoes or tomato puree, one medium can of macédoine of vegetables, one large can of plums or apricots, one medium can of blackcurrants, one sixteen-ounce can of prunes, one small can of evaporated milk, a one-pound can of cooking fat (lard, suet or dripping).

The August 1939 edition of *Ideal Home* magazine contained an article on 'Emergency Preparations'. It said that stocking food:

should be done now and not left until an emergency arises, and no one will think you an alarmist or a hoarder if you store enough food to provide the family with sufficient and well-balanced meals for a week to ten days. . . .
   A good general rule . . . is to transfer some tins to the larder each week and replace them so that the freshest possible food is available in the event of an emergency.'

Besides a similar list to the one above, the magazine article added: two large cans of spaghetti, four cans of milk pudding, one can of steamed sponge pudding, eight large cans of unsweetened evaporated milk, two medium cans of cream, one can of coffee or cafe au lait, two cans of jam or marmalade, two one-pound cans of butter, and a one-pound can of cheese. It continued: 'In addition to the above, McDougall's flour can be bought in large cans, and Ryvita Crispbread is available in sealed tins, so that with a good supply of tea and sugar (kept in Clamptite metal containers) one could be completely independent of outside food supplies.' It is surprising not only that goods were available which we might have assumed to be modern (crispbread, tinned beans and spaghetti) and that the range of items sold in cans included cheese, flour and butter, but also that 'product placement' is not new.

On 8 September 1939 the Government set up a new ministry, the Ministry of Food (MoF), under W.S. Morrison MP. To prevent profiteering, prices of the most important foods were to be controlled and straightaway the MoF issued the first in a series of lists setting out the maximum retail price for eggs, butter, condensed milk, sugar, canned salmon, flour, potatoes and dried fruits. Fresh fruit, on the other hand, was never subject to such controls, which led to some amazing prices being charged for exotic fruit; in the summer of 1944, for example, pineapples were on sale for 5 guineas (£5 5s) each.

The Squander Bug, created for the National Savings Campaign, was a bad influence, encouraging people to waste money on things they did not need, instead of buying National Savings Certificates.

A TAXING TIME

Sir John Simon, the Chancellor, introduced his War Budget on 27 September 1939. Income tax was set at 7s 6d in the pound, and there were increases on duty; a penny each on a pint of beer, a packet of cigarettes and a pound of sugar, and 1s 6d on a bottle of whisky. Apart from the sugar, on which a tax seems very odd today, the rest of the list is depressingly familiar. The increase the tax represented was actually very high; taxes and war insurance added between 10 and 30 per cent to the cost of most items. Still, there was little protest, either from Parliament or the public.

On 21 October 1940 purchase tax was introduced for many goods, at rates varying from 16 to 33 per cent. There was a two-fold reason for this; first, it was designed to cut back consumption and, secondly, it would bring in desperately needed revenue.

In the April 1941 budget the Chancellor, Sir Kingsley Wood, raised basic income tax from 8s 6d to 10s in the pound, and super tax to 19s 6d in the pound.

In May 1943 purchase tax went up once more; to 100 per cent on certain luxury items.

REGISTRATION DAY

On Friday 29 September 1939 the entire nation was registered; every house-holder had to fill in a form giving details of everyone who lived in the house. Next day these forms were collected, and the collectors filled in an identity card for everyone, man, woman and child.

Issuing the first ration books, based on the National Registration ID cards, was a massive task. (Imperial War Museum)

Using the information gleaned from the National Registration, ration cards were prepared for everyone in the country, and these were issued from the second week in November 1939. To get a ration card, or to exchange your old one, your identity card had to be produced and stamped on the back with an MoF stamp.

During the course of the war, separate books were issued for different items and the introduction of a furniture ration book in 1943 brought the number to four: petrol, food, clothes and furniture. Ration books were a vital part of family life, and there was a thriving trade in forged or stolen books.

The MoF also took control of all food imports, and at first made attempts to introduce standard brands of margarine and tea but there was an outcry against this, especially over tea. A standard margarine was sold at 6*d* per lb, containing vitamins A and D to bring it up to the vitamin value of butter, but soon the proprietary brands were back on the shelves again.

On 1 November 1939 it was announced that butter, which was by this time a pooled blend called 'National Butter', and bacon (including ham) would be the first foodstuffs to be rationed but not before the middle of December. In the meantime, everyone was asked to register themselves with a retailer of their choice. The MoF broadcast that: 'The ration for both bacon and butter will be four ounces per week for every individual consumer, i.e. one pound of bacon and one pound of butter for a family of four persons.' He went on to say that if consumption of sugar was kept to 1 lb a week per head, then there would be no need for it to be rationed for some months, but once again, consumers were asked to register with a supplier. There was little commotion as everyone had expected and talked about rationing for some time.

In fact, rationing was a very popular idea, especially among the poor who knew that, otherwise, in times of shortage, they would be the ones to suffer most. A 'free-for-all' on limited supplies would have been anything but, as wartime prices soared. During the First World War, the Government had been reluctant to introduce rationing and had eventually done so only in February 1918.

Early rations, including 'National Butter', and a ration book. (Imperial War Museum)

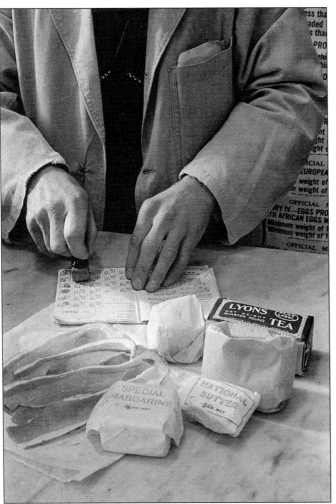

By that time, the Government faced civil unrest as prices soared and many of those that could afford to, bought and hoarded as much food as they could. Pressure from the right wing held up the introduction of rationing: this kind of 'fair shares for all' was sometimes known as 'war socialism' and was therefore not popular with them. Now, however, even they only grumbled a bit; this was less than had been expected and later than had been expected.

On 29 November 1939 Mr Morrison announced that rationing would begin on 8 January 1940. On 28 December it was further announced that sugar was also to be included on 8 January, and the ration was set at 12 oz a week for each person. This was, of course, below the level the Minister had spoken of, but, as he said in his statement, 'Sugar is an important and convenient source of energy, but the same energy is available in alternative foods, especially in potatoes and other vegetables which provide valuable protective elements as well.' Here is a second feature of the MoF's work. They not only tried to preserve supplies by rationing, but also promoted healthy eating by encouraging consumers to convert to more readily available alternatives.

1940

The year began with the introduction of rationing; people were, on the whole, quite resigned to it. After all, they had had one ration-free Christmas, and not too many had expected that. Ration books were to be issued; at first eight categories were envisaged:

Making the rations stretch – an ever-increasing problem. (Imperial War Museum)

General, for adults and children over six.

A child's book for those under six.

Travellers, for use by salesmen, lorry drivers, actors, etc.

Adolescent supplementary, for boys (not girls) between thirteen and eighteen – these contained extra meat coupons.

A heavy worker's supplementary, also with extra meat coupons.

A seaman's weekly ration book.

An emergency book for those bombed-out.

A service personnel book for use while on leave.

In the event, the adolescent boy's and heavy worker's supplementaries were not issued. Each category had its own colour, the main two being buff for the general book, and blue for the children's. All contained coupons for the rationed foods, plus further coupons for meat and cooking fats.

Once the ration book had been received, the consumer was to register with a supplier for each of the rationed items. The supplier then removed a counterfoil from the book which allowed him to apply to the local Food Officer

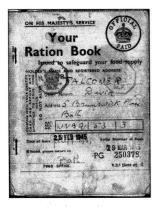

A ration book issued in February 1945.

for a warrant to buy the necessary supplies to cover all his customers. The customers could then receive amounts of these foods on production of the relevant coupons, and of course, the appropriate money. Babies, young children, expectant and nursing mothers also received orange juice, cod liver oil, and extra milk through the welfare system. Children often hated taking the cod liver oil, but resourceful mothers found a use for it after July, when cooking fats went 'on the ration'.

The rationing scheme was more successful than the Government had hoped – it even began to produce surpluses. In the middle of January certain types of bacon could be sold without coupons and, by the end of the month, the ration for bacon had been doubled to 8 oz.

Meat became subject to shortages, and was rationed from 11 March. This was not by weight, which would have been impossible given all the different cuts and animals but by value. The ration was 1s 10d worth per person, per week (half for children under six), although this did not include sausages. As the war went on even sausages became harder to get and, on the whole, it was probably best not to guess at what they contained – if you were lucky, they might include meat!

So how much did you get with the meat ration? In January 1940, 1s 10d would buy you almost 3 lb of beef, pork or mutton, or 2 lb of stewing steak, or about five pork chops; by 1942, the meat ration was down by almost a half.

On 3 April Mr Morrison became Minister of Shipping and his old position of Minister of Food was taken by Lord Woolton, Frederick Marquis, a well-known businessman after whom the 'Woolton Pie' was named.

Along with growing food and rationing food, a third campaign was

LORD WOOLTON PIE

Potato, swede, cauliflower and carrot make a good mixture.

Take 1 lb of them, diced, 3 or 4 spring onions, if possible, 1 teaspoonful vegetable extract and 1 tablespoonful of oatmeal. Cook together for 10 minutes with just enough water to cover. Stir occasionally to prevent the mixture from sticking.

Allow to cool, put into a pie dish, sprinkle with chopped parsley and cover with a crust of potato or wheatmeal pastry.

Bake in a moderate oven until the pastry is nicely browned and serve hot with a brown gravy. Enough for 4 or 5.

The ingredients of Woolton Pie could be adapted to fit what was available at the time. This was reflected in the name, which varied from the socialist sounding 'Woolton Pie', through 'Lord Woolton Pie', to the almost messianic 'The Lord Woolton Pie'. The original recipe was, in fact, created by the chef at the Savoy Hotel, who called it 'Lord Woolton's Vegetable Pie'.

The difference mentioned in this advert is the addition of 'flavoursome, appetising and nourishing' Vita-Gravy. Many of the recipes recommended by the Ministry were wholesome but boring, so sauces, pickles and gravies were often used in (not always succesful) attempts to perk them up.

promoted nationally – 'Food is a Munition of War'. This was about making the most of food and not wasting it. Along with other ministries, the MoF began to appeal directly to the public through the newspapers. This took the form of 'Food Facts', notes and hints for the housewife. The first was a message from Lord Woolton:

> This is the emblem of the Ministry of Food. It is the banner under which you, too, are fighting; helping to defeat the enemy's attempt to starve us out.
>
> Through rationing, price control and other measures, the Ministry of Food sees that all get a fair share of essential foods at fair prices.
>
> But nearly half of our food comes across the sea. The U-boats attack our food ships, and although most arrive safely, some are lost.
>
> Now, here is your part in the fight for Victory. When a particular food is not available, cheerfully accept something else – home produced if possible. Keep loyally to the rationing regulations.
>
> Above all – whether you are shopping, cooking or eating – remember 'Food is a Munition of War'. Don't waste it.

The first of many Ministry of Food bulletins: Food is a Munition of War – Don't Waste It. (HMSO)

The MoF also produced War Cookery leaflets, which pointed out that 'potatoes should be eaten in place of bread and other cereals'. Potato pastry could be used instead of ordinary pastry, either for sweet or savoury dishes, and grated potatoes could be used instead of suet. People quickly discovered that pastry cooked with potato suet had to be eaten immediately, as it soon went rock hard. The ministry tried to get people to eat more oatmeal and they encouraged its use in many ways, particularly mixed with diced or minced meat to make it go further.

There were plans to base rations on an idea for a national 'basal' diet. This was to be 1 lb of potatoes, 12 oz of bread, 6 oz of vegetables, 2 oz of oatmeal, 1 oz of fat and just over ½ pint of milk, plus a few small luxuries. The plan was vetoed by Winston Churchill, who was ambivalent about the whole subject; in a letter to Lord Woolton, he wrote: 'The way to lose the war is to try to force the British public into a diet of milk, oatmeal, potatoes etc. washed down on gala occasions with a little lime juice.' It is said that on another occasion Churchill heard that people were complaining about the size of the meat ration and asked why. He was shown a week's ration and remarked that it would be quite enough for him – he thought it was the ration for one meal!

Also in May 1940 – on the 27th – as the news of the military situation worsened, the sugar ration was cut from 12 to 8 oz. The butter ration was halved from 8 to 4 oz on 3 June, and, one week later, the bacon ration likewise was halved from 8 to 4 oz. On the same day, in a move to stop profiteering, another list of articles whose prices had become controlled was published. These included clothes, hardware, furniture and a whole range of household goods. For a short while, extra sugar could be obtained to make jam, so that the summer's fruit crop would not be wasted. You had to undertake to use the extra sugar for jam making but this was, of course, impossible to police.

In July tea was rationed at 2 oz a week, as were cooking fats and margarine.

In September came another huge blow to food distribution. On Saturday 7 September, the London docks were the subject of a massive air raid. Thousands upon thousands of tons of food went up in smoke as warehouses blazed along the whole of the Thames waterfront. There is a

Jam making and fruit bottling made the most of summer surpluses.

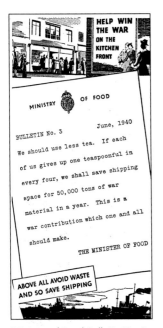

HELP WIN
THE WAR
ON THE
KITCHEN
FRONT

MINISTRY   OF   FOOD

BULLETIN No. 3   June, 1940

We should use less tea. If each
of us gives up one teaspoonful in
every four, we shall save shipping
space for 50,000 tons of war
material in a year. This is a
war contribution which one and all
should make.

                THE MINISTER OF FOOD

ABOVE ALL AVOID WASTE
AND SO SAVE SHIPPING

Ministry of Food Bulletin No. 3.
This was serious – the British
were being encouraged to drink
less tea. Well, it was June 1940
and France was falling. (HMSO)

story that streams of molten sugar ran down the gutters as Tate and
Lyle's warehouses blazed and that, the next day, canny East End
housewives arrived and broke the hardened mass into chunks which they
took home, reboiled and sieved ready for use.

By Christmas 1940 the meat ration, which had actually risen to 2s 2d,
was reduced again to 1s 10d, although for the holiday period tea was
doubled to 4 oz and sugar increased from 8 to 12 oz. The public were
warned that after Christmas further belt-tightening would be necessary.

There would be no more bananas until after the war, no lemons, and no
fresh or tinned fruit would be imported, except a few oranges; the shipping
space was badly needed for war materials. Dried fruit was price controlled
in three categories: dates at 7d per lb maximum; currants, raisins,
sultanas, etc., at 9d per lb; and peaches, apricots, pears, etc., at 1s per lb.

Ration books changed now too. The system had required that the
retailer cut out the coupons from each book. This had taken up vast
amounts of time and was dropped; all the shopkeeper had to do was cross
out the coupons in pen. By now, paper was so short that this had the
added advantage that coupons could be much smaller.

1941

During 1941 the Government took increasing control of what was
manufactured. Variations were ironed out as production was
standardised; the operative words were 'National' and 'Pool'.

One week's rations from 1941,
including points items of
biscuits, chocolate and tea.
(Imperial War Museum)

In February 1941 a standard wholemeal loaf containing 'National Wheatmeal' flour of 85 per cent extraction was introduced. This meant that only 15 per cent of the wheat was discarded as chaff, and the resultant flour was much coarser and browner. At the same time, bread prices were brought under Government control.

After the Christmas holidays, the meat ration was cut again on 6 January, this time to 1s 6d each, and this included meat such as offal, which had previously been 'off ration'. People had hardly started to complain when one week later it was cut again, to 1s 2d. Worse was to come; at the end of March, it fell once more to a mere 1s, though offal was once more placed off ration.

This was the lowest point of food shortages. Even onions became scarce, and the price of fish rocketed to over four times its pre-war level. The Government was forced to bring fish on to the list of price-controlled food. After this, supplies improved as the Navy had more success against the U-boats. Also in March 1940, the first Lend–Lease agreement with the USA came into effect, and the first consignments of food – cheese, canned foods and lard – arrived in May. As well as the usual foods such as tinned sausage meat, there was new and exotic fare such as Spam, Mor (sweetened ham) and Soya flour. The latter caused great confusion; it was not a substitute for wheat flour, but a sweet ingredient.

The arrival of the Lend–Lease goods actually created a problem. Although these new supplies were most welcome, the goods varied and delivery was unsure, so they could not be rationed. The Government could not guarantee that there would be enough for everyone, and rationing was only welcomed by the people on the basis of fair shares for all. The solution was an extension of the personal points system used in clothes rationing. As well as the specified rationed foods that continued to be supplied on a fair shares basis, there were other shortage goods that would be placed 'on points'. Each ration book now contained a number of points coupons (sixteen a month per person); these could be used to obtain any of the goods on points, from any supplier. This had several advantages: it introduced an element of choice in how you spent your rations – you could save them up for luxuries if you wanted – and further, you were not tied to a single supplier and could shop around to see who had anything new in.

Points rationing commenced on 'Points Day' – 1 December 1941. It had been planned for 15 November, but had to be delayed because of a shortage of points goods in the shops; tinned meat, fish and beans were all on points. In February 1942 the number of personal points was raised to twenty a month.

In March 1941 the butter ration was doubled to 4 oz, but in June it went back to 2 oz. Also in March jam, marmalade, syrup and treacle were rationed at 8 oz a month (in total, not each). In June it was announced that the sugar ration would be doubled for the four weeks beginning at the end of June, although on this occasion no undertaking was required that it would be used for jam making, as had been the case the year previously. The MoF arranged for supplies to be delivered to various women's organisations, such as the Women's Institutes, the Townswomen's Guilds and the WVS, for jam making so that fruit would not be wasted.

From 5 May 1941, cheese joined the growing list of rationed foods – a mere 1 oz a week per person was allowed, although this was doubled at

Don't hoard

—not even a little

BOVRIL

An advertisement from November 1941 – Don't hoard. Wartime propaganda leads us still to believe that everyone worked selflessly for the good of the nation; ads like this indicate that this was not always so.

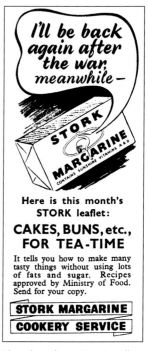

I'll be back again after the war, meanwhile –

STORK MARGARINE

Here is this month's STORK leaflet:

CAKES, BUNS, etc., FOR TEA-TIME

It tells you how to make many tasty things without using lots of fats and sugar. Recipes approved by Ministry of Food. Send for your copy.

STORK MARGARINE
COOKERY SERVICE

This advert from 1944 is really for the latest Stork margarine cookery service leaflet rather than the margarine itself, which was not available. The leaflets offered tips on how to bake without using lots of fats and sugar.

Women's Institute members bottling jams and preserves. The Government encouraged this in order to make maximum use of seasonal fruit harvests. (Imperial War Museum)

the end of June. Many shopkeepers said it was impossible to measure this amount accurately, and issued a month's ration at a time. A special ration of ½ lb of cheese was given to miners and farm workers. Vegetarians could register as such and were given extra cheese instead of meat.

In June 1941 'shell eggs' (the term was used to differentiate fresh eggs from powdered eggs) were rationed; one egg as often as supplies permitted, which averaged out to about three a month. Children, expectant mothers and invalids got more, about twelve a month. Those who kept chickens on a small scale could trade in their egg coupons for chicken meal instead.

On 8 December, the Vitamin Welfare scheme was started; children up to the age of two were given free cod liver oil and blackcurrant puree or syrup. The following year, the latter was replaced by Lease–Lend orange juice, although this had to be paid for.

1942

In March 1942 Lord Woolton announced that all flour production would henceforth be 'National Wheatmeal', although the 'Wheatmeal' part was to be dropped from the title thus creating 'National flour'. 'White' bread would no longer be available. In a reflection of the fashion swings in food, today we would think that this was healthier and, probably, more expensive. However, in the 1940s people thought that good quality bread meant a white, sliced loaf. On 6 April, the sale of white bread became illegal except under special licence. Thus for most people the only bread available was the 'National Wholemeal' loaf or other authorised brown bread.

In March it was declared illegal to hoard more than four weeks' supply of unrationed foodstuffs. Breakfast cereals and condensed milk were put on points, and office tea rations were cut from 1 lb to ½ lb per week for every twenty workers.

In July the tea ration for under fives was abolished, the idea being that it should be replaced by free orange juice, which was far better for them. It is another example of how rationing altered the eating habits of Britain, often for the better.

Then for some, especially children, came one of the worst days of the war. From 26 July 1942, chocolates and sweets were rationed at 2 oz a week; four weeks later it was raised to 3 oz. Special ration-sized chocolate bars were produced, although the milk shortages meant that milk chocolate was not always available, and when it was it was often of poor quality, commonly referred to as 'candle grease chocolate'. Plain chocolate versions of many favourites were produced. Innovative as ever, children found various ways to get round the rationing, buying cough sweets and lozenges which were not rationed.

New, simplified, food ration books came into use at the end of July. Personal points were reduced from 24 to 20, and syrup and treacle, previously part of the preserve ration, were now on points, along with biscuits. At the same time, the cheese ration was temporarily increased to its wartime highest of 8 oz (double for those engaged in heavy work), although this was not to last: that July, the shortage of milk meant that it too was brought under control. As with other basic foods, you now had to register with a supplier, usually the milkman who served your road. Each

A Mars advert which seeks to address sweet rationing. In fact, most children preferrred to use their coupons on smaller boiled sweets, so as to stretch the ration.

Make MARS last longer

CUT IT UP

INTO

SLICES

Every Mars Bar is so richly satisfying in flavour and goodness that — now they are rationed — you'll want to make the most of every one. So cut that chewy, chunky bar into slices and s-t-r-e-t-c-h your enjoyment of it, piece by toothsome piece. **2½ᴰ.**

Mars GRAND FOOD—GRAND FLAVOUR!

road had only a single milkman; choice would have meant a plethora of dairies' floats making deliveries in every street, which would be a waste of fuel and manpower. Thus the various dairies were each allocated their own areas. At the same time, the Government introduced the 'National Milk Scheme', under which small children, and pregnant women, received 1 pint of subsidised milk a day. The scheme was later extended to nursing mothers, adolescents and invalids. What milk remained was to be shared equally among the rest of the milkman's customers, averaging about 3 pints a week. The commercial production of ice-cream and cream from cow's milk was prohibited, and cheese-making dropped to a very low point. Some adventurous souls kept goats for milking, although rarely in their gardens.

In August biscuits were placed on points. Fats were now rationed as a whole, 8 oz in total, with no more than 2 oz of butter. The meat ration stayed at 1s 2d, but 2d of this had to be taken in corned beef.

In the summer of 1942 rationed supplies of powdered egg were made available. A packet, equivalent to twelve eggs, cost 1s 9d, and the ration was about one packet every eight weeks (double that for children under six). The MoF War Cookery leaflet no. 11, on the subject of powdered eggs, included instructions on 'How to

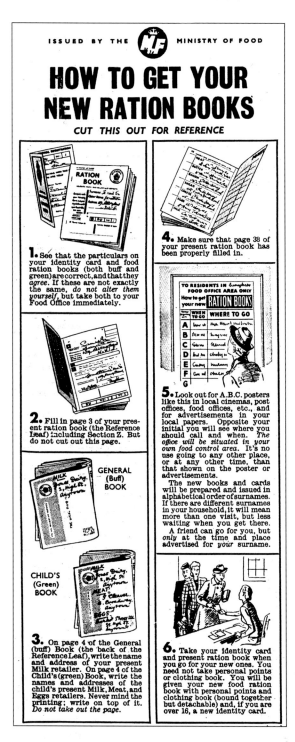

ISSUED BY THE [MF] MINISTRY OF FOOD

HOW TO GET YOUR NEW RATION BOOKS

CUT THIS OUT FOR REFERENCE

1. See that the particulars on your identity card and food ration books (both buff and green) are correct, and that they *agree*. If these are not exactly the same, *do not alter them yourself*, but take both to your Food Office immediately.

2. Fill in page 3 of your present ration book (the Reference Leaf) including Section Z. But do not cut out this page.

GENERAL (Buff) BOOK

CHILD'S (Green) BOOK

3. On page 4 of the General (buff) Book (the back of the Reference Leaf), write the name and address of your present Milk retailer. On page 4 of the Child's (green) Book, write the names and addresses of the child's present Milk, Meat, and Eggs retailers. Never mind the printing; write on top of it. *Do not take out the page.*

4. Make sure that page 38 of your present ration book has been properly filled in.

TO RESIDENTS IN [*Lunyhrm*] FOOD OFFICE AREA ONLY
How to get your new RATION BOOKS

	WHEN TO GO	WHERE TO GO
A		
B		
C		
D		
E		
F		
G		

5. Look out for A.B.C. posters like this in local cinemas, post offices, food offices, etc., and for advertisements in your local papers. Opposite your initial you will see where you should call and when. *The office will be situated in your own food control area.* It's no use going to any other place, or at any other time, than that shown on the poster or advertisements.

The new books and cards will be prepared and issued in alphabetical order of surnames. If there are different surnames in your household, it will mean more than one visit, but less waiting when you get there.

A friend can go for you, but *only* at the time and place advertised for *your* surname.

6. Take your identity card and present ration book when you go for your new ones. You need not take personal points or clothing book. You will be given your new food ration book with personal points and clothing book (bound together but detachable) and, if you are over 16, a new identity card.

A Ministry of Food advert from June 1943 explaining how to get your new ration books. At first, ration books lasted for six months only, but the bureaucracy involved in issuing the entire civilian population with books was so great, as is evident from this advertisement, that this was extended to twelve months. (HMSO)

reconstitute dried egg', and several recipes incorporating dried egg. People were resistant at first, complaining that they were rubbery in texture. However, by 1945, when the supply of powdered eggs dried up (sorry!) with the end of Lease–Lend, there were protests and a great deal of regret.

In November Lord Woolton was made Minister for Reconstruction, being replaced at the Ministry of Food by Colonel Llewellin.

1943

In 1943 the board of Trade announced that in 1942 700,000 clothing books had been replaced having been reported stolen, despite the warnings that books might not be replaced. In August 1943 the board warned once again that lost or stolen coupons would not be replaced and advised the public to keep them in a locked drawer. This also applied to identity cards and, by 1943, the problem had become so acute that between May and July of that year all the old cards were called in and replaced with one in a completely new design, although the old colour scheme of green for adults and buff for under-sixteens still applied.

From July this year, expectant mothers were entitled to three packets of dried egg per month.

FUEL

Petrol was rationed almost from the start of hostilities. On 16 September 1939 branded petrol was replaced by pool petrol, with the price controlled at 1s 6d a gallon. On the 22nd of the same month rationing was announced. Each motorist was allowed between 4 and 10 gallons of petrol a month, depending on the horsepower of the car. A large proportion of the petrol for civil use was set aside for commercial vehicles; this was dyed red to stop it being used by private motorists. Suspect cars would have their petrol inspected by the police. Several ingenious methods were employed to remove the dye, usually involving a type of filtration system and which included passing the petrol through a gas mask filter. The black market thrived on supplying petrol in the first winter of the war. Most motorists knew a friendly garage where petrol could be got without coupons, but at a price – about 6s a gallon, four times the legal cost. The motor industry tried to fight back by introducing new models with low fuel consumption but by the middle of December, half a million cars had been laid up because of rationing and heavy taxation.

In October 1940 the 'free lifts' scheme was brought in. Window stickers were provided by the RAC and AA, and motorists displaying them were entitled to an extra petrol ration. The bicycle reappeared, and other alternative forms of transport were dreamed up. One – the gas-powered car – may well have come straight from the imagination of Heath Robinson. Cars and vans were converted to run on ordinary household gas. The drawback was that a vast amount of gas was needed. This was carried in a large balloon, almost as big as the car itself, which rested in a wooden cradle on the roof. It held the equivalent of just about 1 gallon of petrol and a chain of supply points were set up for refuelling. This delightfully silly scheme came to an end in 1942, when shortages of all types of fuel made it unworkable. In that year, too, even the basic petrol ration was stopped.

Coal was in short supply from as early as November 1939. Like many other manufacturers, Mitchell Russell, who produced stoves, played on the shortages, using patriotism in their advertising: 'It is your National Duty to economise in fuel! Coal goes further with the Courtier Stove.'

By 1941, stocks of fuel were low. There had been suggestions for rationing from the outset but the question was how to accomplish it fairly. Coal could be rationed, but how could this be done for electricity or gas? Targets were set for different fuels, and people were asked to ration themselves. Hints were given here also; eat breakfast in the kitchen, or stop draughts (this was something of a joke to people who had had all their windows blown out – or worse). One useful tip was to cook using a hay-box.

The basic petrol ration was completely stopped in March 1942, and from that date only those who could prove they needed petrol for the war effort, or people such as doctors, were given permits.

The '5 inches of water' campaign encouraged people to use less bath water and so save on fuel, while cutting back on fuels such as gas, electricity and coal was proclaimed as being not only very patriotic for Britain, but also a help for the country's allies. (HMSO)

THE HAY-BOX

These were home-made contraptions. You needed a stout box with a lid, lined with about twenty sheets of newspaper, fastened with drawing pins. Next, about 5 inches of hay was spread in the bottom, and a mattress of hay made, the same size as the box (though not as tall). When a saucepan of soup or stew was hot, it could be placed into the hay-box, straw packed around the sides, the mattress put on top and the lid closed. This kept the food hot, and had the effect of slowly simmering it, without the need to use more fuel of any sort. Another fuel-saving device were half-moon saucepans, two of which could be heated at the same time over the same ring on the cooker.

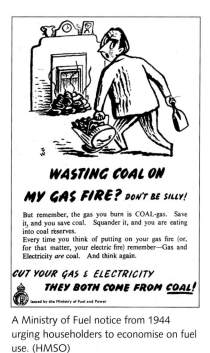

A Ministry of Fuel notice from 1944 urging householders to economise on fuel use. (HMSO)

To save on fuel housewives were encouraged to fill up the whole oven. (Imperial War Museum

Demands on transport became increasingly heavy, and Government controls were extended. Pressure was increased on civilians to refrain from using transport; this included a poster campaign, one of which, Bert Thomas' 'Is your journey really necessary?', was to become one of the most famous posters of the war.

In an attempt to save fuel, in 1942 the Government introduced the 'five inches of water' scheme and being dirty became patriotic! People were encouraged to bath in no more than 5 inches of water to save heating; like many such 'drives' the scheme was accompanied by a short cinema film, in the usual jokey style, featuring a man who had a line marked 5 inches up his leg, so that he could measure his bath water.

Fuel shortages and petrol rationing meant bus travel became a must, and even then, would-be passengers were urged to 'Walk short distances'. The amount of people waiting for buses became huge, and in April queuing became compulsory. Bus and train fares soared to several times their pre-war levels.

RULES ABOUT FUELS

Because of the fuel rationing and shortages during the war, the Government issued several fuel-saving tips:

How To Make Coal Last Longer: Dissolve a tablespoonful of common salt in half a pint of water and sprinkle this over a small scuttleful of coal. The coal will not burn away so quickly and will give a solid red glow.

How To Light a Fire Without Wood: Take a whole sheet of newspaper, roll it from corner to corner, and then roll it round the finger and tuck the end in (neither of the rollings should be tight). Lay the fire (lightly) in the usual way, using about five of these paper 'lighters' for a sitting-room grate, and seven for a kitchen stove.

How To Keep A Fire In: Large lumps of chalk give out a great deal of heat if placed in a fire which has already been started some time. The chalk becomes as red and glowing as coal, and lasts a considerable time, thus saving much firing.

Small coal or slack, sawdust, and clay may be mixed together until they are about as thick as mortar. The mixture should then be moulded into convenient brick-like shapes, afterwards leaving it to dry; or the slack can be mixed with sawdust slightly moistened with paraffin and shaped into balls as big as an orange. You cannot light the fire with such bricks or balls, but they will keep a fire going a long time, and will give out strong heat if placed at the back of a grate with coal in front.

CLOTHES RATIONING

On 1 June 1941 Oliver Lyttelton, President of the Board of Trade, broadcast that clothes rationing would be introduced the following day, followed almost immediately by rationing of furnishing fabrics and carpets. This was accomplished by using twenty-six spare 'margarine' coupons in the food ration books as the first instalment of the sixty-six coupons allotted for the next twelve months of rationing, followed by a card containing forty coupons which was issued at Post Offices in August that year. Unlike food rationing, where each person got the same amount of food, clothes were to be rationed using the points system used by Germany during the First World War. Thus, instead of each person being allowed to buy one pair of shoes every six months, he or she was given a certain amount of points which could be used on any of a number of rationed items. Knitting wool for service comforts, along with uniforms for certain civilian groups such as the Red Cross, and some working clothes were exempted.

The first ration books made specifically for clothes were issued on 1 June 1942. These had grey covers; later versions were in red. They were intended to last until the end of July 1943, although this was later extended until the end of August. They contained sixty coupons; twenty each of green, brown and red. In addition, some people received a supplementary sheet of ten brown coupons (for children or workers in certain jobs), or one or two sheets of ten green coupons for certain older children. But working out who these 'certain older children' were was a real nightmare:

> Children born on or after 1st August 1926 have already had, with their clothing book, a supplementary sheet of ten coupons. To provide for the special needs of those who have grown to a stage where they have to buy most of their clothes in 'full coupon' sizes, the following additional issues will be made later on:– Children born between 1st August and 31st December, 1926 (inclusive) or in 1927 or 1928; children born in 1929 or later who are 5 foot 3 inches or more in height or 7 stone 12 pounds or more in weight when measured on or before 31st October 1942 – 20 extra coupons besides the 10 they already have – making 30 extra coupons in all.
> Children born between 1st January and 31st July, 1926 – 20 extra coupons.
> Children born between 1st June and 31st December, 1924 (inclusive) or in 1925 – 10 extra coupons.'

Expectant mothers received sixty extra coupons on production of a certificate, available after the fourth month of pregnancy, signed by their doctor. Mothers of newborn babies would receive a food and clothes ration book for the child, with the amount of coupons depending on the date the baby was born. Within a family, (but only within a family) clothes coupons could be pooled – that is, the mother or father's coupons could be used to augment those of their children, and vice versa – but otherwise coupons could not be given away or sold.

Losing your ration book, whether food or clothing, was serious. If it was due to bombing then it could be replaced by applying to the local Assistance Board, but if it were lost in any other way, replacement was unlikely, unless you could prove 'exceptional need'.

The clothes rationing rules were so complicated that the HMSO issued a booklet, *The Clothing Quiz* to try to help people understand the system. Literally hundreds of different articles of clothing were each allotted their

Cuts introduced in September 1945, as Harrods so helpfully pointed out, meant that each adult received the equivalent of only three clothing coupons a month. Labour shortages meant prices rocketed, especially for non-rationed items. As an alternative to paying high prices for hard-to-find garments, clothes and fabric shops offered remaking services, such as turning last season's coat into a new two-piece suit. The problem for most women was that last season's coat was this season's too.

These typically cheerful wartime print dresses needed coupons. Abuse of the original system meant that clothing could not be bought with loose coupons. Instead, the shopkeeper cut the coupons from the book, as shown here. Despite the limitations imposed by rationing, all three of these women show how it was possible to look very smart.

own number of coupons, which varied according to material and size, such as: 'pair of men's half hose – not woollen, or pair of ankle socks not exceeding eight inches from point of heel to top of sock when not turned down – 1 coupon.'

Among the more obscure articles were 'leggings, gaiters or spats' – 3 coupons for adults, 2 for children; 'Cassock, non woollen' – 7 coupons for adults, 6 for children (woollen, 1 more); cotton football jersey – 4 coupons for men, 2 for boys; kilt – 16 coupons for men, 14 for women, 8 for children. Even babies clothes were covered, such as 'knitted bootees' – half a coupon.

The coupon system lasted well into the war. In *Picture Post* in 1944, Anne Scott James advised on 'Some clothes for your coupons': 'February has brought you 24 new coupons. . . . At this stage of the war your choice of clothes is a serious matter. Most of us have extremely few clothes left . . . you can't afford a single failure.'

Some of the latest styles in Utility and other clothes for women, pictured in the same issue, were the Atrima (say it slowly) Utility suit at £3 5s and 10 coupons, which compared favourably to the non-Utility Dereta scarlet corduroy jacket alongside it, which cost £8 4s 8d and 12 coupons.

The unbelted Utility coat made fashion virtue out of necessity in these lean times and this 1944 collection featured a bright red version with a single button and a minimum of trimming. It cost only £4 and 18 coupons. The cheapest item on offer in this selection was the Rembrandt Utility dress, in a 'golden stripped rayon that looks like linen'. This illustrates another wartime fashion feature which was fabrics that, with varying degrees of success, were made to look like more expensive and scarce materials. The Rembrandt dress cost £2 13s 7d and 7 coupons, and was available from John Lewis.

Some goods did not require coupons, and for obvious reasons, such as ankle supporters, surgical stockings and hernia belts. It is more of a mystery why other items were 'coupon-free', such as ballet shoes, ecclesiastical garments (not including cassocks), academic robes, 'headgear other than nurses' squares or officers' caps and other than that made from scarves or incorporating handkerchiefs' and 'apparel made of paper or feathers'.

The rules for second-hand clothes were also complicated. Private sales were exempt, but clothes from dealers were only exempt if they were sold at a price worked out by a complicated formula. They had to cost less than the amount of coupons that the item would require new, multiplied by a set price, which varied according to the article! For example: 'a pair of women's shoes which require 5 coupons if new can only be sold as second-hand without coupons if the price is not more than 1s 6d per coupon, i.e. *7s 6d.*' Who on earth sat down and decided all these things, and quite how they did it, is not known.

Clothes could also be hired, for which coupons were not required, but only for a period of fourteen days or less.

Making your own clothes was encouraged, but this was really only a partial solution as the materials required to make them were also rationed. Knitting wool was rationed, one coupon for 2 oz, and cloth was also rationed (even upholstery material, which, like curtain material, could be used for clothing), depending on its size and the type of material. As an example, single texture cloth, or double texture cloth woven in one process, between 33 and 40 inches wide required 3 coupons per yard. Small pieces of cloth, and short lengths of wool for mending, were coupon free, as were fur skins and lengths of lace.

Utility Clothing

The 1942 Civilian Clothing Order was the start of Utility clothing. The Board of Trade asked for designs for four basic outfits, and eight designers, including Digby Morten, Hardy Amies and Norman Hartnell, responded. The outfits were a top coat, a suit, an afternoon dress and a cotton overall dress. As a result, the Board of Trade had thirty-two outfits to view in September 1942. From this selection, the Board of Trade had the most suitable styles mass-produced, conforming to the regulations of the Utility scheme. These first Utility clothes were in the shops by the

Below, left: One of the original thirty-two designs submitted to the Board of Trade by the London Society of Fashion Designers, this coat has all the hallmarks of later Utility designs. Patch pockets and belts in the same material as the main garment were especially popular features of the scheme. (Imperial War Museum)

Below: Another of the original thirty-two LSFD designs, this smart suit is typical of Utility's well-cut, fitted style. Utility permitted a maximum of three buttons on a jacket, and features such as the cutaway front saved on material. (Imperial War Museum)

Dyeing old or faded garments was one way of re-using old clothes, thereby saving precious clothing coupons.

following spring, in 1943. Carrying the distinctive CC41 label of the scheme and made from Utility fabrics, they were a great success.

The Utility scheme was intended to ensure adequate supplies of durable good quality clothing at reasonably low prices. At the heart of the scheme was the need to save on cloth and labour, and in order to fulfil that condition all wartime clothes were made under various restrictions set out by the Making of Civilian Clothing (restrictions) Orders. For instance, in 1942 an order was made prohibiting the manufacture of men's double-breasted coats and turned-up trousers; a limit was put on the amount of pockets and buttons; men's shirts were to be shorter and pyjamas were to have no pockets. (This order was revoked at the end of January 1944.)

All Utility clothes, fabrics and shoes bore the official Utility mark, CC41, which stood for Civilian Clothing 1941. While they were not the only clothes available, Utility garments had one big advantage to the consumer in that maximum prices were set for all Utility cloth and garments. As the war went on, these styles made up an ever-increasing proportion of the clothes available.

UTILITY

This advert for fur coats incorporates the CC41 'cheeses' logo. Fur was obtained from a variety of domestic sources; rabbits were especially vulnerable, their pelts exotically labelled 'Lapin' or 'Sealine' in the shops – which fooled no one.

One of the best known symbols of the Second World War was the Utility label 'CC41', which stood for Civilian Clothing 1941. It was introduced in September 1941 as part of the 'Limitation of Supplies (Cloth and Apparel) Order', although the scheme grew to cover far more than just clothing. The scheme was launched by Sir Laurence Watkinson of the Board of Trade. The designer Reginald Shipp was told to incorporate the double C in the logo in such a way that the public should not recognise the letters as such, and he came up with the two wedges, known at the Board of Trade as 'the cheeses'.

The origin of the use of the word 'utility' is hard to pin down. Its first official use seems to have been in the 'Utility Cloth (Maximum Prices) Order' of October 1941, but it was certainly widely used before that time to denote standard or basic styles.

It is no surprise that a great deal of Utility furniture and cloth survives, some of it still in everyday use; it is a tribute to its craftsmanship. Yet it cannot be denied that for many who lived during the war, or just after it, the term 'Utility' became synonymous with austerity, shortages and rationing. John Vaizey, in the introduction to the catalogue for the Inner London Education Authority's Utility exhibition in 1974 said: 'The poor, it seemed, had a thirst for frills and furbelows which gimcrack producers satisfied with shoddy, cheap and nasty things. The system was as ugly as it was wasteful.' In fact, no sooner had rationing and the Utility system gone than people returned to their old habits. It was not just a desire for 'frills and furbelows', it was a desire for change. Having lived through the limitations of the war (and, for many people, of two world wars), now they wanted a change of furniture every year, so who cared if it fell to bits in two years?

Adverts for Utility furniture, from *Picture Post*, 1944 and 1945.

FURNITURE RATIONING

On 3 July 1942 the President of the Board of Trade, Hugh Dalton, announced the extension of the Utility scheme to furniture (to be made available from January 1943), pottery, cooking utensils, suitcases, umbrellas, cutlery and household textiles. Utility cooking utensils included an enamelware combined saucepan/kettle; this was like a kettle, but with straight sides and a large lid, so it could be used easily as a saucepan too.

The manufacture of domestic furniture was completely prohibited from the beginning of November 1942. At the same time, it was announced that all furniture other than Utility which was presently being made must be finished by the end of January 1943, and sold by the end of February. All new furniture sold after that date had to be Utility. At first called 'Standard Emergency Furniture', which had originally been announced in early 1941 in an attempt to conserve valuable timber stocks, Utility furniture could only be obtained with permits similar to ration coupons. These permits were issued to newly married couples and people who had been bombed out of their homes. From March 1943 this was extended to married couples with children who were setting up home for the first time.

Successful applicants for Utility furniture coupons would be assessed and issued with a certain number of 'units'. For example, a couple with no furniture would receive 60 units, and an additional 15 for each child. A sideboard would be around 8 units; a table – 6; armchairs – 5; dining-chairs – 1 each; and a bed settee – 15.

Furniture rationing was introduced at the beginning of 1943, when the first Utility furniture catalogue appeared. By August 1943 the Utility furniture scheme, which so far had applied only to the mainland, was extended to Ulster.

TROWBRIDGE

NEW & SECOND HAND

FURNITURE

Choice of 3 **Mahogany Pedestal Office Desks.**   **£9 10s. 0d.**

Modern Dark Oak Welsh Dresser 4' 0" wide, fitted with 2 cupboards and 3 dresser shelves.   **£17 10s. 0d.**

Attractive **Queen Anne Wing Easy Chair**, re-upholstered in brown tapestry.   **£9 18s. 6d.**

Old Brown Oak Corner Cupboard, 6' 0" high, upper section composed of cupboard with 3 shelves, 2 small drawers in centre, and cupboard below with 1 shelf. A useful and attractive piece of furniture. **£12 10s. 0d.**

4' 9" Hide **Settee** with 4 loose cushions in brown velvet.   **£15 0s. 0d.**

Mahogany 3' 0" panel-end **Bedstead** with box spring by Heal.   **£17 10s. 0d.**

Light Oak Dining Room Suite comprising 5' 0" Sideboard, fitted with 2 drawers, cellarette and 2 cupboards with shelves, oval shaped Dining Table, size 4' 0" x 3' 6" with 1 leaf, 4 Dining Chairs with stuffed seats. **£35 0s. 0d.**

2 Modern Solid Oak "D" end panelled **Bedsteads**, complete with Vono-type spiral springs and hair mattresses.
    £22 0s. 0d.
    the pair.

Modern Solid Oak Bookcase with glazed front, double doors, 4' 2" high x 3' 6", with adjustable shelves.   **£12 10s. 0d.**

Set of Rush Seat Ladder Back Chairs, 6 smalls and 2 arms.
    £25 10s. 0d.

H. J. KNEE LTD.
MARKET PL., TROWBRIDGE
Phone 260

New and second hand furniture advertised in the *Bath and Wilts Chronicle and Herald*, May 1942.

Paper shortages affected more
than just the food packaging
industry. This logo appeared in
a book first published in 1941.

Even toothpaste tubes, which
were made of metal, were
recycled.

OTHER COMMODITIES

Pre-war stocks began to run out, leading to shortages of just about everything. This was very noticeable with wartime packaging; Swan Vesta match-boxes carried admonitions to 'use matches sparingly'. (By the end of 1941, the shortage of matches had created a great demand for petrol lighters. Various Government designs, often made of plastic, were produced at the controlled price of 6s 6d each.) Wood was always in short supply. Orlox suet pudding was now sold in plain packets bearing the words 'This is an Orlox plain suet pudding in a wartime jacket', which was later changed to 'a utility jacket', and Gibbs' toothpaste was 'Now in battledress refills' – many goods were sold in refill packs to save materials. People were even encouraged to return their used toothpaste tubes to their retailer, the proceeds from the sale of the recycled metal going to the Red Cross and St John's. Paper shortages meant that shoppers were expected to take their own wrapping paper with them to the shops.

Cigarettes too were always scarce, and barley was needed for bread, so beer was not always available, nor whisky, nor other spirits. In April 1942 came the 'Sacrifices for Victory' budget; cigarettes went up from 1s 6d to 2s for twenty. At this, many people took to growing their own tobacco. To begin with this practice was illegal without a licence, but by the end of the war this requirement had been dropped if the crop was for personal use.

Domestic soap was rationed from February 1942 because of the shortage of fats used in its manufacture. The choice was either 4 oz household soap or 2 oz toilet soap per person per month. This included soap for washing-up although, surprisingly, it did not include men's shaving soap, and many people washed their faces with this. The ration was set at 16 oz a month.

In May 1942 both new and second-hand furniture prices were brought under control, although anything pre-twentieth century was regarded as an antique rather than a piece of furniture, and so was exempt. Also in May, women were asked not to wear stockings in the summer months; leg make-up became the in-thing, either ready made or home-made using such things as onion skins to dye the leg and an eye-brow pencil to mark the seam.

Rubber came from the Far East, where we were at war with Japan, and this was soon in short supply too. Either the country of origin was overrun, or the long supply routes were too fraught with danger for ships to pass. What little there was was needed for the services. Consequently, wellington boots, rubber gloves and similar items were almost impossible to get. If they were 'essential' to your job (and this word was stressed), you could apply to the Factory Inspectors (in the case of industrial workers) or the War Agricultural Committee (farm workers) for a buying permit. Even then you still needed coupons – 4 for wellingtons, 2 for ankle-length boots. It was illegal to sell such rubber boots to anyone without a permit. The same applied to rubber gloves, although permits for these could also be obtained from the Ministry of Health in the case of medical workers.

In April 1942 the Board of Trade ruled that pottery designs had to be chosen for simplicity of design and resistance to breakage, and from the beginning of June the price of domestic pottery was controlled and the manufacture of decorated and inessential items was banned. From now on, everything produced had to be plain 'whiteware' or in natural colours; cream or brown.

Probably the best of them was Wedgwood's 'Victory Ware', designed by Victor Skellern. Besides being attractive, the pieces in the range were intensely practical. The teapot lid had a recessed handle for durability and also fitted on top of the jugs and teacups. All these items had low centres of gravity for stability, therefore lessening the risk of breakages. Even the serving dishes were so designed that one could be inverted to fit over another, thus forming a covered casserole. Spode's Utility teapot doubled up as a jug once the lid was removed. It was important for these pieces to be interchangeable as the number of variations was small; of the sixty-seven different types of cups produced pre-war, only three were still being produced during the war.

THE BLACK MARKET

The black market is (and was) a somewhat confusing term; one contemporary cartoon showed two 'old dears' asking at an information desk for directions to the black market. The term, of course, referred to the illicit trade in articles such as foodstuffs, raw materials, clothing, petrol, cosmetics, furniture, cigarettes, spirits and fuel; in fact, just about everything that was rationed or whose price was controlled. This trade could be from the butcher supplying a little extra 'under the counter', through the street corner 'spiv', epitomised by Private Joe Walker in *Dad's Army*, to the wholesale robbery of warehouses and Government storehouses carried out by armed gangs.

All but the most patriotic were aware of and, if they could, took part in petty 'fiddles'; meat that had been condemned following bomb damage being cleaned up and sold, a bottle of scotch, a bit of knicker elastic, or a pair of stockings sold from a suitcase in the pub or down an alley. One has to qualify this with 'if they could', because the black market was a bit like 'free love' in the 1960s – everyone had heard of it but it was often nowhere to be found. Of course, for those who had access to farms, a few eggs or milk might be available, but for many in the suburbs, with travel restricted, this might as well have been a million miles away.

The variations in the scale of black marketeering were reflected in the penalties incurred. In March 1942 Herbert Morrison announced that the maximum penalties for black market activities had been raised to one year's imprisonment on conviction of small-scale trading going up to fourteen years' penal servitude for organised large-scale offences.

There were other wartime crimes too. Burglars were busy while homeowners were in the shelters. In spite of Government

After bombing raids, when residents had to leave their damaged homes, looting was a problem. This notice warns that the crime carried the death penalty. (Imperial War Museum)

Above: Sorting household rubbish into various categories of salvage – tins, wastepaper, cardboard, etc. (Imperial War Museum)

Above, right: Putting out the salvage. Wellingtons, hot water bottles and even toy water pistols were all a valuable source of vital rubber, as the advancing Japanese forces threatened to cut off supplies. (Imperial War Museum)

propaganda to the opposite, looting of bombed or evacuated property took place. Notices warned that the penalties included death or penal servitude for life. Sadly, it was not unknown for members of the rescue service, fire brigades or police to help themselves in damaged buildings. In some areas, the Auxiliary Fire Service had the reputation for being the refuge of army-dodging petty criminals. Even in the 1943 British film *The Bells Go Down*, a wartime tribute to the AFS, one of the characters is just such a crook.

SALVAGE

Salvage, or recycling as we would call it today, was essential. People were asked to save their scrap paper, food waste for the pigs, rags, bottles, bones for soap and fertiliser, and scrap metal, including milk bottle tops.

Lord Beaverbrook had started the first salvage campaign – the 'Saucepans for Spitfires' campaign – in July 1940 when he had broadcast: 'Women of Britain, give us your aluminium. . . . We will turn your pots and pans into Spitfires and Hurricanes.' Sadly, little of it was of a high enough quality for aircraft production but in propaganda and morale-building terms the exercise was a success – people felt they were doing something towards the war effort. Later campaigns were far more vital as stocks really were running out. Children especially played a vital part in collecting salvage, either individually or as part of a group such as the scouts; their efforts were often co-ordinated by the WVS who set up the Cog in the Wheel campaign, where children could earn plastic Cog badges, or become Salvage Stewards. Posters encouraged you to 'Save your Scrap for the Scrap', or to 'Waste Littler, Paste Hitler', or told you that 'Rags for salvage will give the troops more blankets'.

SIX

THE WARTIME
KITCHEN

Many books and magazines gave advice to the new homeowners of the 1940s. Every part of the house was covered, but the kitchen drew more column inches than all the others. The quotes in this section are from several such publications and show how, while much advice was common sense and practical, other helpful hints ranged from the amusing to the downright baffling.

FURNITURE AND DECORATION

Stove/Aga

Coal or anthracite cooking ranges were supplied to houses of moderate size. Finished in enamel, they were always much in demand – 'extras' included a heat-resisting glass window and a side boiler for kitchen hot water. The August 1939 edition of *Ideal Home* magazine looked briefly at the problem of wartime cooking in an article on 'Emergency Preparations', and promoted the use of anthracite:

An Aga cooker advertised in the 1930s. (*Good Housekeeping*)

> when it might be difficult to obtain solid fuel, and gas and electricity might be temporarily unavailable. Anyone who is thinking of taking advantage of summer coal prices and at the same time of laying in a larger stock of solid fuel against emergency should consider the claims of anthracite. . . . Anthracite sufficient to fuel an Esse Minor cooker burning continuously for a year can be stored in a cellar 4 ft square.

Gas or electric cookers were equally popular in homes as both forms of energy were routinely included in suburban housing developments by the time war broke out. Cookers made in the thirties have a smooth, mottled patterned, vitreous enamel finish. Electric cookers especially could be economical if they were fitted with a small

THE AMAZING EFFICIENCY

OF THE MOST MODERN COOKER

The Aga Cooker combines the merits of a coal range with the ease and cleanliness of electricity. Provides all the oven and hot plate temperatures you need. Cooks for two or sixteen. Burns coke or anthracite. Need be refilled only once and riddled only twice every 24 hours. Burns incessantly day and night — and so is ready for use first thing every morning! So cool, so clean, so compact — the Aga makes life in the kitchen a joy, and cooking light and easy work. *Insulated with Bell's Asbestos.*

A QUARTER'S FUEL FOR YOUR AGA COSTS LESS THAN £1

Come and see the Aga Cooker in use, or write for fully illustrated booklet.

BELL'S HEAT APPLIANCES, LTD
157, QUEEN VICTORIA STREET, LONDON, E.C.4

West End Demonstrations at 5, Newman Street, Oxford Street, W.1
The Aga Cooker can be installed on Deferred Payments system for an initial payment of £5.10.0

A 'modern' kitchen from *The Housewife's Book*. This features a gas stove and coke boiler combination, lino, and a double sink.

Services were provided by a wide range of suppliers, including local councils, as this 1930s gas advertisement from Perth demonstrates.

boiler for hot water, and oil-powered cookers were also still popular. But overall, cookers were far less accurate as regards temperature control, less well insulated and far more wasteful in the way they used energy than today.

Cast-iron vitreous enamel ware, often white inside and brick coloured outside, was used routinely on electric or gas appliances. Aluminium ware, especially made with quarter-inch bottoms, was ideal for electric, especially when fitted with fully insulated and heat resistant Bakelite handles.

The following is a list of utensils recommended for the kitchen from a 1930s book of household management:

several mixing bowls
  – preferably china
	set of cake tins	set of saucepans
		  and fry pans

set of basins	several baking sheets	set of pie dishes
kettles	1 dozen patty tins	steamer
1 cook's knife	1 dozen bun tins	frying basket
1 palette knife	flour dredger	fish kettle
1 vegetable knife	sugar dredger	fish slice
1 chopping knife	pastry board	cook's fork
1 fruit knife	pastry brush	receptacle for bread
1 grater	rolling pin	2 sieves
1 egg whisk	oven thermometer	– 1 hair and 1 wire
several wooden spoons	set of pastry cutters	tin opener
several iron spoons	graduated measure, preferably glass	storage ware of assorted sizes

It further suggested a mincing machine, an omelette pan, stew pans or casseroles and assorted whisks and beaters. Optional extras would include a cream maker, a waffle iron, an egg poacher, a knife rack, potato, tomato and grapefruit knives, a butter curler and an egg timer.

This advert from a *Slonetric* catalogue shows some of the attachments available for an electric mixer in the late thirties.

Electrical Gadgets

Besides the traditional utensils, an increasingly wide range of electrical gadgets was available for the kitchen. The 1937 *Slonetric* catalogue included electric coffee percolators (£1 5s to £2 5s), electric porringers (17s to 23s 6d) and egg poachers (£1 to £1 2s), electric saucepans (£1 9s to £2 1s 6d), and toasters (19s 6d to £1 15s 6d). The latter still involved some work though as it only toasted one side at once, so the bread had to be watched and then turned over. A toaster did exist that was more like the modern versions, able to toast the bread on both sides at once and with an adjustable timer-switch that turned it off automatically. However, it was much more expensive: the two-slice model cost £13 10s and the four-slice £18 10s.

Another idea that lasted was the electric 'mixing machines', or food mixers as we would call them today. The 'Kitchen-Kit' (£5 15s) had a range of optional attachments (costing from 1s 6d to 22s 6d) including beverage mixer; flour sifter; buffer for polishing silverware (silver, or at least silver-plated cutlery was much more popular then); can opener; shredder and slicer; mincer;

SLONETRIC

Electric Mixing Machines

"MIXMASTER."

The "Mixmaster" gives a perfect mix because beaters go right down into bowl. Motor tilts back, and bowls are easily removed. Bowls of special coloured glass revolve by themselves on ball-bearing platform feeding all the food into the beaters. Easy to clean, beaters just pull out. Completely enclosed dust-proof motor has ten different speeds, won't tip over. Electricity consumption 60 watts. Supplied for Universal A.C. or D.C., 200-220, 230-250 volts.

Height overall 17"
Width overall 13"

What the "Mixmaster" will do—

Mashes Potatoes, Turnips, etc.

Mixes Cakes and Batters.

Squeezes Oranges and Lemons.

Beats Eggs and Whip Cream.

Allows the motor to be used apart from the stand.

Price (Q).... £6 6 0

Complete with motor, stand, fruit juice bowl and reamer, 2 mixing bowls (one measures 9¼" diam. by 4½" deep, the other 6½" diam., by 4" deep), double beaters and straining devices.

For extra attachments please refer to opposite page.

Please state voltage when ordering

Makes Mayonnaise and Salad Cream. (Special oil dripper device supplied).

'A refrigerator is a
necessity' The
Homeowners'
Handbook, 1938

coffee grinder; ice cube breaker; knife grinder; pea sheller and bean slicer. The 'Mixmaster' (£6 6s) had several integrated features – such as the orange and lemon squeezer – as well as optional attachments like the potato peeler (£1 4s) and the freezer unit (£1 2s 6d) for making ice cream (you did, however, also need an ice-cream freezer). You could buy separate electric ice-cream makers which, like the traditional home ice-cream maker, had to be packed with ice and salt. However, whereas the traditional version required repeated and lengthy spells turning the handle (the responsibility of the kitchen staff), the electric model did it for you. Electric fridges of various sizes ranged in price from £23 2s to £81 18s, the former with a capacity of 2½ cubic feet, and the latter of 9 cubic feet. This also had 'ice capacity 84 cubes, fitted door racks, vegetable bin, crisper [and] automatic lighting'.

Walls and Floors

Where possible, tiles completely covered the walls, but this could be expensive. The recommendation was that they be used at least round the sink and stove and, if possible, part way up all walls at least 'to elbow height', the remainder of the wall being painted with distemper or, better still, washable finishes such as oil, enamel or gloss paint. Imitation tiles were also available, one of the most effective being zinc sheets that were enamelled to look like tiles. Some washable papers were sold as suitable for kitchen use, but it was usually recommended that they be varnished after hanging. Pastel colours were fashionable; white, cream, apple green, pale grey and powder blue were particular favourites.

For the floor, buff or red quarry tiles were easy to clean but could be hard on the feet. Composition floors were the most popular, being 'ideal for kitchens . . . warm, draught proof and considerably more resilient than tiles'. They could be laid in black, green, brown and red, and two colours were often used. Composition floors were recommended for the kitchen as they covered up scuff marks, as did marble-, jasper- or granite-patterned linoleum.

THE WARTIME KITCHEN CUPBOARD

It is tempting to believe that women in the thirties and during the war spent all their time bent over the cooker, conjuring up delicious home-made meals. But the labour-saving movement was as strong in the area of cooking as it was in cleaning. For those who could afford it, or whose busy schedules dictated – and there were ever more of those in the war – convenience foods were the answer.

Most of us would probably be surprised at what we would find in the wartime larder: items like crispbread, baked beans and tinned spaghetti have more of a feel of the fifties, but they were all available during the war. Tinned convenience foods were always popular. These included Fray Bentos meats and Smedley's peas. Throughout the war, Heinz continued to produce their 57 varieties. Favourites were oven-baked beans with pork and tomato sauce, baked beans, vegetable or tomato soup (they offered a

Good cupboard accommodation is important in every labour saving kitchen. If fitted cupboards are carried up to the ceiling, dust cannot accumulate on the tops, and the upper part, which may be reached by the aid of a pair of steps, can be used for the storage of articles not often required. Where the general arrangement makes it satisfactory, it is possible to have the refrigerator built in as part of the cupboard space. A long cupboard for brooms, the vacuum cleaner, and other long-handled articles should be provided.

wide range of soups, including asparagus, spinach, kidney and mock turtle), salad cream, and mayonnaise. The latter two were especially useful for adding flavour to an otherwise plain rationed meal; alternatives included HP, Daddies or OK sauce, Pan Yan pickles or Yorkshire relish. Treats might include Hartley's jams; Senior's fish and meat pastes; Weston's or Huntley and Palmer's Biscuits; Chiver's jelly; Green's or Bird's custard; Carnation milk; and, for the family dog, Winalot or Spiller's biscuits.

The main problem of food in the war was not the possibility of starvation – there was generally enough food – but boredom. The use of oatmeal, a domestic crop, was promoted by the Government, which subsidised its price. People were encouraged to use it instead of flour, and to add it to meat meals to bulk them out. The range of food available was often very limited, and staples like potatoes made up an increasing proportion of the food people ate. It was therefore important to add variety. For this reason, sauces and pickles were never rationed.

Certainly as the war went on and rationing and shortages intensified, some products became harder to find. Adverts acknowledged this, such as the Nescafé coffee promotion which said, 'when you *do* get a chance to

buy a tin'. Other supplies did dry up altogether as raw materials became impossible to get. Sometimes they just faded away, sometimes they were advertised as being no longer available until after the war. However, some managed to soldier on: beef cubes, such as Oxo or Brooke Bond, meat extract like Bovril, and gravy powders like Bisto remained and gave meals a meatier taste during meat rationing.

Nerve tonics were heavily advertised. For some, a good night's sleep was enough, and this could be achieved more easily, people were told, with Horlicks, Bournvita, Ovaltine or Rowntree's, Bournville or Fry's cocoa – perhaps Guinness, Bulmer's cider, or VP wine if something stronger was required!

With decreasing availability and increasing Government controls, branded breakfast cereals that were commonplace before the war – such as Shredded Wheat, Weetabix, Kellogg's Wheat Flakes, Quaker wheat and Quaker rice – had to be replaced with exclusively home-grown items. The Government ban on white bread did not stop Hovis, Vitbe or Allinsons producing their brown bread and flour. McDougall's self-raising flour, Trex and Spry cooking fat were available only during the early stages of the war, whereas Brown & Poulson's Cornflour, Borwick's baking powder and Green's sponge mixture were obtainable throughout.

Another big change was in packaging. To save paper, metal and labour, wartime wrapping became plainer and smaller, often bearing the words 'wartime economy pack' or 'wartime emergency pack'. Some packaging, like that of Mazawattee tea, declared itself to be 'gas-proof'. New additions included tins of butter, dried egg and dried milk from Canada and America. Most were unusual in that they carried no labels, the wording and design being printed directly onto the can.

Opposite: A selection of wartime adverts for items of food, some of which were available on points rationing. Several products, including Nescafé and Shredded Wheat, were difficult to get or were available only in certain 'zones'. Others, like OK sauce, were advertised as giving flavour to boring rations. Many adverts played on the initials ARP, like this Oxo ad.

> *Never waste bread. Keep crusts and odd pieces in an open tin until stale, then crush for breadcrumbs. A tin of readymade breadcrumbs is a useful asset to cooking.*

FEEDING THE FAMILY

The Food Front

During this time a series of short information adverts called 'Food Facts' were started which appeared in newspapers almost every week until the early 1950s. Early slogans such as 'Let your shopping save our shipping' were backed up with practical tips and recipes, which were often topical. Recipes used new types of food, explanations were offered on how to make the best use of what was available at that time, and suggestions made for seasonal ideas such as Christmas recipes. Because they were so practical, these adverts were very popular with hard-pressed housewives. The MoF also issued War Cookery leaflets, which covered a wide range of food, and a book *Food Facts for the Kitchen Front*, full of wartime recipes and tips.

Cartoon characters were used to appeal to children, as they still are in food ads today. One popular chap was Potato Pete, born in 1941, a rustic potato, with a piece of straw in his mouth, a green hat and gaiters. Doctor Carrot pointed out the healthy side of that particular root, especially for seeing in the blackout, but he was replaced by Walt Disney's

War Cookery leaflet no. 11: dried eggs. The leaflet explains, among other things, how to reconstitute the eggs and how to use and store them.

"SHARE MY ENERGY"
says Potato Pete

In your home do potatoes mean only *boiled* potatoes? There are so many easy ways to make them into a delicious main meal. You can fry them for breakfast as is done in Devonshire; you can make them into scones for tea, or into pies for supper. More potatoes and less bread are good for you and the Nation too!

POTATO PIE

Cooking time : 20 minutes. *Ingredients :* 2 lb. potatoes, 1 onion or shallot, ¾ pint of milk or household milk, 1 dessertspoonful flour, 1 teaspoonful fat, salt and pepper. *Method :* Grease a piedish with fat. Scrub potatoes and slice. Chop onion or shallot. Arrange potatoes in alternate layers in dish with the onion, flour and seasoning, finishing with a layer of potatoes.

Place the remainder of the fat on top in small pieces, pour milk into the dish. Cook in moderate oven for 20 minutes.

FREE — ask at any of the Food Advice Centres or Bureaux for a free copy of the Potato Pete Recipe Booklet, or write direct to the Ministry of Food, London, W.1.

POTATOES KEEP YOU *FIGHTING* FIT

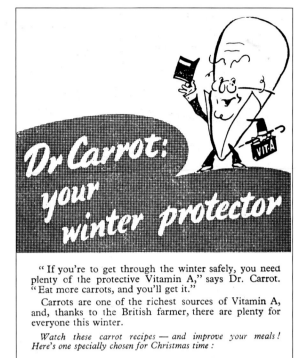

Dr Carrot: your winter protector

" If you're to get through the winter safely, you need plenty of the protective Vitamin A," says Dr. Carrot. " Eat more carrots, and you'll get it."

Carrots are one of the richest sources of Vitamin A, and, thanks to the British farmer, there are plenty for everyone this winter.

Watch these carrot recipes — and improve your meals! Here's one specially chosen for Christmas time :

Mincemeat

Cook 1 lb. carrots, chop finely with 1 lb. apples, cored but not peeled. Add 4 ozs. dried fruit (previously soaked and chopped if dates, figs, or prunes are used), 2 ozs. shredded suet, ½ teaspoonful mixed spices, pinch nutmeg, few drops lemon juice substitute or vinegar. Mix together thoroughly. A pleasant filling for Christmas tarts — and it *takes no sugar*. (It will not keep more than a week or so.)

Two wartime cartoon characters, Potato Pete and Doctor Carrot, encouraged people to eat these home-grown, unrationed foods. They are a great example of how much propaganda was influenced by advertising – even a modern- day sales campaign for frozen vegetables might well centre around such characters. (HMSO)

creation 'Clara Carrot'. Perhaps, in his wing collar and top hat, Doctor Carrot was just too old fashioned.

On 25 June 1940 the BBC introduced the 5-minute long *Kitchen Front* radio programme. This was broadcast throughout the war, after the morning news at 8.15 from Tuesday to Friday. The programme format varied, as did the presenters. Probably the most popular were 'Gert and Daisy', comediennes Ethel and Doris Walters (sisters to actor Jack Warner, later famous as Dixon of Dock Green). Gert and Daisy gave the programme a comical slant in a series of sketches based on the characters of two char-ladies. They were such a hit with the public that *Gert and Daisy's Wartime Cookery Book* was produced. Another comedy format was the *Buggins family*. The programmes could be serious, as when another radio personality, Dr Charles Hill, 'the Radio Doctor', presented a series on healthy diets. Later, the name was changed to *The Household Front* to allow the scope of the programme to be widened but food continued to be the major topic.

The MoF set up food advice centres in the larger towns, staffed by home economics advisers, and cookery demonstrations by various experts were always popular. In April 1940 the Nation Food Education Campaign was launched jointly by the Ministries of Food, Agriculture, Health and Education. Its three aims were to show how people could be fed using home-grown food, to demonstrate waste-free cooking methods, and to show how to keep healthy on a wartime diet. These remained the central core of food campaigns throughout the war and after.

'Food Production is Vital' from a wartime gardening book. Britain nearly lost the Battle of the Atlantic, which would have meant the loss of the war as the country could not have survived without the supplies that were being brought in by merchant ships.

Meat

Probably the single biggest cause of complaint about food rationing was meat. In all but the poorest pre-war households, meat made up a far larger proportion of meals than it does today. Advice on how to stretch the meat ration included serving it with potatoes and vegetables. Official advice was to dice or mince the meat, and then mix it with pulses or oatmeal. Some meat was not rationed, such as heart, liver and kidney, tongue, calves' and sheep's heads, ox cheek, ox and pigs' tails, rabbit, tripe, trotters, heels, chitterlings (pig's intestines), sausages and chicken (never rationed, but just about impossible to buy). Wartime recipe books included recipes such as baked stuffed sheep's hearts, sheep's head roll, brawn, cow heel with parsley sauce, stewed ox cheek, rabbit dumplings, curried tripe or brains on toast. One of the least nauseating, perhaps, was hot potato and kidney pie.

Like other non-rationed items, these cuts of meat were often only available 'under the counter'. This meant that they were not kept on show, but were literally brought out from under the counter and offered to favoured customers only. Unlike the black market, this was not illegal – the goods were not rationed, but scarce – it was more a form of nepotism which meant that butchers and grocers became persons of some standing. Many women would go to great lengths to keep in with their butcher. The Government also found it necessary to point out that children from the age of six upwards needed the same rations as adults for healthy growth, and that their rations should not be given to adults.

Corned beef became almost a staple. Once again, the MoF worked hard to come up with ways to make it interesting, including corned beef and oatmeal pudding, and potato and corned beef pancakes.

Alternatives to meat were sought continually. Stock cubes were advertised as a way of adding meat flavour to vegetables. Rabbit was widely used. Tripe was introduced (unsuccessfully) in the south and, in 1943, horsemeat, or horse flesh as it was called, was commonly available, though rarely popular. 'Mock' became the operative word, with recipes for

An Oxo Home Guard advert from November 1941.

HOT POTATO AND KIDNEY PIE

8 oz potato pastry (see p. 107)
8 oz ox kidney
about 1 lb potatoes
pinch of herbs
salt and pepper

Remove fat and skin from kidney – cut it into small pieces. Dice the potatoes and mix together with herbs and seasoning. Add a good tablespoon water. Roll out the crust thinly, and cut into sufficient rounds to use two for each pie. Grease good-sized deep patty pans, line with pastry, then fill with kidney mixture. Damp edges well, and cover with another round of pastry, pressing edges well together so the juice will not escape. Brush over with milk. Prick a hole in the centre of each, and bake in moderately hot oven for about 30–35 minutes, or longer if necessary. Test filling with skewer. (Serves 4–6 people)

MOCK GOOSE

1½ lb potatoes
2 large cooking apples
4 oz cheese
½ teaspoon dried sage
salt and pepper
¾ pint vegetable stock
1 tablespoon flour

Scrub and slice potatoes thinly, slice apples, grate cheese. Grease a fireproof dish, place a layer of potatoes in it, cover with apple and a little sage, season lightly and sprinkle with cheese, repeat layers leaving potatoes and cheese to cover. Pour in ½ pint of stock, cook in a moderate oven for three-quarters of an hour. Blend flour with the remainder of the stock, pour into dish and cook for another quarter of an hour. Serve as a main dish with a green vegetable.

MOCK CHICKEN CUTLETS

2 cupfuls breadcrumbs
1 good cupful ground walnuts
mix together with a good pat of butter
1 good tablespoon onion juice
½ teaspoonful mace

Melt 1 oz of butter in a good-sized saucepan, work ½ oz flour and add gradually 2 cupfuls fresh milk. When this boils add nuts etc., one beaten egg, salt and pepper to taste. Stir well, turn out into bowl to cool, add a teaspoonful lemon juice, shape into cutlets, dip in egg and bread crumbs as usual and fry crisp. Serve with bread sauce.

mock duck, mock oyster soup, mock venison and mock goose.

For many this meat-free cooking was very new but the vegetarian movement had thrived in the pre-war years. Health food specialist shops existed even then, and the National Association of Health Stores produced books such as *Health-giving Foods and How to Prepare Them* full of wartime recipes. These used proprietary meat alternatives such as 'Pitman Nut Meat', 'Rissol-Nut', 'Nuttolene' and 'Nut Meat Brawn'. It also included recipes such as cheese and parsnip roast, steamed nut savoury and mock chicken cutlets.

Fish

Fish was an alternative to meat but it could also be in short supply. New types of fish were introduced to the British public (one newspaper cartoon showed a sea-serpent lying on the fishmonger's slab, with the fishmonger telling a customer, 'We 'ave to take what we can get these days'). Whalemeat, on sale in 1942, had a very fishy taste (very few liked it). Exotically named fish such as megrim, saithe and witch appeared alongside Icelandic salt cod, or fresh salted cod. The MoF told the fishmonger that salted cod had to be soaked in water for 24 to 48 hours before they sold it. The housewife was told that it was; 'almost free from bones, it's easy to cook, and there's no waste. Above all it's cheap – the maximum retail price is 9d a pound.' Admittedly its low cost was a main advantage, but perhaps it is not surprising that, no matter how long you soaked, it still just tasted of salt and nobody liked it!

Bread

Bread was not rationed until after the war, but it was the subject of much work by the MoF. People were encouraged to eat more potatoes instead of bread. From the very beginning of the war, millers were ordered to produce 'National straight-run flour', which used 70 per cent of the wheat. In February 1941 this was increased to 85 per cent and the National Wholemeal Loaf was introduced. This became the National Loaf when the production of white bread was prohibited in March 1942. To make up for the deficiency of vitamin B1 in the wartime diet, synthetic B1 was added to the bread. But the bread was never very popular; it had a greyish colour rather than brown, was too moist to cut properly when fresh, but soon went hard. Above all, people just couldn't get used to the taste.

Potatoes

Potatoes are easily grown in Britain so they played an important part in the wartime larder. The MoF's War Cookery leaflet no. 3 was entirely about potatoes, and gave the following information: 'They contain the same vitamins as oranges, and three-quarters of a pound a day will give over half the amount of vitamins needed to prevent fatigue and help fight infection.' There were general hints on cooking: '1) Always cook them in

FOOD FACTS

Brighter Breakfasts help to start the day right

Fish Fritters make a pleasant change
4 oz self-raising flour, or
4 oz plain flour and 2 level teaspoons baking powder
1 level teaspoon salt
¼ level teaspoon pepper
2 to 3 dried eggs, dry
2 to 3 tablespoonfuls water
¼ pint milk
2 to 3 oz flaked cooked fish
1 level teaspoonful chopped parsley
fat for frying

Mix flour, baking powder, salt, pepper and egg. Make to a thick batter with the water and milk. Beat well. Add fish and parsley. Drop spoonfuls into a little hot fat in a frying pan and fry until golden brown on both sides. Serve at once. This makes 8 fritters.

'Eggy Bread' is popular with children. Reconstitute 1 dried egg and season with salt, pepper and a pinch of mustard. Dip slices of bread in the egg, and fry in smoking hot fat till brown. Chopped fried bacon, chopped cooked vegetables or baked beans can be served hot with the slices.

A Ministry of Food 'Food Facts' bulletin from May 1941, one of a regular series of articles giving tips and often encouraging the use of non-rationed foods. (HMSO)

their skins. 2) If you must peel them, peel thinly. 3) After peeling, cook at once. Avoid soaking in water if possible.' Finally, the leaflet contained recipes – in addition to the usual baked, mashed or stuffed potatoes, there was potato salad, potato scones, and, with the shortage of flour in mind, savoury or sweet potato pastry.

People were encouraged to make as much use of potatoes as possible. The MoF produced *Potato Pete's Cookery Book*, full of recipes starring its eponymous hero. An expanded version of the War Cookery leaflet, the book contained similar tips: 'Remember to save the water in which potatoes have been boiled, as it is a useful foundation for a soup.' There were a great many more recipes, including Irish potato cakes, Champ (just mashed potato and vegetables), Fadge (Irish potato bread), pink and green puree (potatoes, carrots and watercress), potato piglets (baked potatoes stuffed with sausage meat) or, if served on a bed of cabbage, pigs in clover, or stuffed with sprats instead of sausage meat. For further excitement, this recipe could be 'Jack in the Box', for which the variation was to – 'Make a head emerge from one end and a tail from the other.'

Among the more exotic (or bizarre) recipes were surprise potato balls. There was even a song, recorded by Betty Driver:

> Potato Pete, Potato Pete,
> See him coming down the street,
> Shouting his good things to eat,
> Get your hot potatoes from Potato Pete.

Digging for Victory – housewives planting potatoes. (Imperial War Museum)

SAVOURY POTATO PASTRY

8 oz mashed potato
4 oz flour
1 oz cooking fat
½ teaspoon salt

Mix the flour with the salt. Rub in the fat and work into the potato. Mix to a very dry dough with a small quantity of cold water. Knead with the fingers and roll out.

SWEET POTATO CHOCOLATE SPREAD

2 tablespoonfuls mashed potato
1 tablespoonful cocoa
1 tablespoonful sugar
Almond or vanilla flavouring

Mash the potato thoroughly. Mix in the cocoa, sugar and flavouring. Use as a spread instead of jam.

Those who have the will to win
Cook potatoes in their skin
Knowing that the sight of peelings
Deeply hurts Lord Woolton's feelings.

The various campaigns worked too well – consumption of potatoes went up by 60 per cent during the war, and in 1945 even potatoes were in short supply.

Vegetables

As meat, fish and cheese became a decreasing part of the week's food, vegetables took over. People were even encouraged to eat parts of vegetables normally discarded, such as cauliflower leaves, pea-pods and broad bean pods. Two famous wartime characters – Lord Woolton, the Minister of Food, and Mr Middleton, the Wireless Gardener – had vegetable dishes named after them. Potato Pete's recipe book included the Middleton Medley. 'Food Facts' gave two alternative fillings to the standard potato mixture: 1) diced cooked carrots and turnips, with a sprinkling of finely chopped parsley;

SURPRISE POTATO BALLS

1 lb cooked potatoes
1 large carrot, grated
1 teaspoon chopped parsley
A little sweet pickle
Salt and pepper
A few teaspoons of milk, if necessary
Browned breadcrumbs

Cook the potatoes and beat them well with a fork. Add the grated carrot, parsley, salt and pepper. Use a little milk, if necessary, to bind the mixture, but do not make it wet. Form into balls. Make a hole in each, drop in a spoonful of pickle, and close the hole.
Roll in the breadcrumbs [cue for a joke!], place on a greased baking sheet, and cover with a margarine paper. Bake in a really hot oven for 15–20 minutes. Serve piping hot with good gravy.

A greengrocer's display. A few oranges have slipped in among the domestic produce. When such delicacies were available, they were often sold, as the notice says, 'for children only'. (Imperial War Museum)

2) small cooked sprouts sprinkled with finely grated cheese or ground mixed nuts. Substitute spinach when in season.

Carrots and parsnips were increasingly used in sweet dishes. Parsnips could be flavoured and substituted for pineapple, or banana, while carrot cake was baked instead of Christmas cake. Carrots were eaten as sweets, sometimes dipped in toffee like toffee-apples.

Onions, so useful for flavouring dull wartime fare, became very much a shortage item as the normal supply lines from France and Spain dried up. Onions were even given as prizes in Warship Week raffles. They became a stock item for those who grew their own food, and alternatives such as spring onions and leeks were also sought after. The shortage continued right up until the last year of the war.

Cucumbers were also scarce, but for a different reason; the Government decided that they were of low nutritional value and banned their cultivation in heated greenhouses. As a result, they all but ceased to be grown by

RIPE TOMATO SAUCE

12 lb tomatoes
1 lb sugar
1½ oz salt
1 pint malt vinegar
pinch of cayenne pepper
1 level teaspoon ground ginger
1 level teaspoon ground pimento
1 level teaspoon ground mace
1 level teaspoon ground cloves

Cook the tomatoes until tender, rub through a hair sieve. Add the spices, salt and sugar dissolved in the vinegar and boil gently in an open pan until the consistency of thick cream. Pour into hot bottles and seal at once.

CARROT TART

This is so delicious that it is recommended in the great chef Escoffier's cookery book.

Cook the carrots with enough water to cover them well, adding, for ½ a pint of water, a ¼ oz of salt, ½ oz of sugar and 1 oz of margarine. Cook the carrots until the water has almost entirely evaporated, then make a puree with the bulk of them, reserving a few for cutting into rings. To make the puree, drain the cooked carrots and rub them through a fine sieve. Stir them in a pan over a good heat until they get drier, adding a small piece of margarine. Then moisten them very carefully with milk or stock until they are creamy in consistency. If a heavier puree is liked, a quarter of the weight of the carrots in rice may be cooked separately, and rubbed through the sieve with the carrots. Line a plate or flan-ring with pastry, and bake this empty. (This, of course, is done by lining the pastry with greaseproof paper and filling this with haricot beans or split peas, which can be used again and again, in order to keep the pastry when cooked in shape.) When the flan is baked, fill it with the carrot puree, and decorate it on top with overlapping rounds of the rest of the carrots. Now reduce the liquid in which the carrots were cooked to a syrup, by letting it boil away quickly in the pan over a good heat. Keep stirring it and do not let it burn. Coat the carrot rings with this, and put the flan back into the oven for five minutes before serving. This tart can be made with parsnips, while rings of carrots would make a livelier decoration.

commercial suppliers. On the other hand, tomato growing was definitely encouraged and market gardeners were forced to turn most of their greenhouses over to their cultivation for half the year.

Milk

When 'Victory Milk', the name for pooled milk, was regulated in July 1940, alternatives were on hand for those who were not considered 'priorities'. One was condensed milk, the other – 'National Household milk'– was dried milk that had had the fat removed; it was rarely popular. Both were distributed by milkmen from 1941 onwards but, by 1942, condensed milk was on points and dried milk limited to one tin per family per month. The prohibition of the use of cow's milk for making cream or ice-cream in July 1940 led to a spate of recipes using alternatives.

Every bit of milk had to be used. Even the last few drops in a bottle could be saved; housewives were encouraged to rinse milk bottles and keep the resulting milk-water for use in making pastry, sauces etc. Milk that had 'turned' was too valuable to be poured away, and there were many recipes using sour milk.

Dig for Victory ad featuring an onion. At one point these were so scarce that one was offered as a raffle prize.

I was front-page news a year ago . . . more precious than gold to those lucky enough to get a pound of me. That was because you relied on having me brought to you from abroad. Yet, if women and older children, as well as men, are sensible enough to Dig for Victory now, you can have me ALL THE YEAR ROUND for only the cost of a packet of seeds . . .

YOU SEE, I AM ONE OF THOSE CROPS YOU CAN STORE

DIG FOR VICTORY NOW!

★★★ *If you haven't a garden, ask your Local Council for an allotment. Send NOW for Free pictorial leaflets "HOW TO DIG" and "HOW TO CROP" to Dept. A.103, Ministry of Agriculture, Hotel Lindum, St. Annes-on-Sea, Lancs.*

ISSUED BY THE MINISTRY OF AGRICULTURE

Make the MOST of MILK

Here's the way to make cocoa with a minimum amount of milk. For each cup you mix a teaspoonful of cocoa and a little boiling water with 1½ teaspoonfuls of sugar into a thick paste. Then fill up with boiling water and finally add two or three teaspoonfuls of cold milk.

Used in this way Bournville Cocoa helps to eke out your limited milk supplies.

And, by the way, it keeps better in a tin

BOURNVILLE COCOA 5ᴰ PER ¼ LB

LESS THAN PRE-WAR PRICE

This ad for Bournville cocoa claims to make the most of milk, which was a controlled product.

A TASTY SUPPER DISH

1) Strain the milk in a muslin bag as for cream cheese.
2) Add a little mustard, pepper, salt and Worcester sauce according to taste.
3) Spread this mixture on slices of toast.
4) Put under the grill to brown and serve at once.

FOR DRINKING

Take a pint of sour milk, add sufficient sugar to sweeten, beat with an egg whisk for 5 minutes, add a few drops of flavouring essence, such as vanilla, strawberry or ginger. Pour into glasses ready for serving.

The Arabs put half sour milk and half water together, then shake well. It makes an acceptable cooling drink for a hot day.

('Acceptable' seems somewhat euphemistic!)

'A Hundred Cheese Recipes' offered ideas to the housewife on ways to use the cheese ration.

Cheese

In May 1941 cheese was rationed as the vast majority of milk production was taken up trying to minimise the milk shortage. People were advised:

Do not throw away sour milk. Keep it in a warm place till it becomes solidified. Then put it in a cloth and hang to drain out the water. Mix the residue with a little margarine and season with salt, cayenne pepper and a little sugar, to a smooth paste. Use for sandwiches.

Sweet cheese can be made by mixing the residue with the yolk of an egg, and adding a few raisins and sugar. This can be used for filling pancakes or cheese tarts.

Cooking Fat

The shortage of cooking fats especially became a problem for many housewives, and the MoF advised saving fat from bacon, chops and other meat to render down; using the fat that collected at the top of stews; sieving and cleaning fat for re-use; and frying fatty fish without oil. After boiling fatty meats and suet puddings, it was suggested that the liquid be allowed to stand overnight to get cold. Then the skimmings could be used for shallow frying, allowed to heat through slowly first until the water had evaporated.

Sugar

Sugar rationing meant wedding cakes, covered in icing, became a thing of the past, although this might not have appeared the case. Wonderfully authentic-looking tiered 'cakes' made of plaster were available for hire. On the side of the base was a hidden door that, when opened, revealed a tiny cake. This was not for eating, but so that tiny cubes could be kept 'for luck'.

FOOD FACTS

If you are short of fat, use this pie crust which is made without fat. Mix together 8 oz wheatmeal flour, 1 level teaspoonful baking powder, a pinch of salt, a pinch of powdered sage if liked. Stir in nearly ¼ pint of cold milk, or milk and water. Roll out the mixture and use it as you would an ordinary crust, but serve the pie hot.

To save sugar when cooking rhubarb or plums, boil the fruit (before adding the sugar) with a little bicarbonate of soda.

A WEEK'S MENU

Of course, there was more to it than finding new and exciting recipes for just one meal, the real art was in putting together a week's meals on limited rations. It wasn't really a question of finding enough to eat, but more of making a menu that was not completely boring at a time when the bulk of food was made up of vegetables, the main varieties of which were available seasonally, rather than daily. As well as ordinary recipe books, there were more adventurous publications. Hurricane books' *Kitchen Parade*, published in 1941, set out menus for whole weeks. It was even published in four editions – spring, summer, autumn and winter – so that the availability of seasonal vegetables could be taken into account. The menus and recipes were written by the Austrian chef I. Diener. 'This book of recipes,' we are told rather grandly, 'by a man who once commanded Europe's finest chefs de cuisine, is planned to help in the first line of defence, the Kitchen Front.' The menus are fascinating especially for their use of non-rationed meats and vegetarian alternatives.

The following is a typical week's programme of main meals, including some recipes for the more interesting items. We are told that the amounts are 'based accurately on the amount of rationed food available for a typical family of five – three adults and two children'.

Sunday

Barley and bean soup
Roast beef, Yorkshire Pudding, Sauté potatoes
Lemon meringue pie

Every Sunday's menu is some form of the traditional roast lunch.

Monday

Leek soup
Housewife casserole
Sago pudding

As was the habit at the time, Monday's main dish was based on Sunday's leftovers.

Tuesday

Peapod soup
Vegetable pudding
Tomato salad
Plum roll

HOUSEWIFE CASSEROLE

Line greased casserole with breadcrumbs. Lay out with sliced raw potatoes and a few rashers of bacon. Mince rest of cold meat from the joint, mix with cut cold cooked vegetables, season. Put into casserole, cover with raw sliced potatoes, sprinkle with dripping and baste for 40 minutes.

VEGETABLE PUDDING

Boil ½ lb of macaroni in salted water with 1 cup of fresh peas until tender. Mix with 1 cupful of breadcrumbs, 2 spoonfuls white sauce, 1 tablespoonful grated cheese. Put in greased pie dish lined with breadcrumbs. Spread 1 oz margarine on top with 1 tablespoonful grated cheese, bake until golden brown.

Wednesday

Cabbage soup
Braised sheep's heart
Steamed potatoes
Trifle

Heart was off ration – not that people exactly rejoiced at this.

Thursday

Potato soup
Hot-Pot
Rice pudding

The Hot-Pot is made of stew 'previously prepared from all kinds of cold meat available – the rest of the joint, bacon, sausages, etc.'

Friday

Lentil soup
Fish cakes
Green peas and carrots
Chocolate balls

Like the traditional roast on Sunday, fish was the traditional meal on Friday.

Saturday

Green pea soup
Stewed rabbit and dumplings
Pancakes

Rabbit was also off ration.

CHOCOLATE BALLS

Soak stale buns or other sweet cakes in milkwater. Press out and form into equal little balls. Dip in breadcrumbs, fry in hot fat till golden brown. Before serving pour hot chocolate sauce over them.

CHOCOLATE SAUCE

Soften 1 bar of chocolate in oven. Mix with 1 cup milk, 1 tablespoon sugar, re-heat, stirring constantly. Alternatively, 2 tablespoonfuls cocoa could be used.

Chocolate was not rationed until the following year.

PETS

One member of the extended family who received no rations at all was the pet. It became increasingly hard to feed animals and the numbers of family pets dipped sharply during the period. As early as 1937, in *The Householder's Handbook*, people were advised to send their pets out of the danger areas, in the case of an emergency, if possible. Many were unable to do so, and when the war came many chose to have their pets put down, anticipating the problems which lay ahead. In the first phase of the war, cats and dogs suffered heavily in blackout road accidents – the RSPCA and other animal groups encouraged owners to keep their pets in during the hours of blackout, making sure they were exercised during daylight.

The relentless mayhem of the Blitz was a nightmare for animals; owners were advised to use bromide or aspirins as sedatives when the warning siren was sounded, but many pets ran away never to be seen again. Animals were banned from public shelters, partly because it was feared they might be driven mad and attack people. In some places, such as Kensington Gardens in London, dog air raid shelters were erected. The bombing claimed many animal as well as human lives. In September 1940, the first month of the Blitz, almost 11,000 bomb-injured animals had to be put down.

The Government, working with the animal charities, set up NARPAC, the National ARP for Animals Committee, whose animal stewards acted

The National ARP for Animals Committee (NARPAC) was set up to co-ordinate the rescue and care of animals injured in air raids. Here a PDSA animal rescue team are searching among the ruins for trapped pets.

Bob Martin's 'Condition Powder Tablets' would help keep dogs fit. (*Picture Post*, 1944)

as air raid wardens for animals, helping to find, feed and identify lost animals, and dig out and treat trapped animals. To help identify lost animals, owners were encouraged to register their cat or dog with NARPAC; they would then receive numbered discs to attach to the pets' collars, to help identification.

As food shortages really began to bite, keeping a pet was an increasing headache and, sadly, the flow of animals taken to the vets to be put to sleep was constant. It was not only the food shortages that affected pet food; before the war, 15 million tins of pet food were being produced each year, using vast amounts of valuable metal. By 1941 pet food tins had been replaced by re-usable bottles produced under familiar names such as Chappie and Kit-e-Kat, along with the less familiar such as Red Heart and Ken-L-Ration. As the war went on, meat became harder to obtain and so too did some of these early alternatives; potatoes, which had become an increasing part of the human diet, were fed to pets too. The RSPCA suggested they be mixed with gravy made from bones as this meant that the bones could still be used for salvage afterwards. 'Horseflesh', as horsemeat was known, could be used, or 'carcase residues' from the butcher.

Offal, when it was not rationed, was one solution for cats and dogs, although the amounts involved could be prohibitively expensive and hard to find. One source suggests 2 lb of meat a day for large dogs such as Alsatians. (Some people still regarded owning these dogs and Dachshunds as unpatriotic, though nowhere near as many as had been of that opinion during the First World War.)

Cookery in Wartime gave some suggestions for pet meals; for cats they suggested a large saucerful of tepid milk for breakfast, and for dinner a saucerful of finely chopped, lightly boiled liver twice a week, stewed rabbit and onions twice, and the meat from a cod's head or tail, simmered in a little milk, on the other days. These had to be mixed with a little stale bread, soaked in gravy, and a little of whatever vegetable the family were having. An alternative was chopped, stewed oxheart, with vegetables and bread or boiled rice. If rationing tightened, the book suggested collecting fish and meat scraps, and mixing 2 or 3 oz with dried stale bread, boiled rice or thick porridge with gravy. 'Keep all meat gravy and fish broth for your cat. Toss cereal flakes, bits of left-over toast, or dried crusts in it. Some cats will take tripe if fried in a little dripping and cooked in a little stock with onion. Always season food with a little salt before cooking.' Milk could be replaced by water, of course, although this should be occasionally substituted by meat stock or diluted gravy.

Dogs, on the whole, are easier to feed than cats. Extra dog biscuits or stale bread soaked in gravy were recommended as a replacement for some of the meat. As with cats, the meat could also be stretched by adding rice, oats, vegetables, toasted scraps of bread and so on. Dog dinners suggested by *Cookery in Wartime* included: stewed liver and onions with boiled rice; tripe with carrot and onion; stewed oxheart with onion, greens and stale bread soaked in gravy; sheep's head broth; stewed rabbit, carrot and onion, with greens and stale brown bread soaked in gravy. Bones were to be given three times a week.

That these recipes were suggested at an early stage in the war is clear because of the liberal use of milk, the specification of brown bread (there was no other bread after March 1942), and the assumed plentiful supply of meat, even if it is only offal, and bones.

DIG FOR VICTORY

The first official use of the phrase 'Dig for Victory' was on leaflets issued by the Ministry of Agriculture and Fisheries in November 1939 calling for '500,000 allotment holders' as part of the Government's Grow More campaign. (The phrase 'Dig for Victory' was first coined in an *Evening Standard* leader.) The allotment scheme was run locally through the borough, parish or district council. Owners or occupiers of land that was not in full use were asked to place it at the council's disposal, either free of rent or at an agreed agricultural rent. Soon every piece of spare ground was being turned over to food production. Householders converted their lawns and flower beds to vegetable crops, and vast amounts of spare land were turned over to allotments, to be worked by those who had little or no garden of their own. The allotments included the moat around the Tower of London and there were even plans to dig up the Centre Court at Wimbledon.

In September 1940 Dig for Victory became a campaign in its own right, complete with posters and leaflets; for some time both Grow More and Dig for Victory leaflets were produced. Once again the Ministry called for allotment holders – another 500,000. During 1940, Defence Regulations permitted all allotment holders to keep pigs, rabbits and hens. In October, the Minister of Agriculture urged every householder to convert part of his or her garden to vegetable growing.

One feature of many wartime gardens was the Anderson shelter; as part of its construction it was sunk into a hole and the earth piled on top to a depth of about half a metre. This was an area ripe for horticulture; some recommended it be turned into a rockery, although it was most

A selection of adverts promoting the idea of digging for victory.

popularly used for growing marrows. Although not so comfortable for people, the dark, damp atmosphere inside the shelter was ideal for mushrooms and rhubarb.

Many of those now growing vegetables had little or no experience of doing so. To help them, a series of Dig for Victory leaflets was issued free by the Ministry. These gave tips on various aspects of vegetable and fruit growing such as: no. 9, 'How to make Bordeaux and Burgundy mixtures in small quantities' (these are fungicides, not wines!), and no. 7, 'How to make a compost heap'. Many of the leaflets covered the more obvious carrots, onions, peas, potatoes, and so on, but they also encouraged growing exotic crops such as celeriac, salsify, kohlrabi, pumpkins and Chinese artichokes. The Ministry soon realised that inexperience was leading to a general failure to plan for all-year round crops, and a new campaign was launched, complete with cropping plans and model allotments set up in local parks.

There was a huge response to the scheme. Not only did it appeal to the love of gardening shared by so many in Britain, it was also, on a more mundane level, just about the only way to supplement the rations. Suburban gardeners pulled up their pretty flowerbeds, dug up the lawn, and began growing food. To help them there was a plethora of books; the *Daily Mail*'s *Food from the Garden in Wartime*, for example, was 'planned and written with the main idea of helping the beginner in vegetable growing'. And it was true to its word; as well as chapters on 'when to sow' and 'what to sow', there was even a chapter on 'how to use a spade and a fork', complete with diagrams. *Country Life*'s *Home Front* range was of a more ambitious nature, with titles such as 'Poultry keeping on small lines', 'Rabbit keeping', 'Vegetable crops under glass' and 'Pig keeping'.

All sorts of groups organised talks on gardening, including the Ministry of Agriculture, local horticultural societies, the WVS and the Women's Institutes. The hugely popular *Food Production Brains Trusts* were a live wartime version of the modern radio programme, *Gardeners' Question Time*, and brought panels of experts to village halls, city schools, and town halls to answer questions from the floor about gardening problems. These talks and panels were often part of local Dig for Victory Weeks, which would also include lectures, films, cookery demonstrations and competitions.

In 1942 the BBC outside broadcast staff adopted an allotment, like today's 'Blue Peter Garden', and listeners were treated to a series of topical programmes, *Radio*

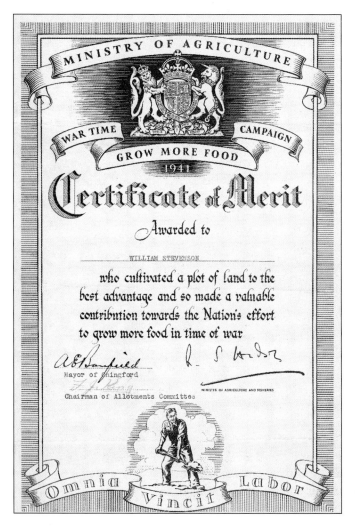

William Stevenson was awarded this certificate by the Chingford Grow More Food campaign in 1941. The initial enthusiasm for Dig for Victory in 1939 soon began to wane, and initiatives such as this were constantly needed to re-vitalise the scheme. (Courtesy Sylvia Harris, née Stevenson)

Allotment, which looked at work in the allotment throughout the year, specifically with the complete novice gardener in mind. One garden broadcaster who had become a star was Cecil Middleton, the 'Wireless Gardener'. Known almost universally as 'Mr Middleton', he had first started broadcasting *In Your Garden* in 1934. The 15-minute programmes continued throughout the war and had an audience of 3½ million. Although Cecil was an excellent broadcaster, his brother later recalled that he was not very successful with his own garden!

In 1942 the Government introduced National Growmore Fertiliser, containing 7 per cent each of nitrogen, potash and phosphates; each allotment holder was allowed 42 lb a year. Gardeners were further encouraged to make compost heaps, a practice that, although common today, was far more unusual at the time.

Having successfully grown the vegetables or fruit, it was most important not to lose them. With this in mind there were several publications such as Dig for Victory leaflet no. 3, 'Storing vegetables for winter use', and no. 10, 'Jam and jelly making'. The latter pointed out that while jam was normally made with 1 lb of fruit to 1 lb of sugar, it could be done using only ¾ lb of sugar to 1 lb of fruit. The result did not keep well, but was 'excellent for immediate consumption'. The leaflet further advised: 'Whenever possible, two batches of jam should be made, one for keeping (using the full amount of sugar), and one for quick use.' Growmore bulletin no. 3, 'Preserves from the garden', included sections on jam and jelly making, fruit syrups, fruit cheeses and pickles.

> 'Let Dig for Victory be the motto of everyone with a Garden'
> Minister of Agriculture, 1939

FRUIT CHEESES

Blackcurrants, damsons, medlars and quinces all make excellent fruit cheeses. The finished cheeses should be firm enough to be cut with a knife and full of the flavour of the fruit used. The amount of fruit used, in proportion to the cheese made, is large, and therefore fruit cheese should be made when there is a glut of fruit. It improves with keeping, and should never be eaten under six months.

Method: Wash the fruit. Put in a preserving pan and nearly cover with cold water. Simmer gently till soft. Put through a hair sieve. Weigh the pulp and allow 1 lb of sugar (loaf if possible) to each 1 lb pulp. Let the sugar dissolve gently, then boil until it becomes stiff (three-quarters to one hour), stirring all the time as it will burn easily. Pour into warm moulds and tie down as for jellies.

Inevitably, the first flush of enthusiasm for digging for victory began to fade after a while and a new campaign – Dig On for Victory – was needed. By 1945, the slogan had become the frankly unimaginative 'Dig for Victory Still'.

LIVESTOCK

People were encouraged to keep animals for food. Suburban gardens now sported ducks, chickens and even goats in their sheds or garages, which did not always please the neighbours. Bacon was one of the first food items rationed, and people began to keep pigs. To help them, the Small

Pig Keepers Club was set up. This helped to convince councils to change their by-laws, and to allow people to keep pigs in their gardens. Pig bins – galvanised dustbins especially used for the purpose – were to be found at the corner of most streets, into which people would place any edible scraps. (The resultant swill had to be cooked for an hour to kill dangerous organisms.)

Rabbits were another favourite, as they were easy to breed, keep and feed. A shed or garage could be converted to hold several of them in banks of cages, and their skins could be used, or even sold to furriers.

Chickens and ducks were kept in the back-yard. Chicken itself was rarely on the menu as a food because eggs were far too important. However, chickens will not lay unless fed well, and obtaining chicken feed was difficult. The product was rationed and the owners could only get it by trading the equivalent egg ration for it. Friends and neighbours formed poultry clubs, all of whom would trade in their rations and share the eggs. On the whole, though, chickens were relatively easy to look after and people were encouraged to keep a few, just enough to feed on kitchen scraps.

The practice of keeping animals in their back-yards gave people the nickname of back-yarders. It was all very well in theory but one constantly recurring theme when talking to people whose parents were back-yarders was that the pig, rabbit or chicken tended to became the family pet. Come the fateful day, it was Dad who had to catch and hold the poor creature and kill it himself; many found that it was far more difficult than they had anticipated to kill an animal that won't stand still. Even if this were achieved, the father of the family would come back to

Below: Pig-swill bins were a common sight on many wartime street corners. (Imperial War Museum)

Below, right: A pig club demonstration at a 'Grow Your Own Food' exhibition staged at Charing Cross. (Imperial War Museum)

the house to find a tableful of weeping children, who could not bring themselves to eat 'Snowy the bunny' or 'Pinky the piglet' and the long-awaited feast became more of a wake.

FOOD FOR FREE

In the 1970s, as part of the self-sufficiency movement, many books of recipes using wild ingredients were published. One of the best, and best known, is Richard Mabey's *Food For Free*. However, like so much else that is 'new', this style of cuisine had been widely known before; as the Second World War went on, every potential source of food was utilised.

Nettles were widely used; young leaves could be used like spinach, topped with a knob of margarine and a sprinkle of nutmeg. *Food Facts for the Kitchen Front* suggested nettles be mixed with potatoes in a variation of Champ. Blackberries and various types of wild mushrooms were collected, and dandelion leaves could be made into a salad: 1 pint of leaves with a diced beetroot in vinaigrette (lettuce could be substituted for the beetroot). Rose and primrose flowers were utilised, and rose hips could be made into jam or syrup.

Old country skills and recipes were also widely publicised. Wine making, using ingredients such as elderberries and elderflowers, was popular at a time when beer and especially spirits could be difficult to get.

Wild produce was not only collected for food; plants for medicinal use were highly sought after too. Rose hips were a great source of vitamin C and widely available, and children were encouraged to pick them. They were paid 3*d* per lb at collecting points, usually run by the WVS or Women's Institutes. A great many of those collected, however, became unusable because of poor harvesting or storage so magazines ran articles giving 'Tips for Hip Pickers':

Snap the berries off – don't pull them . . .
    Look for varieties with large hips – quicker work and better vitamin content . . .
    Wear thick gloves, old clothes, and no stockings. If you have no gloves, make a fingerless shield like a hedging glove for the left hand from thick fabric yourself . . .
    It's a lovely job for a bright, crisp, autumn day, but if you do get bored with it – think of the delicate children whose health depends upon vitamin C . . .

Other widely used medicinal plants included foxgloves, belladonna, dandelion roots, sphagnum moss and stinging nettles.

Food Facts for the Kitchen Front contained recipes that made the most of every available ingredient.

Rowan Berries (Mountain Ash) make a preserve with a pleasant tang, admirable to serve with cold meats. You can make the preserve with the berries alone, or with a couple of apples to each pound of berries.

SEVEN

'IF THE INVADER COMES'

Shortly after the end of the First World War Britain had begun to make contingency plans to deal with another war. But the horrors of that conflict meant that the dominant feeling was determination not to repeat 'the war to end all wars'. This lead to appeasement, and to a view in some quarters that any preparations for war, even defensive ones, were inherently provocative. More prosaically, another reason that few preparations were made was because of the costs involved and, throughout the twenties and early thirties at least, the population generally hoped that if it ignored the threat of war, it would go away.

HELP YOURSELF

By the latter half of the thirties the mood was changing and people were increasingly, if reluctantly, coming to the conclusion that war was coming. This belief spread dramatically after the Munich Crisis of September 1938. Slowly at first, a series of Government leaflets, commercially produced books, booklets, radio talks and magazine articles appeared on how to prepare yourself and your home for air raids, which were expected on a massive scale. The subject matter and information in these publications changed as Government plans developed, and as people learnt from the experience.

Early advice emphasised self-help; W. Heath Robinson, hugely popular at the time with his drawings of unfeasibly complex machines performing strange functions, would have been impressed by some of this. At first, the main perceived threat was from poison gas, the terror weapon of the First World War, and most of the advice was centred around that. Early Government booklets such as *Personal Protection against Gas*, issued by the Air Raid Precautions (ARP) department of the Home Office in 1937, stated that 'every household must have its own gas protected room'. The booklet gave brief instructions on choosing a suitable room: the room should, if possible, be a cellar or basement, or otherwise on the ground floor; it should also be on the side of the house least exposed to the prevailing wind; the windows should be small and face soft ground since 'the blast of an exploding bomb may be more smothered than if they face a paved or metallic surface'. Doors and windows should be protected, the former with a blanket. So far so good, but it went on to talk, in vague terms, about forming an air lock – which was well beyond the ability of most people.

Male and female Fire Guards; the helmet and armband were the only uniform that most of them received. The woman is carrying an interesting privately produced gas mask case. (Imperial War Museum)

ARP

ARP – Air Raid Precautions – were a series of measures designed to cut down the casualties and damage done by air raids. These 'precautions' included air raid warnings, lighting restrictions (better known as the blackout), shelters, gas-masks and evacuation.

The ARP unit involved a number of organisations who were, in effect, a massive expansion of the emergency services, but whose work was aimed specifically at preparation for air raids and dealing with the after-effects. Along with the existing emergency services, the police, fire brigade, and casualty services, they made up the Civil Defence Services.

ARP was controlled centrally by the Home Office, under Wing Commander Eric Hodsall. Its early work centred around making the general public aware of the problems of air raids, and encouraging them to take whatever measures they could. This included producing many pamphlets and booklets.

At first the great majority of ARP workers were part-time, unpaid volunteers. Those who were full time were paid £3 a week for men, £2 for women. During the Phoney War this caused a great deal of complaint, as people said ARP personnel were being paid for doing nothing but interfering. ARP wardens were often greeted with abuse, and some councils even laid people off. But when the Blitz came, the moaning stopped, literally overnight in many places. Soon there weren't enough ARP workers, and by the beginning of 1941 the Ministry of Home Security was forced to issue the first Civil Defence Compulsory Enrolment Order. This stated that all males aged sixteen to sixty, not already doing civil defence or home guard duties, must do up to 48 hours fire-watching a month.

Over the course of the war 2,379 civil defence workers were killed in the line of duty and another 4,459 were seriously injured.

It was quite common for first aid posts to be set up in front rooms, disused shops, anywhere with sufficient space. (Imperial War Museum)

A member of the Home Guard cleans his rifle in the kitchen of his home under the watchful gaze of his young son. (Imperial War Museum)

AIR RAID SHELTERS

In 1937 the Home Secretary told Parliament that it would be impossible to make existing buildings bomb-proof. Purpose-built public shelters would be constructed, although the Government was unsure how these shelters would be designed. A heated public debate ensued; many on the Left, notably prominent members of the Communist party such as the old Etonian scientist J.B.S. Haldane, favoured large, deep shelters. The Government's policy was one of dispersal; they feared that the carnage caused by a direct hit on a large shelter would have a devastating blow on morale, far worse than a steady trickle of casualties from hits on small shelters. The Government and its supporters further argued that it would take too long for a large number of people to reach and enter a large public shelter, especially at night during a blackout. Many would be left in the open when the raid started, or crushed to death in the rush. (Sadly,

STOCKING THE REFUGE-ROOM
*Particular attention should be paid to stocks of food, water both for drinking and extinguishing fires,
first-aid outfit and tools for digging a way out.*

An illustration from a DIY book of the late thirties showing some of the items needed in a refuge room.

There was a fear that the enemy would attack with poison gas, and shelters would therefore need to be 'gas-proof'. This drawing shows a 'filtration plant'; run by electricity, it could be worked by foot power if supplies were cut.

this actually happened in March 1943 when 173 people, including 62 children, were killed in the rush to enter an underground public air raid shelter in Bethnal Green, London.) The Left countered that the Government's main motive was cost, and that inner-city dwellers had no space for individual shelters. As a result, several large underground shelters were built in London later in the war.

The dispersal scheme assumed that most people would shelter at home. In 1938 the Home Office produced a booklet entitled *The Protection of Your Home against Air Raids*, which sold for 1*d*. One of its main themes was the creation of a 'refuge room', which was basically a shelter against bombs and especially gas. The advice given was similar to that in the earlier ARP department booklet, but more detailed. To make the refuge room gas proof, cracks and crevices were to be filled in with putty or soggy newspapers, paper pasted over cracks in the walls or ceiling, and the fireplace sealed by pushing newspaper up the chimney. 'Do not, of course, light a fire in the grate afterwards' the householder was warned! The room could also be protected against 'explosive bombs' by fixing braces from floor to ceiling: 'Stout posts or scaffold poles are placed upright, resting on a thick plank on the floor and supporting a stout piece of timber against the ceiling, at right angles to the ceiling joists, i.e. in the same direction as the floor boards above.' How much protection all this would really have given is, at best, questionable, although these measures made a valuable contribution to morale. Although people were not unconcerned about aerial bombardment, most remained unimpressed by these suggestions. Some people probably did build a gas-proof room, but we've never come across any of them.

No shelter or refuge room was complete until it had been properly stocked. The 1938 Home Office booklet *The Protection of Your Home against Air Raids* contained the following advice:

These are some of the things that will be useful in your refuge room. Keep them in mind and begin collecting those things you haven't got, one by one. Put them in a box, or in a drawer, in the room you have chosen for your refuge room. Candles and matches, hammer and nails, scissors, old newspaper and brown paper, some clean rags, needles, cotton and thread. A candle lamp or an electric hand lamp, suitable material to protect the windows from the blast of an explosion, gummed paper and adhesive tape, plywood for blocking the fireplace, a few tins or jars with air-tight lids for storing food, a bottle of disinfectant and a box of first aid supplies.

'As soon as the Government warns you of a threat of war' a second set of items had to be added to the shelter room. This included a list of all who should be present, tables and chairs, crockery and cutlery, plenty of water for drinking, washing and fire-fighting, tinned food with a tin opener, a food chest of some size to protect other food against contact with gas – airtight tins or jars would do – a wash-stand or basin, washing things, soap, towels, chamber pots, toilet paper, disinfectant, a screen for privacy, books, writing materials, cards, toys for the children, a simple hand pump, and sand with a long-handled shovel, gummed paper for pasting paper over cracks in walls and window panes, pickaxe and shovel (to dig your way out).

Last came a list of items to be taken in from the rest of the house only 'when you hear the air raid warning'. This was comprehensive and included mattresses, overcoats, blankets, eiderdowns, rugs and warm coverings, the wireless set, gramophone with records, mackintoshes, galoshes, gum-boots, and an electric kettle. Even if the average suburban home had a single room that could hold the family, these and all the other items deemed essential, the idea that the family could drag down its mattresses, bedding, gramophone and so on when the siren went could have seemed feasible only to those who had absolutely no practical knowledge of air raids.

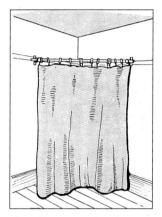

These illustrations show how to gas proof a fireplace, and a modesty-screen across a toilet area.

The Anderson Shelter

With war approaching fast, the Government at last introduced a small shelter for family use. At first it was intended that this should be inside the house, but this proved impractical. An amended version could be erected outside, usually in private gardens, between 6 and 15 feet from the house. The shelter was officially called the 'sectional steel shelter', universally referred to as 'the Anderson'.

Andersons were supplied free of charge to the poorer inhabitants of danger areas, and for a fee to anyone else; from £6 14s to £10 18s depending on size. They were the perfect shelters for the suburbs: they needed a back garden, which many inner-city dwellers did not possess, and the standard shelter took four people, six at a pinch, easily accommodating the average suburban

A REAL GNOME FROM GNOME?

Having constructed it, many people began to personalise their Anderson, growing flowers on it or covering it with turf. Some even decorated it with stone gnomes or sea shells. The Government, being of a more practical inclination, advised vegetable growing.

An illustration showing the Anderson shelter covered with the earth from the hole in which it has been erected.

The remains of an Anderson shelter after a near miss. Three children survived inside it. (HMSO)

family. Delivery of the Andersons began in February 1939 and by mid-1940 over 2¼ million Andersons had been supplied. Later, a larger version was designed that could take up to twelve persons.

As the official name implied, this shelter was delivered in sections made of corrugated iron and had to be put up by the householder. First, a large hole had to be dug, at least 3 feet deep. The shelter had to be erected inside the hole and the earth from the hole spread over the completed shelter to a depth of at least 15 inches so, in effect, the shelter was buried underground.

Being partially underground, Andersons often became filled with water and were, at best, damp, draughty and cramped. In 1941, with the experience of the Big Blitz to draw on, the 1940 Ministry of Home Security booklet *Air Raids – What You Must KNOW, What You Must DO* was re-issued, 'completely re-written'. There was a large section on the problems of Andersons, and how to cure the damp. This could be done by constructing runnels to draw away surface water. Failing this, the earth covering could be removed, the joints between the iron sheets sealed with strips of tarred rag or hessian, and the earth replaced in layers of 4 or 5 inches, well rammed down. Should the joints still leak they could be caulked from the inside with rope or old rags soaked in heavy oil or tar. Condensation could be lessened by painting the inside walls with paint or shellac varnish, and throwing dry sawdust on the paint while it was wet. Alternatively the inside could be lined with lino, plasterboard, felt, or even wallpaper.

Although not the perfect solution, and certainly not capable of withstanding a direct hit, Andersons did provide good protection from a near miss or bomb splinters that would wreck many houses.

The Morrison Shelter

The Anderson had proved successful in saving lives, but it required space – such as a garden – to be put up in and many in the inner cities, where most of the raids were concentrated, had no garden. At the end of 1940, the Government introduced a shelter for indoor use, primarily for those who did not have a back garden. Once again, these shelters were free to anyone earning less than £350 per annum, or could be bought for £7 by anyone else. Officially called the table shelter, it was soon nicknamed the 'Morrison' after Herbert Morrison, the Minister of Home Defence. One of the first Morrisons was installed at No. 10 Downing Street.

A low, steel cage, 6 feet 6 inches by 4 feet and 2 feet 9 inches high, its top was of sheet metal and its sides covered with wire mesh. It was designed to hold two adults and one child (or two very small children). Later, a double-decker version was brought out. When not in use, the mesh sides could be swung inwards and, covered by a cloth, it would double up as a table.

As with the Anderson, the Morrison was delivered in pieces and had to be assembled by the householder. So, in April 1941 the Ministry of Home Security produced a booklet, *How to Put Up Your Morrison Shelter*, which took you through the procedure with the aid of diagrams. People who

A Morrison shelter; the wire mesh could be removed so that the frame could form a table. (Imperial War Museum)

"By the way, did you remember to feed the canary?"

A Sillince cartoon depicting a Morrison shelter. The war proved a rich vein of humour for cartoonists and comedians.

were not able to construct the shelter for themselves – those who were frail or sick – could contact youth groups like the Scouts or Boys' Brigade, who would help.

Morrisons were not used exclusively by those who had no garden. Many in the suburbs bought, or were provided with Morrisons; some even had both a Morrison and an Anderson shelter.

Another indoor shelter, 'the timber framework type', was based, as its name suggests, on a frame erected inside a room, 'almost ceiling high, so that it leaves the householder the normal use of practically the whole of the room'.

In spite of all these variations, even in the suburbs many people never had their own shelters, choosing either to use the public shelters, or to take refuge in the cupboard under the stairs or even under a table.

Shelter Life

Throughout the course of the war the level of enemy activity varied enormously. Before the war, air raids were expected to be immensely destructive but to last only a short time. This would have meant that time spent sheltering would also be limited, so there was no anticipated need for comfort in a shelter. In the event, entire nights were spent 'under warning', so it was soon realised that the Anderson would need provision for sleeping.

At the start of the Blitz, for those who didn't have a spare mattress, advice included putting an airbed on the floor, or a rug covered with an eiderdown. Some people even built their own cabin-style beds, or made hammocks out of old tennis nets. Later, the bunks that became a feature of so many Andersons were introduced. At first, they had to be put up by the householder – one booklet explained how these could be easily made from:

a few feet of timber (2 inch by 2 inch) and some suitable lengths of canvas, hessian or stout wire netting. The standard 6½ feet Anderson provides sleeping room for four adults and two small children (or four babies), and with extensions, any number up to twelve persons. Bunks for the adults should rest on the angle irons inside the shelter, and two smaller bunks (about 4½ feet by 2 feet, on legs about 14 inches high) should be placed at the ends of the others, in such a way that the feet of the adults occupying the larger bunks pass under the smaller bunks.

If you could afford them, bunks were available commercially; later, local authorities supplied bunks.

Shelters could only be lit with electricity because naked lights used up air, and could cause fires, especially in such a small space, although people were advised to keep candles or lamps for emergency lighting. Heating posed a similar problem; the main forms of coal, gas and oil fires could not be used, so alternatives were suggested.

Hot drinks were one solution, contained in Thermos flasks or 'hay bottles' – woollen bags packed with newspaper or straw with a bottle inside. Warm clothing would help, as would sleeping bags, which could be made from two blankets. A hot brick, heated in front of a fire for two hours and then wrapped in a woollen cloth or old vest, made a bed warmer.

Building and equipping air raid shelters and refuge rooms became big business after the Munich Crisis. These adverts show just one of the many types of commercial shelters that were available, along with some of the furniture that might go inside.

Londoners sought shelter in underground stations. Here, people are even bedding down between the rails. Obviously this could only happen when the trains had stopped running and the live rails switched off. (Imperial War Museum)

One of the most original ideas was the 'flower pot heater'. This was made by fixing a candle at the bottom of a flower pot by the drain hole (without blocking up the hole), and then placing a second flower pot upside down on top of the first. After a while this arrangement gave off 'considerable warmth'.

Food and drink had to be taken to the shelter and, to start with, this was usually in the form of snacks, biscuits and a flask of cocoa. But as time and the raids went on, and on, shelter provisions became an elaborate and specialised picnic. Books suggested soup or broth, in a flask or a hay bottle, sandwiches, pasties or pies, and biscuits or cakes. People often had a suitcase or bag ready, containing the family's ration books, identity cards, gas masks, insurance policies, books, games, magazines and comics, so that these things were immediately to hand. Other advice included taking in eau-de-cologne and smelling salts, to 'freshen up' – the *Daily Sketch* of 29 August 1940 pointed out that Atkinson's of Bond Street sold 'special little air raid shelter packs', containing a small bottle of each.

At the height of the Big Blitz in November 1940, a shelter survey found that 27 per cent of people were sleeping in private shelters, and 13 per cent were in public shelters including the underground. Of the rest, many were determinedly fatalistic – 'If it's got your name on it, that's that.' Some took shelter indoors, under the stairs or the table, and many were just too tired; the prospect of a night in their own bed was just too tempting to make the shelter bearable.

CIVIL DEFENCE

In July 1939 four pamphlets on Civil Defence, issued by the Lord Privy Seal's Office, were delivered to every household in the country. No. 1, 'Some things you should know if war should come', gave brief notes under the headings of air raid warnings, gas masks, lighting restrictions, fire precautions, evacuation, identity labels, food and instructions to the public in case of emergency. The warning system, first set out in May 1938, consisted of a 2-minute warning, sounded by police using sirens and reinforced by policemen and wardens blowing their whistles. The country was divided into 111 districts so that warnings could be localised, the warning being sounded when enemy aircraft approached a district. In practice, this meant that warnings were often sounded in an area with no subsequent raid as the bombers passed overhead on their way to another town. The enemy learned quickly from this, and single German aircraft would fly around setting off warnings in several areas; the effect on morale and on production – factories would stop as the workers went down to the shelters – was significant. People began to hate the sound of the sirens almost as much as the bombs themselves, so the warning was cut to 1 minute, and efforts made to cut down on the number of warnings. This counter-measure was sometimes over-zealous too, as some areas were bombed without the warning being sounded at all.

Leaflet no. 2 dealt in detail with 'Your gas mask', looking at how to store it and how to put it on, and 'Masking your windows'. This part covered the blackout, explaining that, on the outbreak of war, all external lights and street lighting would be switched off, 'but this will not be fully effective unless you do your part, and see to it that no lighting in the house where you live is visible from the outside'. It suggested that the most convenient way of doing this was to use close-fitting blinds, which could be made of any thick, dark coloured material such as glazed

" Now, dear, you're quite clear what you've to do in the event of invasion, or gas, or high explosive, or incendiary bombs, or a combination of any two or more of them? . . ."

This Langdon cartoon pokes gentle fun at the plethora of pamphlets, leaflets and advice that was given to the householder.

Road accidents soared during the blackout, so manufacturers responded with a raft of 'luminous' gadgets, which, as the drastic price cuts imply, proved to be ineffective and consequently unpopular. (Imperial War Museum)

Above: Removing the blackout. You can also see the anti-blast tape on the window to prevent flying glass. (Imperial War Museum)

Above, right: Early advice rightly identified flying glass from windows as a major source of danger. As usual, manufacturers saw the selling opportunities, in this case for stick-on leaded lights as ARP equipment.

October 1941 saw the introduction of a new character – Firebomb Fritz – and a new service – the Fire Guard. Millions of civilians were directed to take part in part-time firewatching. (HMSO)

Holland, Lancaster or Italian Cloth. Thick curtains would also serve if they fully covered the windows with a bit of cloth to spare all round. Alternatively, you could fix up sheets of black paper or thick dark brown paper mounted on battens. Readers were advised to test material for suitability: 'Hold up a piece against an electric bulb. If no light shows through, or only scattered pin holes of light are seen, the material will do. If a patch of light shows through, it is no use.' Instructions were given for treating blinds that were not opaque, using a mixture of 1 lb of concentrated size, 3 lb lamp black in powder form, ½ a gill of gold size thoroughly mixed with 2½ gallons of boiling water. This produced enough to cover 80 square yards of material.

The leaflet went on to point out that it was most important not to forget skylights, fanlights, or glazed doors: 'You may find it simplest to make these permanently obscure by applying sufficient coats of some dark distemper or paint, or pasting them over with thick brown paper.' Back and front doors should be able to be opened without showing lights. This might be done by forming a 'light lock' in the hall or passage with a blanket, or by turning the lights off before the door was opened. It concluded with these remarks:

Do not leave things until the last, but get together the materials which you think you would need. If you wait, you might find that you had difficulty in getting what you wanted. Besides, your help is wanted in making effective the 'blackouts' for the ARP exercises which are being arranged to try out our defences from time to time.

Indeed, a series of blackout exercises did take place, one involving large areas of south-east England in August 1939.

Windows also featured in another form of air raid precaution; bomb blast would shatter glass, the pieces being blown through the air, adding to the casualties. People were encouraged to cover windows in sticky tape, stuck on in a criss-cross fashion, especially large windows. Trains and

buses often had netting pasted on to the windows, limiting the view. Once again, manufacturers saw an opening; lead strip had been sold as part of the thirties' craze for DIY, to create latticed windows or leaded lights. Now it was labelled as ARP protection for windows, and would work as well as any sticky tape.

Booklet no. 3 was on 'Evacuation – why and how?', and gave details of the Government's scheme. No. 4, 'Your food in wartime', included details of the food supply and rationing scheme. A fifth booklet, issued in August 1939, 'Fire precautions in wartime', was mainly about the incendiary bomb and methods of combating it, a task for which everyone was encouraged to take some responsibility:

> However strong the Fire Brigade may be, an outbreak of many fires close together and beginning at the same time would be more than it could successfully deal with unless the householder himself and his family took the first steps in defending their home.
>
> In Civil Defence EVERYBODY has a part to play. This is especially true of fire-fighting. In every house there should be one or more people ready to tackle a fire bomb.

The leaflet explained that most incendiary bombs would hit the roofs of houses, where they would penetrate, stopping at the first boarded floor: 'Fires will therefore mostly break out in roof spaces, attics and upper

A classic wartime picture; children with labels, teachers with armbands, and parents (not all of whom look unhappy). (Imperial War Museum)

Using a sandbag to extinguish an incendiary. (Imperial War Museum)

floors.' Incendiaries could be dealt with using water, but not thrown from a bucket, as this would have the effect of scattering molten metal, making things worse. The recommended method was a form of stirrup pump, a hand-operated pump designed specifically to fight incendiary bombs. They could also be smothered by dry sand and could then be scooped up, dropped into a bucket containing about 4 inches of sand, and removed.

The section 'What you should do now' contained the following advice: 'Clear your roof spaces and attics of any old "junk" that you have collected there.' This measure was later formalised by the wonderfully titled Clearance of Lofts Act 1940:

Make sure that you can easily get into your attic or roof space.

Have ready at least four large buckets, a shovel and a scoop, preferably with a long handle, and a fair quantity of sand or dry earth. Provide also what appliances you can; if possible, a stirrup hand pump with the special nozzle giving either a jet of water for playing on a fire, or spray for dealing with the jet itself. Failing this, a garden syringe would be useful, or even old blankets soaked in water.

The householder was advised, as soon as war seemed likely, to 'Fill at least two large buckets with water and see that they are kept filled.' This was fine for the average home, but less practical was the advice to 'Have a bath or tank kept full of water to refill the buckets in case of need'. We are sometimes given a glimpse of the privileged lives of the senior civil servants who wrote these leaflets; only they would think it practical to have a spare bath full of water for fire-fighting.

'KEEP CALM – DON'T PANIC'

In a popular book produced at the time, *ARP – A Practical Guide for the Householder and Air Raid Warden*, a section entitled 'Hints for householders – to prepare for an emergency' included the following:

Always carry your Respirator [the official name for the gas mask] with you whenever you leave your home or place of business, and an identity label on which your name and address are clearly written.

Don't let the children play with their gas masks.

STIRRUP PUMPS AND THE REDHILL SCOOP

Owners of stirrup pumps could get cards from their local council bearing the words 'Stirrup Pump' or just SP to display in their windows. Many places of work organised staff rotas to act as Fire Watchers – taking turns to watch the building at night, or at the weekend, usually armed with a tin helmet and a stirrup pump, ready to attack any fire bombs. For many it was a welcome source of overtime.

Civil Defence leaflet no. 5 also described the use of the Redhill scoop, hoe and container. This very useful (for its purpose) long-handled shovel and hoe were used to pour sand from the container onto the bomb without getting too close. The bomb could then be pushed onto the scoop with the hoe and tipped into the metal container. Householders were encouraged to buy some of this equipment themselves, either alone or with their neighbours to share the cost.

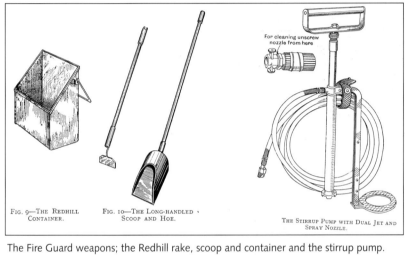

FIG. 9—THE REDHILL CONTAINER.

FIG. 10—THE LONG-HANDLED SCOOP AND HOE.

For cleaning unscrew nozzle from here

THE STIRRUP PUMP WITH DUAL JET AND SPRAY NOZZLE.

The Fire Guard weapons; the Redhill rake, scoop and container and the stirrup pump. These put out many of the hundreds of thousands of incendiary bombs that were dropped on Britain. (From the *Fire Guards' Handbook*, published 1942, HMSO)

A three-person stirrup pump team demonstrates its use. Only the one on the 'business end' enters the burning room, making use of whatever cover is available. (Imperial War Museum)

Don't wear glasses or, if a woman, a hair net, when you have put on your Respirator. [Wearing glasses over your gas mask might impair its efficiency, but a hair net?]

A second section, 'Hints for householders – during a raid', set out what the ordinary householder was expected to do on hearing the warning.

If you are at home, at once close all doors and windows. . . . Take the necessary extras into your refuge room.

Turn off all gas at the meter, put out all fires and, at night time, darken all lights visible from outside.

Assemble in the refuge room, call the roll of those who should be present, see that each has a respirator, and seal the room up.

This exercise was to be completed in the seven to ten minutes it was estimated that people would have before the Luftwaffe arrived. Another hint now irresistibly brings to mind Corporal Jones of *Dad's Army*: 'Keep calm – don't panic.' Some of the hints verge on the surreal: 'Don't rush into the street if you hear an explosion near by. . . .'

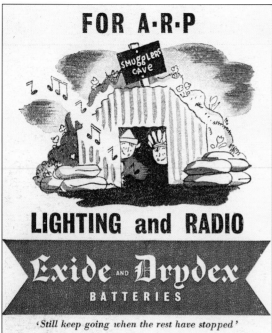

In the early days of war, the ordinary citizen was bombarded, not by bombs, but by advice from the government and others, and advertisements for various ingenious devices. Both the advice and the devices proved to be of variable value.

ANIMAL INSTINCTS

The family pet also had to be prepared for the coming raids. Dogs and cats were not allowed into public shelters, and people were advised to send their pets to the country if possible, although for many this was not an option. In the first week of the war, vets were overwhelmed with people wanting their pets put down, and there were quite literally piles of bodies outside some surgeries. If you kept your pet, you were advised to take your dog for walks near home so you would have time to get back if the warning sounded. The official advice was to keep dogs on a lead in your own shelter, with a muzzle on if possible. Tranquillisers or bromide from the vet were also recommended, as was putting cotton wool over the dog's ears. A dog's gas mask was produced, but it proved difficult; dogs come in such a wide range of shapes and sizes – even those it did fit struggled hard to get it off. As for cats, an ARP broadcast in 1939 recommended: 'Don't worry about your cats. Cats can take care of themselves far better than you can. Your cat will probably meet you when you get into the shelter.'

A mixed group of male and female wardens search through the rubble of a bombed out building. (Imperial War Museum)

ANIMAL SHELTERS

The *Handy Wartime Guide* by S. Evelyn Thomas gave the following advice on pet shelters. Small animals (dogs, cats, rabbits, etc.) can be adequately

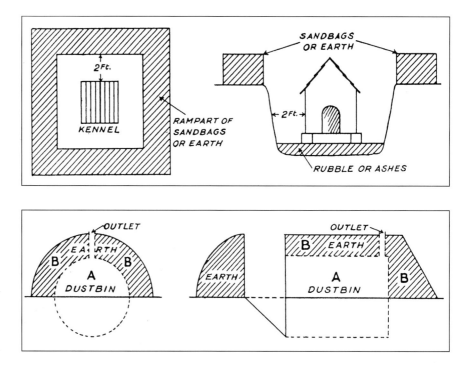

protected against high explosive blast and splinters in kennels and similar devices placed in the centre of a hole in the ground. The hole should be large enough to allow a space of at least two feet all round the kennel, and deep enough for only about one foot of the kennel to appear above ground level. To avoid or reduce dampness, place a good covering of broken bricks or ashes in the bottom of the hole, and place a brick under each corner of the kennel. Earth dug from the hole, or sandbags or boxes of earth, can be used to build a mound or rampart round the edge of the hole up to the level of the top of the kennel.

Kennels could be made gas-proof by adding a close-fitting door with felt or rubber round the edge. The point was then rather defeated by drilling air-holes in the door. The animals, (dogs, cats, rabbits, etc.) could then be shut in and the kennel made gas-proof by having a blanket draped over it which had been soaked, either in water, or preferably, a solution of one teaspoon of glycerine and one teaspoonful of washing soda to one pint of water, or in a solution of one ounce of permanganate of potash to a pint of water. Let the blanket trail on the ground all round the kennel, and fasten it tightly round the bottom of the kennel with string. If permanganate of potash is used, the dog must be muzzled so that he cannot chew the blanket, otherwise he might be poisoned!

A sort of pet's Anderson shelter could be made by burying a dustbin in the ground, as shown, with the earth dug out of the hole used to cover the dustbin, and to form a blast-wall to protect the entrance. The added benefit of this idea, which for some reason was described as being for use in an emergency only, was that the dustbin lid could be used as a door. For this reason an air outlet was added. Like the rather less sturdy-looking kennel in a hole idea, the dustbin-shelter could be made gas-proof with the addition of a soaked blanket draped over it.

EIGHT

FASHION

LADIES' CLOTHES

By the end of the 1930s, women were wearing a vast selection of styles. A room full of well-dressed women of the time would include revivals of everything from classical Grecian to Edwardian dress. Romantic and nostalgic images such as shepherdesses would be seen alongside sleek, modern styles. The desired body shapes could be padded or slimline, but the most fashionable was the curvaceous figure-of-eight shape, which emphasised the bust and the hips.

Dresses required corsetry again and some even had bustles in a retrospective nod to the style of the Victorian era. Advice for women over the age of forty appeared in the magazines and journals of the time; *Women and Beauty* carried corsetry advertisements that urged its readers to 'spend more time choosing your corset than any other item in your wardrobe'. But the necessary undergarments women now wore were in lightweight, elasticated fabrics, far more comfortable than the Victorian and Edwardian equivalents.

The key word in thirties fashions had been 'allure' and this continued to define the smart woman. It meant longer skirts and a gentle, curving shape from the shoulder to a high waist, replacing a straight line from the shoulder to a low, hip-level waist which had been so popular in the twenties, and a shapely bosom replaced the classic twenties flat chest. Femininity replaced androgyny.

From the mid-thirties onwards, in the immediate pre-war years, women's off-the-peg clothing had benefited enormously from the arrival of Jewish tailors and cutters from Vienna and Berlin. Previously, size labels could be vague: W for average sized women; SW for small women; and WX for large women. These new arrivals brought with them the techniques which led to British female clothing adopting the more accurate sizing method of 10, 12, 14, 16 and 18 that we know today. The techniques were eagerly adopted by the English women's wear trade as they also meant fabric lengths could be used more economically.

Huttons, advertised here in the 1930s, offered frocks for all activities – holiday frocks, garden frocks, house frocks and the 'all-day-long' frock. Before wartime restrictions war began, the dresses were available in many colours and fabrics.

MEN'S CLOTHES

Men's fashions, in terms of collections and designer labels, were a phenomenon that would not appear for many years. True, from the twenties certain styles had enjoyed temporary popularity with younger

LEAFLET No. 1192
MAN'S CARDIGAN

Copley's

Price 3d   Leaflet No. 1192   40 inch chest

4-ply "EXCELSIOR" Wool

L. COPLEY-SMITH & SONS LTD.   MANCHESTER

This wartime knitting pattern shows the 'casual' look – trousers, sweater, but still shirt and tie – which shortages forced upon men's fashions. That it is wartime is shown by the cartoon bellboy (upper left) pictured wearing a helmet.

men, such as the wide-legged trousers known as Oxford bags (after the students who wore them), cravats and plus-fours. The Prince of Wales, briefly Edward VIII, had continued that important royal tradition of 'Clothes Horse to the Nation', but in Britain generally, women wore fashions but men wore clothes. The suburban male wardrobe generally included a three-piece business suit, shirts with detachable collars, tie, overcoat or raincoat, and a hat, the style reflecting the owner's occupational status. On weekdays, suburban streets were filled with men wearing bowlers and Homburg hats.

Only a few men such as lawyers or doctors, in very traditional professions, still wore a black morning coat and waistcoat, with grey pinstripe trousers. Ties were worn by everyone, although the suit jacket might be replaced by an overall-type coat, and the hat might be a trilby or a flat cap.

Suits consisting of a jacket, waistcoat and trousers had become the uniform for most middle-class men from the turn of the century. Everybody still regarded London, with its Savile Row tailors, as the centre for men's clothing in the way Paris dominated women's clothes. Most middle-class men's suits would be made to measure by tailors and a hand-written label would give the owner's name, the date the suit was completed and the tailor's address. Trousers were high-waisted and roomy. Waistcoats were sometimes replaced by woollen pullovers, often knitted in a fancy stitch or in multi-coloured fair isle.

The lounge suit was especially popular with middle-class men who travelled to the towns to work. The development of the suburbs popularised the ticket pocket in their jackets. This was a small pocket in the jacket, exclusively for holding the wearer's return train or tram ticket.

Jackets were generally short and double-breasted in style. At the beginning of the thirties, the style was for three pairs of buttons but fortunately, in terms of the wartime need to cut back, this had been reduced to two pairs by the end of the decade. By the outbreak of war, jackets had become so short the popular term was 'bumfreezer'.

In the thirties, shirt collars were soft or stiff, detachable or fixed and, in the absence of anything more serious to talk about, debate had raged over which should be worn, when and where. In evening wear, the tuxedo, a black or white short jacket named after the Tuxedo Club in the United States, was part of a more relaxed, bare-headed approach to men's evening and formal wear, replacing the top hat, white tie and tails lauded in song by Fred Astaire.

FASHIONS IN WARTIME

Women's Wardrobes

Like everything else, clothes suffered from shortages in materials and labour. The pre-war women's shape continued to be popular in wartime, adapted for the shorter skirts and close-fitting jackets that were economical with material, to give a box-like silhouette. Some styles were no longer so easy to justify. Fashions that focused on legs meant that silk or nylon hosiery needed to be worn to draw attention to their finer features and to disguise blemishes. Styles that emphasised hips did so with full skirts, which required much more material than was necessary for practical purposes. Raw materials for such styles were increasingly conspicuous by their absence. Silk stockings and bias-cutting, so popular pre-war, went the way of chocolate and cosmetics – just fond memories.

Trousers had become part of the smart woman's wardrobe as a result of the First World War, when women wore them especially while working in factories and on buses. In the 1920s they became fashion items, especially as 'pyjamas', variations of which were worn on the beach, around the house, while smoking and, for the first time by women, in bed. In the thirties, trousers grew in popularity as the fashion for sports activities increased. Film stars, most notably Katherine

This photograph was probably taken at the beginning of the war – the jackets and coat have far too many buttons for Utility clothing, which was the only clothing in production by 1943. Popular wartime features are the short jacket of the suit worn by the woman on the extreme left; the two large feathers, from domestic birds, in the hat of the woman next to her; platform shoes on three of the four women; and the large clutch bag carried by the woman on the far right. The woman second right is dressed in a style more typical of the 1930s.

These women wear the ubiquitous 'overall' as they work in a munitions factory in 1941. Note the neatly curled hair of the girl sitting behind. (Imperial War Museum)

Hepburn, Marlene Dietrich and Greta Garbo, all wore men's styles in clothing and this too made trousers more acceptable. But in the main, women during the Second World War wore trousers for practical reasons and in some settings, especially factories, they were part of a compulsory uniform. But they were still not acceptable everywhere and at all times. Even in the auxiliary services, women were sometimes not permitted to wear trousers when off the camp, so as not to offend civilians. Women also wore suits as they were practical and could be used for many occasions.

So wartime fashion emphasised the aesthetic appeal of restraint and simplicity, with just a little 'trimming'. Plain clothes were embellished by decorating faces, hair and bodices. Bright red lips were popular, despite the scarcity of make-up. Hair was arranged on top of the head, decorated and restrained with combs or ribbons. Brooches and other jewellery, or decorations such as home embroidery, were worn on the bodices of plain dresses and blouses.

Military Influences

In November 1939 *Women and Beauty* magazine carried a special advertising supplement, 'You Mirrored for Winter'. Its advice for women in their twenties reflected the popular pre-occupation with the possibility of aerial bombardment. 'When you are out of uniform, keep your ensemble homogenous . . . don't go in for lots of frou-frou bits and pieces – he'll want to be proud of you and he can't be if you go round looking like what's left of an air raid!'

One-piece, zip-up siren suits, so called because they could be quickly pulled on when the air raid siren went, were very much part of the fashion scene as the threat of war made military styling popular in the run-up to, and first phase of the war. In Richmal Crompton's 'William' books, early on in the war, William Brown's sister Ethel, ever the touchstone for what was 'in' and what was 'out', is featured wearing her siren suit around the house because it suits her so well. Churchill, whose dress sense might be politely termed 'eclectic', was influential in this respect, being regularly pictured in a siren suit. He famously had one made in red velvet.

Models in advertisements for women's clothing were frequently pictured with servicemen and the military connection was further emphasised in the garments themselves, which one advertisement described as *avec l'air militaire*. Clothes in this style were square cut and masculine in shape with pockets, buttons and other trimmings to imitate military uniforms. The advertisement's French slogan was a pipe-dream, however. For Britain, the invasion of France had inevitably meant the end of Paris' influence and supplies, and all links with its haute couture designers and its fashion houses were severed.

In 1941 the Cotton Board's Design and Style Centre commissioned a group of illustrators and designers to produce a range of fabrics with a Government subsidy. The results were shown in Vogue – which approved, as it also did of the Utility scheme. Contributors included Fougasse, Duncan Grant, Ben Nicholson and Graham Sutherland. The Fougasse cartoon from his poster for the 'Careless Talk Costs Lives' campaign was printed on Jaqumar silk and was typical of the continuing fashion for topical pictorial designs.

When the most common shade was grey, anything that added colour or livened up garments was welcome. Another famous fabric, produced by the

This pre-war pattern is for a 'Unity' suit – clearly a variation of the siren suit that became so popular later. The zip could be replaced by buttons and the suit can be worn while working in the house and for emergencies.

"Dayella"

The finest Utility cloth you can buy—

Here's a cloth that is completely reliable — it carries the famous " Day & Night Wear " guarantee of quality. 'Dayella' is shrink-resisting and hard-wearing, and washes beautifully. Because it comes in plain colours, dainty pastels, pretty patterns and woven designs, you can make dozens of things for your babies and your older children with this soft, absolutely dependable utility cloth.

VIYELLA HOUSE
DAY & NIGHT WEAR
NOTTINGHAM

This advert for Dayella fabrics demonstrates the quality and range of Utility fabrics. This was especially important from 1943 onwards, when the only new clothing made in this country was manufactured under the Utility scheme.

Calico Printers' Association and used mainly for headscarves, was the 'V for Victory' design. This featured aeroplanes and bombs and was especially topical because the Battle of Britain had been fought in September of 1940. The written version of the Morse Code 'V' was printed round the edge of the fabric.

The firm of Jaqumar produced a series of propaganda prints by one of their own designers, Arnold Lever. They were made into aprons, dresses and blouses designed by Bianca Mosca, featuring slogans such as 'The Navy's Here', and 'Dig for Victory'.

Digby Morten created a dress with large pockets typical of the time, for one women's magazine. The design was sold as a Bestway paper pattern, priced at 4s ½d. Under the headline 'Joined Up', it promised: 'the gay defiance of plaid, importance of military pockets, allied to Fashion's youthful swinging line are all combined in this easily made dress for wearing on those occasions when femininity is just as important as efficiency.' What this meant was a knee-length dress with long, cuffed sleeves, a bodice made mainly from plaid, large, button-down pockets and a fabric bow at the neck.

As the war went on, overalls were increasingly worn by men and women as industries employed a growing workforce of directed labour.

Menswear

Civilian men's clothing was as bound by restrictions as women's: the Utility scheme initially permitted double-breasted suits and contrasting checks but turn-ups on trousers were banned. However, a pair of trousers too long in the leg had to be turned up, rather than trimmed to the correct length, so a clear line dictated by fashion – turn-ups or no turn-ups – was out of the question. London had long been the centre for men's tailoring but men's clothes were not subject to the whims of passing fashions to the extent that women's were, not least because, in wartime, uniform was the thing for a man to be wearing.

Many civilian men usually wore overalls as they worked in engineering or construction. Wartime put many more civilian men into overalls and other uniforms, such as the Home Guard and as civil defence workers. For those who continued to dress in 'civvies', the three-piece suit began to be replaced by trousers, sports jacket and jumper (usually hand-knitted).

As the war progressed, it was discovered that men's suits were very versatile, especially the by-now unfashionable and unused evening dress. These could be cut up and re-sewn into (for women!) a matching skirt and jacket, the tails being useful for a longer length jacket. Dress shirts could be made into a wide range of items for women and children in the family and the scraps too worn for anything else used for handkerchiefs.

Underwear and hosiery for men and children at this time was knitted in fine wool. Interestingly, a wartime study by 'Mass Observation' found that, on average, a man owned only one pair of underpants, suggesting that in reality many men wore none at all under their trousers. But the colder rooms of that time, which became even colder once coal was rationed, meant that most men wore woollen vests and 'long johns' were popular in winter.

WVS children's clothes exchange. Rationing made life very difficult for parents of growing children, so the WVS set up clothing exchanges to help ease the problem. (Imperial War Museum)

Children's Clothes

Babies wore a lot of white clothing, girls wore skirts and blouses, and dresses, and boys wore short trousers. In the United States, the concept of the teenager, complete with teenage fashions, had arrived. But in wartime Britain, as they reached the teenage years, boys went into long trousers and girls would adopt the styles of their older sisters and mothers. Fashion played no part in it – children's clothes were advertised to appeal to the adults who bought them and, in the main, chose them.

Pre-war, the typical school uniform for girls would be a blouse and tie; gymslip; blazer and felt or straw hat, each with a school badge; black shoes. In the summer a gingham or poplin dress and ankle socks would be worn; as the war took hold, stockings were quickly replaced with ankle socks all year round. Boys wore a similar traditional shirt and tie; blazer; short trousers, or longer versions for older boys; and a school cap. Hand-

These young people are returning to England in 1945 after being evacuated to Australia for five years. Most are teenagers but their clothes are simply scaled-down versions of what their parents might wear. (Imperial War Museum)

In the absence of teenage fashions, older boys' clothes were a combination of those worn by their younger siblings, such as the shorts, and those worn by their fathers, such as the pullover. Pullovers from this period were short as trousers were high-waisted.

me-downs within families and 'make do and mend' barely coped with the demand from growing children of school age.

Always a problem, children's clothes became an even greater headache during the war. One legitimate answer was the clothing exchanges and these were especially useful for growing children. Clothing exchanges appeared all over Britain and were essential for families who, regardless of their income, simply could not clothe their growing children from rationed and home-made clothing. Clothing exchanges enabled people to swap clothes of all sizes for all age groups. Donations from overseas, especially the American 'Bundles for Britain' campaign, ensured massive stockpiles of clothing in the early part of the war. These were distributed via exchanges or by groups such as the WVS to people whose own clothing had been lost in bombing raids or similar action.

Children from poorer homes were often sewn into their only set of winter underwear at the appropriate time of the year, a revelation to those with whom they were billeted when they were evacuated.

Hats

Hats were an accepted and expected part of a civilian's day-to-day outfit before the war, and it would have been viewed as almost an oversight to leave home without one.

When the war began, however, hats, especially those for women, quickly changed from what might be seen as frivolous decoration to essential, practical headgear. Early on during the war, the ultimate fashion accessory, for men as well as women, was the steel helmet, which could be bought in many hat-shops – Bakelite versions were available too.

Men's trilby-type felt hats, immensely popular before and during the war, were just one item hit by the need to economise. Brims and crowns became smaller; the width of the hat-band shrank from a norm of $1\frac{1}{2}$ inches to $\frac{1}{2}$ inch; the felt became thinner, so that the hats were less stiff, and the fabric rougher. The quality of workmanship was also affected: before the war, most hats had binding sewn around the edge of the brim but this quickly disappeared in the drive to save labour and materials.

By 1944 enthusiasm for plain and economically cut clothes was easily balanced by despair at the worsening situation – in Anne Scott James' case, hats were the problem: 'The necessary shortage of good shoes and accessories, and the unnecessary price of hats make it difficult enough to look well-dressed. . . . No amount of excuses from either the hat trade or officialdom will convince us that the price of hats is anything but exploitation.'

Straw hats were almost impossible to find and magazines pictured various ways of altering and adjusting last year's models. One headline proclaimed that 'Berets are back' – and probably not for the first time.

THE HUMBLE HOMBURG

Throughout the thirties, Anthony Eden, the British Foreign Secretary, was regarded as something of a dandy and hatters frequently placed photographs in their shop windows of the MP wearing his Homburg. He resigned in 1938, unable to support Neville Chamberlain's policy of appeasement. The most important consequence of this for men's outfitters was that the Homburg rapidly fell from grace and was replaced by the bowler hat, later made popular by Churchill.

Just over a year later, in March 1945, things were, if anything, worse; *Picture Post* showed the efforts of two actresses who had remodelled last year's headgear using old ostrich feathers, starchy needlework and coarse lace insertions. One concoction in feathers and flowers, using twelve precious hairpins and looking suspiciously like it was held in place for the camera, labours under the caption: 'Perhaps you too can wear a nonsense hat like this of Harriet Johns'!

Shoes

By the 1930s shoes had generally replaced boots as the chosen footwear of the professional classes. The term 'correspondent's shoes' was applied to shoes in two-tone leathers, so named because they were of a style likely to be worn by the sort of man who might imaginably be cited in a divorce case. They are now regarded as iconographic of the time, but they were rather too ostentatious for respectable, middle-class men who regarded a coloured or striped shirt as slightly daring.

Anne Scott James, writing in *Picture Post* in October 1941, said that the 'news in shoes' was that they should be practical. They should make use of new materials such as sealskin, elk, suede, canvas and chenille, and new styles featured combinations of two or more materials, allowing makers to use smaller off-cuts and recycled pieces. Calf leather had all but

Clothing rations did not include coupons for hats, which were therefore expensive and difficult to find in the shops. Most women made their own and knitted turbans were especially popular as they held the hair off the face. This hat shop has a wide range of designs that would have been popular in the thirties, from wide-brimmed, masculine styles and heavily decorated fripperies, to the Cossack style worn by the lady in the check suit. The shop's lino, incidentally, is also very thirties.

Portland take Utility in their Stride

Portland Shoes have always been designed for service. They established themselves because they gave such good value for money, such style with perfect comfort, and such long wearing quality

Portland

STYLE · COMFORT SHOES

No. P6556.
In Black, Brown or Navy Blue Glacé Kid, also in Black Suede Kid. Lightweight. Shape 30. Extra wide fitting. Louis heel, 1⅝" high.

● *Because of war restrictions you cannot be sure of getting any one particular model at your Portland Stockist's, but you can be sure of getting full-time comfort from whichever style you select.*

Send for the address of your nearest Portland Stockist :—
T. ROBERTS & SONS LTD. (DEPT. 83), PORTLAND SHOE WORKS, LEICESTER.

It is a tribute to the obsessive nature of the advertising industry that Portland shoes were still promoted, even when the ads themselves admitted it was unlikely they could be obtained. The advert for Wearra shoes displays the Utility clothing CC41 logo.

disappeared as military demand took precedence over civilian tastes. Crêpe-soled shoes were recommended as they were 'more damp-proof and broken glass-proof than leather. An excellent wartime trend.'

Standard shoes were already a hot topic. The rumours in the shoe trade were that such footwear would be introduced in six months' time. The idea of the 'standard shoe' was not to give everyone the same footwear but to simplify and limit styles – which the Utility scheme, introduced in the following spring, effectively achieved. Among the scheme's regulations, peep-toes were banned and heels could be no more than 2 inches in height. Shoes were low-heeled and square-looking, partly because the restrictions meant that there was little alternative, partly because of fashion, and partly because high heels were utterly impractical for the demands of wartime working.

Wedge heels were a new idea whose novelty gave them added appeal. The high-fashion shoe designer Salvatore Ferragamo claimed to have invented the wedge in 1938, as well as the platform, but most women saw them for the first time in the early forties. Among the most sought-after were Joyce shoes. Particularly popular were plain slip-on versions with small platform soles and moderate wedge heels, which came in a variety of colours. Queues would form outside any shoe shop rumoured to have taken delivery of them. Not that Joyce shoes were cheap: a 1941 advertisement for a pair of chenille house shoes with tartan linings and wedge heels stated the cost as 35s – much more expensive than plainer and more versatile footwear.

Clogs needed no coupons and as leather was one material in particularly short supply, they became an everyday sight. A variation on the clog was the introduction of wooden soles on shoes, hinged at the instep to provide flexibility.

Stockings and Socks

Sheer nylon stockings, tantalisingly invented in 1939, were known of but virtually unobtainable through legitimate sources before American GIs arrived bearing gifts. Stockings made of wool, wool mixture or artificial fibres could still be found on the domestic market, but they were hard to get. One answer to the persistent shortage of stockings was to paint your legs with one of a number of specially prepared leg make-ups and, using an eyebrow pencil, to draw a 'seam' up the backs of the legs. The 'seam' was best done by a friend, as a straight line was difficult enough to achieve even then.

Alternatively, in the absence of proprietary leg make up, home-made substitutes such as gravy browning could be used. A 1943 advertisement for leg cream contains the following advice:

> Beauty goes to extremes . . . here's a tip for stockingless legs. If you can't buy stocking make-up, sponge the legs with a few grains of permanganate of potash dissolved in warm water. Be sure to test on the sole of one foot first because it won't wash off for days. Do this before a special occasion on which you want to look your nicest.

Ankle socks made one of their regular but ultimately futile bids for fashion credibility. Women did not like wearing them with dresses and they looked ridiculous with smart suits. However, ankle socks were practical, and went well with the clumpy shoes, which again, for practical reasons, had become fashionable. They could also be worn under trousers.

Hair

War work certainly made popular styles that took hair off the face but although many women went for shorter hairstyles, still more preferred to pin or tie longer hair back, using turbans, combs or the increasingly rare hair grips or 'Bobby Pins'. The Victory Roll, in which the hair swept over a band round the crown of the head, was popular.

By late 1942, magazines were advertising the:

> Liberty Cut . . . an ideal hair style for wartime. The secret of the attractive upward sweep lies in the hair being 'tapered' as it is cut. This takes the weight from the crown. . . . It can be shampooed and set at home quickly and economically – and today it is especially important to adopt a hair style which keeps the hair clean and tidy easily.

But there were limits to all this self-help. Women were urged to 'Take these illustrations to your hairdresser. Do not try to cut your hair yourself. Only an expert can make a success of this cut.'

Make-up, Perfume and Jewellery

At first it was seen as unpatriotic for women to be heavily made up. In January 1940 *Picture Post* ran this letter from a reader, F.C. Meredith (schoolgirl), Palace Hotel, Jersey, Channel Islands:

In the absence of stockings, special make-up was available for legs. It had to be painted on with a steady hand – and a friend to help with the seam.

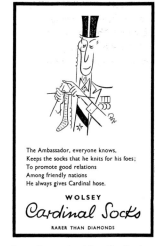

A wartime advert for Cardinal Socks, from *Picture Post*, 1943. Note the legend – 'Rarer than Diamonds'.

This model has the classic wartime hairstyle – long but swept back off the face – and make-up. Cosmetics were scarce but lips and eyes were often heavily made up to add a touch of glamour to plain styles and drab colours.

I wish the war hadn't started as it has put women in uniform. . . . You should see them parading about the town in Somerset where I go to school. I think that they believe this is a time for an extra layer of make-up and an expensive, though not attractive, permanent wave. Most of the blondes seem to have joined something or other. What is more, they smoke cigarettes and wear high heels on duty. Is this what you call serving your country?

But slowly, people came round to the view that looking good helped everyone's morale, and make-up and jewellery were the best ways to liven up otherwise practical and sometimes drab outfits.

Women in the Forces were allowed to wear discreet make-up, after some initial controversy and resignations, and an orange-red shade of lipstick called Tangee was eventually created especially for those in the ATS, to tone with their khaki uniforms. The Ministry of Supply went so far as to give its female munitions workers a booklet, *R.O.F. Beauty Hints. Look to Your Looks*, along with a special high-grade foundation and face powder. These were great improvements on beetroot juice and calamine lotion, just two of the substitutes used by women.

War workers' endorsement was mentioned in the society magazine, *Tatler and Bystander* (as it was known in 1942). M.E. Brook, in an article entitled the 'Highway of Fashion', said that the fragrance Tweed '. . . is a mental tonic when applied behind the ears and over the temples. It is economical as a little goes a long way. War workers revel in it as it ever freshens the atmosphere suggesting the great outdoors.'

Jewellery, especially that using precious metals or stones, was also too scarce to be an ever-changing item of fashion. In a magazine column on 'Jewellery from the Tea-table', Moshe Oved, artist and connoisseur in precious jewels and metals, told women to wear their jewellery rather than hide it away. In these times of increasing shortages, he advised helpfully that: 'Silver is better for some women than gold, jade and turquoise more successful than diamonds.' His comments accompanied a photo of a model wearing a necklace, bracelet and earrings made from Victorian and Edwardian sugar tongs.

Home-made jewellery became a common gift, made from pieces of Perspex, aluminium or brass, often by factory workers in an odd quiet moment or by servicemen in a reflection of the trench art of the First World War. Common themes were a V for Victory, a unit badge or initials.

This post-war advert for Tangee make-up announces that this pre-war favourite is back again. After wartime restrictions, the lipstick was now available in 'beguiling pinks' and 'bewitching crimsons'.

These two 'jumpers' are nothing of the sort. Called 'gilets', they are knitted fronts, each completed with half a yard of net for the back. Gilets were a practical variation on the fashion, common since the twenties, for separate fabric fronts worn under dresses. Adapted for wartime, these knitted versions were popular worn under jackets and with suits, especially as they could be made from oddments and scraps of wool.

Shortages

The clothing trade was severely cut back soon after the outbreak of war. Many factories and workshops in the traditional centre of the 'rag trade' in the East End of London were closed down or went over to producing uniforms at breakneck speed. Some companies moved out of London to avoid the worst of the bombing. A few were directed to producing civilian garments for export only, and thrived as a result, with an occasional item finding its way on to the home market.

Wool, the major home-produced textile, was immediately in demand for military clothing, just as it had been in the First World War. Jaeger produced knitting patterns into the late 1930s, offering various gifts to knitters for sending in tabs or labels from balls of Jaeger yarn. According to the number they sent in, knitters could receive in exchange a print, a velvet calf-leather knit pack, a doll, a case of knitting needles or a bendy toy lamb. But almost as soon as war was declared, the offers were overstamped 'Suspended During War'.

Home knitting had been popular before the war but now, just about every female and a good few men knitted whenever and wherever they could. Pre-war, the main problem with shop-bought knitting wool was that it shrunk; now it was almost impossible to find and had to be paid for with precious coupons. By 1944, Lavenda wools were advertising their yarn with a drawing of a skein of wool and the wistful legend, 'Beautiful wool of pre-war quality'.

Instead of buying wool, old knitwear beyond repair was unpicked and re-knitted and soon, short-sleeved, multi-coloured jumpers were the fashion norm. Even old, matted wool could be cut and sewn as cloth, and used for waistcoats, children's coats and slippers. Unpicked wool knitted up thinner than it had originally, so the official advice was to weigh wool and test the tension. Dresses or blouses could have knitted sleeves attached to bodices and vice versa; worn, hand-knitted socks could be made into ankle socks or the undamaged parts sewn together to make a new pair. One of the most bizarre ideas was to replace a worn stocking foot by knitting an ankle sock on to the stocking leg. And the recipient might have disagreed that the worn-out tops of a pair of wool stockings could make 'cosy underpants for a small boy'.

Knitting and sewing circles thrived. These groups met in each other's homes to work on garments and knit together. Circles worked to supply themselves and the forces, for whom they knitted socks, balaclavas and gloves. The wool and patterns were delivered by the organising group, such as the WVS or Women's Institute. The garments that were knitted were collected and re-weighed, to make sure that none of the wool went astray during knitting.

Like wool, silk was in demand for military purposes right from the start, especially for parachutes – wartime work in a parachute factory was one way to get hold of silk off-cuts to make underwear. Another surprising source for civilians were unexploded German land mines, which were dropped on green silk parachutes; in heavily bombed districts you might have found a predominance of green underwear, and more than one bride walked down the aisle in green. In 1941 the commercial use of silk for stockings and other women's clothing was banned so all supplies could be preserved for parachutes and other war equipment.

Artificial silk, made from cellulose, had been popular since the twenties and now it was one of the few fabrics generally available. It was known as 'Rayon', after a competition to find a name in 1924. Viscose rayon, the most common type of rayon, had been patented as early as 1892 by three British chemists and had been produced by the British firm Courtaulds since 1905. Its cellulose fibres, derived from wood pulp, were used in most types of garments.

Underwear needing elastic and other rubber-based products for fastenings was also difficult to come by; fully elasticated knickers were replaced by ones with a 2-inch piece of elastic and a button fitting. Metal fastenings from this period tend to be of poor quality, and so more likely to rust, as metal too was in short supply.

An advert for 'Vedoknit' utility underwear, from 1945, described as 'top grade utility'. (*Picture Post*)

These women practising their rifle shooting wear a variety of wartime styles: the woman on the extreme left has her hair in a snood, the woman next to her has her long hair curled and pinned away from her face; footwear ranges from stout lace-ups to summery sandals. The woman on the second right's uniform shows that she is an ARP driver. Officially, women were not to bear arms but as the threat of invasion grew, many set up their own civilian organisations and learned rifle shooting as well as unarmed combat and first aid.

THE END OF THE WAR AND AFTER

Woman magazine's Anne Edwards had this advice for women leaving the auxiliary forces and returning to civilian life:

> . . . service girls have learned to value good grooming so highly.
>
> Some of the wartime fashion experts predict that the one thing a service girl will do when she gets out of uniform is to plunge for veils and fripperies and high heels, in a wild reaction from the simplicity of the uniform . . . having learned how important good grooming is, how comfortable and sensible low-heeled shoes are, how much it pays to have the details right and simple, too, you'll keep that knowledge inside your pretty heads and will not be led away by the effects of screen glamour.

The reality was that women craved something decorative and the cinema, dominated as it was by American films, featured long-haired and glamorous heroines such as Veronica Lake, with her Peek-a-Boo hairstyle that draped seductively over one eye – a style which would be impossibly dangerous on the factory floor. By 1944, the 'Thin Man' series made a welcome return to the screen and Judy Garland made the lavish musical *Meet Me in St Louis*. One of the most popular films of 1945 was the *Ziegfeld Follies*. So there were plenty of examples of screen glamour to dream about, if not to copy.

The more ludicrous and less popular US films were usually those set in occupied Europe – one of the 'best' has to be *Mademoiselle France*, in which Joan Crawford is a heroine of the French resistance. Even in these pictures, the Hollywood heroines turned out with the full benefit of wardrobe, make-up and hairdressing. And everyone knew it looked wonderful as Britain waded through yet another year of Austerity, Utility and exorbitant prices for scarce and shoddy goods.

The war dragged slowly to an end; men transferred or released after at least six months in the services were issued with a set of civilian clothes, including the famous 'demob' suit. They were also allowed to keep certain items of their service dress. On 18 June 1945, large-scale demobilisation began and the garment industry was as busy as ever.

In September 1945, four months after the end of the war, the clothing ration was cut still further to thirty-six coupons for an adult each year. This time the reduction was because of shortages of labour in the mills. The new Labour Government tried to boost exports as part of its strategy for a thriving peacetime economy. Clothing exports went quickly into a post-war boom. In 1938, British fashion export earnings totalled £98,000; by 1946, this had risen to £507,000.

Fashion featured heavily in the 1946 'Britain Can Make It' exhibition at the Victoria & Albert Museum in London. It showed the latest designs from the Incorporated Society of London Designers, many of them using fabrics created by artists who had completed similar commissions in 1941. But these garments were available for export only. At home, clothing was rationed but the restrictions gradually eased. The wedding of the 21-year-old Princess (now Queen) Elizabeth in 1947 was an opportunity for more celebration and 'glad-rags'. The British fashion industry was given another boost when Norman Hartnell designed her wedding dress.

Wartime had set an entire range of conditions that defined and determined fashions. As a result, people were so sick of these parameters that it was no surprise that fashion longed for excess. This excess was eventually given tangible and coherent form in Christian Dior's New Look. Called the Corelle Look by its inventor – the New Look was the name given by an American fashion journalist – Christian Dior's 1947 collection picked up where pre-war styling was heading in 1939: yards of material, an hourglass figure and high heels that were as impractical as they were uncomfortable. However, High Street versions of the New Look had to work within the limitations of rationing, which still dominated supplies.

The last clothing coupons were issued in September 1948. In February 1949 the home fashion market was given a boost when the number of coupon-free garments was greatly extended. Styles and lines were more diverse – skirts, for example, could be slim cut and tight fitting, or fully flared. The Utility scheme was still in operation, controlling price and quality among garments for people of all ages but it was a far cry from the all-embracing scheme running at the height of the war. Utility involved fewer and fewer restrictions and the scheme was wound up in 1952. By then it was applied mainly to clothing which was exempt from Purchase Tax but which, in those post-war boom times, few wanted.

NINE

ENTERTAINMENT

The Greatest
Love Story of
our Time

Paramount's presentation of
ERNEST HEMINGWAY'S

"FOR WHOM
THE BELL TOLLS"

STARRING
Cooper-Bergman
GARY   INGRID
IN TECHNICOLOR

CARLTON
THEATRE · · · · HAYMARKET

DAILY · · · · · · ·   2.30, 6.30
SATURDAYS · · · 11.0, 2.30, 6.30
SUNDAYS · · · · · · ·   5.45
ALL SEATS BOOKABLE at Theatre
and usual Ticket Agencies only

Cinemas remained open during the war, although they were initially instructed to close. This film was showing during the winter of 1943. (*Picture Post*)

Soon after the Prime Minister had declared war, the radio, somewhat inevitably, broadcast a list of new regulations. These included the announcement that: 'All cinemas, dance halls and places of public entertainment will be closed until further notice.' Not only that but 'Football matches and outdoor meetings of all kinds which bring large numbers together are prohibited until further notice'. The newspaper headlines put it more succinctly: 'All sport brought to a halt'. All that was left were the pubs and the radio, and even on the airwaves only one BBC station, the Home Service, would be broadcast.

This was at a time when the official and general belief was that mass bombing would begin immediately. As soon as it became obvious that this was not going to happen, the restrictions were loosened. Wise heads in Government soon recognised the importance to morale of entertainment; indoor entertainment soon resumed, although outdoor events continued to suffer. Floodlit events were obviously out of the question, although afternoon events were allowed, to limited crowds, as long as raid spotters were employed. These were people, trained in aircraft recognition who would keep a look out, sounding a siren or some other form of warning if they saw aircraft approaching. The same system was used in many armaments factories to avoid unnecessary disruption of production.

Later, notices would tell theatre and film audiences that 'An Air Raid Warning has been received'. If they chose to, people could take shelter, often in the basement, but the show would continue for others. As the war continued, more and more audiences, out of fatalism, familiarity or even stubbornness, chose to see the performance out. (The willingness of the audience to stay could also be an indication of the quality of the performance.)

THE GREAT ESCAPE?

During the war, cinema-going was at an all-time high in Britain, whether to see flag-wavers such as *Went the Day Well*, *Henry V* or *Millions Like Us*, or escapism such as *Dumbo* or *Gone With the Wind*. Hollywood continued to dominate and the most popular films were those from the United States, offering escapism with lavish costumes and Technicolor. But Hollywood's wartime attempts to reflect the realities of life in occupied Europe and Britain, such as *Edge of Darkness* with Errol Flynn and *Mrs Miniver* with Greer Garson, were met with understandable derision and contempt.

SPORT

Soon after the initial ban, a limited programme of friendly football matches were introduced with the size of crowds limited to 15,000 in safe areas and 8,000 elsewhere. From the end of October 1939, the league was suspended and a regional competition was set up comprising of eight groups, thus reducing the amount of travelling involved. The FA cup was also suspended, and in March 1940 a 'War Cup' competition was introduced. The football pools continued, though like much else in wartime Britain they were themselves 'pooled' – there was one single competition in place of the various pre-war providers.

Cricket changed into one-day games, played by new teams such as the British Empire XI, and the London Counties XI. Rugby and golf still went on, but again, they were restricted by the number of players either called up or volunteered.

HOME ENTERTAINMENT

Most entertainment took place in the home. In 1939 and throughout the war, the radio was the centre of home entertainment.

Radio

Like all the most successful inventions, radio was not just a great idea, or an amazing technology; it was an idea of its time, fulfilling a great need. The growth of the suburbs, with their central theme of privacy within the one family dwelling, created a routine where every weekday morning Father left at the same time to catch the train to his office, the children followed soon after for school, leaving Mother alone to do the housework with the aid of her labour-saving devices. Inevitably, with the closing of the front door behind them, the house was silent; boredom and loneliness set in for a great many suburban housewives, and there was no better solution than the 'wireless'.

Radio had been around in one form or another for some time, but it was during the First World War that the military had come to rely on it more and more. Thousands of men had been trained in its use, and on their return to 'Civvy Street' many of them retained their interest. Like other things in the twentieth century, its potential had been developed in the USA, but Britain was not slow to follow. In June 1920 the *Daily Mail* had sponsored a wireless concert of songs by the hugely popular Dame Nellie Melba, broadcast from the Marconi Works. The British Broadcasting Company Limited was formed at a meeting of radio manufacturers and shareholders in October 1922. Wasting no time, the BBC began broadcasting from stations in Manchester, London and Birmingham just one month later, joined in December by Newcastle (the Corporation didn't actually receive its licence until January 1923). In that year, following the Sykes Committee report, the Government introduced a listeners' licence and by the end of the year almost 600,000 had been issued.

A Unity Pools coupon from May 1945. The football pools carried on! Even during the Blitz there was always the dream that it might be your turn to scoop the jackpot this week. Like petrol and butter, the pools were pooled.

*P*APER is short and sets are short, so I'll be short. This Company has three jobs to do in wartime — as much direct war effort as we can contribute . . . A strong attack on exports to build up British finances abroad . . . The care of the Home Market. We are trying to do our duty in all three. These sets, which have been designed and made for wartime conditions, show you how we have tackled your claim on our efforts. You will see that we have given you greater Short Wave facilities than ever before. You will see that the cabinets are still as distinctive and solid as ever. You *won't* see, but I will tell you, that the things that we have always put first in our sets are still first — reliability and truthful reproduction. We believe that in this time of war, each wireless set we make has a great national job to perform in someone's home — perhaps yours. We have tried to design and make sets worthy of their job, sets which will be a comfort and a stand-by to you in these days.

E. J. POWER, *Managing Director.*

'Standard' TABLE SUPERHET

An all-wave superhet with a fine "station-getting" performance, especially on short waves, and a high standard of reproduction. Press-button wave-band selection and a special short wave logging scale are important features. Pick-up connections (A.C. model only) and switched external speaker sockets are provided. The cabinet is highly polished and has an all-silk front with a black bakelite escutcheon for the scales and controls. Wave ranges covered :
15.7-50 METRES   190-550 METRES   970-2,000 METRES
Cash Prices: A.C. MODEL £11 10s.   D.C./A.C. MODEL £12

SHORT-WAVE 'Station Master'

This set is the year's short-wave "Special." There are 95 short-wave station names marked on the scale, and, with the aid of Electrical Band-spreading, tuning on the short waves is as easy and as *certain* as it is on the medium and long waves (where, of course, the high standard of Murphy performance is fully maintained). Eight Push-buttons control the wave-band switching. Pick-up and switched speaker sockets are fitted. The quality of reproduction is typical of Murphy sets. Cabinet in warm brown polished oak with fluted black bakelite control panel.
Wave ranges covered :
(SHORT WAVES) 13 M., 16 M., 19 M., 25 M., 31 M., 41-50 M. bands. (MEDIUM AND LONG WAVES) 190-550 METRES. 970-2,000 METRES.

Cash Price: (A.C. ONLY) £15 15s.

BATTERY-OPERATED 'Station Master'

This is the Battery version of the Mains Station Master set described above and illustrated on the right. This model incorporates all the most important features of the mains set, and for the first time gives the battery set user the advantages of really advanced short wave performance. Wave ranges covered as on the Mains Station Master.

Cash Price (without Batteries) £14 10s.

'Standard' RADIOGRAM

All the radio features of the Standard Table set described above are combined in this all-wave superhet Radiogram with record reproduction of much higher quality than has hitherto been available in a set at this price. This is largely due to acoustic design pioneered by Murphy Radio. Push-button wave-change, short wave logging scale and switched speaker sockets are incorporated. The cabinet is distinguished by the all-silk front and bakelite escutcheon. The gramophone has a flush motor-board, and the pick-up is of a special design which considerably reduces record wear. Wave ranges covered as on the Standard Table Model.
Cash Prices: A.C. MODEL £26   D.C./A.C. MODEL £27 10s.

'Economy' BATTERY SUPERHET

Minimum running costs and a moderate price give this set its well-earned name. The circuit provides a wide choice of stations on the short and medium wave-bands with high quality reproduction and simplified tuning controls. "Low drain" valves allow longer use of the accumulator between charges, and automatic grid bias ensures maximum life from the H.T. Battery. Dark polished oak cabinet with silk front and Zebrano wood control panel. Wave ranges covered :
16-50 METRES   190-550 METRES
Cash Price (without batteries) £7 15s.

All Murphy sets, exclusive of valves and batteries, guaranteed for one year. Prices do not apply in Eire. Hire Purchase Terms available.

Murphy Radio Ltd., Welwyn Garden City, Herts.

★ ★ ★ ★ ★ ★ ★ ★ ★ ★ ★ ★

'Standard' ALL-WAVE TABLE SET

'Standard' ALL-WAVE RADIOGRAM

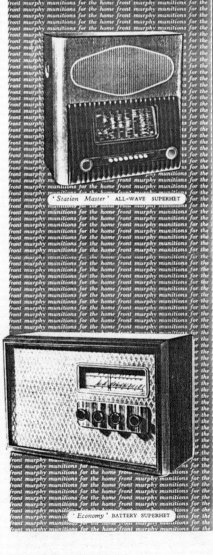

'Station Master' ALL-WAVE SUPERHET

'Economy' BATTERY SUPERHET

A lot of commercial sets were available at the time, but many people preferred the fun of making their own crystal set with headphones, through which, depending on atmospheric conditions, a solitary listener could receive stations from across Europe or even the USA. The loudspeaker turned radio from a solitary to a family pleasure.

In May 1923 the directors of the BBC decided to launch *Radio Times*, because newspapers wanted to charge the BBC advertising rates to publish details of its programmes. The first copy of *Radio Times* was produced in September. By the end of the decade, it was regularly selling more than a million weekly copies, during which time the British Broadcasting Company Limited was replaced by the British Broadcasting Corporation (1927).

The wireless came into its own during the Second World War; all the great events of the time were covered on it. Many people listened to Neville Chamberlain's declaration of war on their radio sets, and on VE-Day, Churchill officially announced the end of the war in Europe to the nation on the wireless, followed later by a speech from King George VI. The audience was huge. In 1939, 9 million wireless licences were issued – with an average family size of four (and taking into account that not everyone bought a licence), this meant that about 90 per cent of households had a wireless. Some in Government, Chamberlain among them, believed that radio also should close down in the event of war. Fortunately, others were aware of the importance of maintaining public morale, and of the part that entertainment, especially radio, would play in this.

Opposite: This Murphy radio catalogue of 1940 clearly shows the type of radios/radiograms available at the beginning of the war.

A Greek refugee family gathers round the wireless, just as so many of their British hosts would do. (Imperial War Museum)

In the first week of the war the radio schedules were changed – a new version of *Radio Times* was rushed out on Monday 4 September which proclaimed:

> Broadcasting carries on! That is the slogan of the BBC in this hour of National Endeavour, when the British Nation is nerving itself for the greatest effort it has ever made. . . . There will even be a children's hour and regular broadcasts for schools.

At first, expecting the worst, the BBC broadcast only music interspersed with news bulletins and Government announcements; Sandy Macpherson played interminably on the 'BBC's Theatre Organ', giving over twenty recitals in the first week alone. On 4 and 5 September *Children's Hour* had been cancelled – it was deemed far too flippant for wartime – but on Wednesday 6 September it was back, cut down to half an hour but retaining its original title. Every day from then on, it was introduced by 'Uncle Mac' (Derek McCulloch), with his famous line 'Hello children everywhere'. Two daily broadcasts for schools at 11.00 and 1.50 were a godsend to those children who had not been evacuated with the rest of their school friends and so had no schools to go to. There were also morning and evening prayers, Government bulletins, including the daily 'Food Facts' programmes, and, of course, the news.

The war turned the news readers into stars. They had always remained anonymous, but in the summer of 1940, they began by identifying themselves: 'Here is the news and this is Alvar Lidell reading it', or Bruce Belfrage and so on. This was all part of the invasion scare. It was believed that the Germans might try to put out fake broadcasts, giving misleading directions or damaging morale. This would be made far more difficult if the news readers, and their voices, became familiar to their listeners. Thus a new type of news reader/radio personality was born. The most extreme example of this was the arrival of Wilfred Pickles, whose northern brogue shocked people who thought the BBC broadcasters should demonstrate perfect Received Pronunciation and sound as if they were wearing evening dress when they spoke. Brendan Bracken, a journalist who became the Minister for Information, encouraged the BBC to use Pickles specifically because his accent would be far harder for a German impostor to imitate.

But the wireless was as much for entertainment as for news, and during the war years it produced some of its finest work. Variety shows were always popular, such as *Hi Gang* starring the American couple Ben Lyons and Bebe Daniels with Vic Oliver. Others were *Happidrome* with its theme tune 'We Three', and *Garrison Theatre*, a music hall show that made a star of Jack Warner. Best-loved at a time when humour was badly needed were the comedy programmes. On Saturdays listeners tuned in to *Bandwagon*, starring Arthur Askey – 'Big Hearted Arthur' – and Richard 'Stinker' Murdoch; Charley McCarthy, a ventriloquist act (sic); and the *Crazy Gang*, featuring Flanagan and Allen.

By far the most popular comedy show was *ITMA – It's That Man Again*. The man in question was Tommy Handley, in charge at the

As nowadays, spin-off goods were produced for the more successful TV and radio shows. This is the 'first' book of ITMA rhymes; was there a second?

Tommy Handley (*ITMA*) and Funf the German spy having fun with Tommy's ration book, from a 1941 *Radio Fun* comic. Comics for older children made great play of the war, with their characters taking on the nasty Hun and winning. (Vin Mag Archive Ltd)

Ministry of Aggravation and Mysteries (a pun on Agriculture and Fisheries). In a Britain constantly complaining of bureaucracy and regulations, the show struck a deep chord, the nearest thing to satire during the war; the unending directions, restrictions and exhortations of so many different ministries, some obscure, some obvious, some downright silly, were a natural source of humour. Handley was supported by a long but familiar cast of characters – each of the performers played several parts, each with their own catch-phrases: the tipsy Colonel Chinstrap (Jack Train) – 'I don't mind if I do, Sir': 'No, after you, Cecil'; the office char-lady Mrs Mop (Dorothy Summers) – 'Can I do you now, Sir?'; and 'It's being so cheerful what keeps me going' and the mysterious spy Funf.

Another success was the *Brains Trust*, a panel show where intellectuals – the 'brains' in question – would discuss topics sent in by the public. Started in January 1941, it was immensely popular. In 1944 almost one-third of the listening audience tuned in to hear the views of such favourites as Commander Campbell, Colonel Walter Elliot, Dr Julian Huxley, Dr Joad, Jennie Lee and Donald McCulloch.

Other huge favourites included Mr Middleton the wireless gardener with his *In Your Garden* talks, and J.B. Priestly, who, in 1940, began a series of programmes called *Postscripts*. These came after the Sunday

LORD HAW HAW

One of the most unexpected radio stars created early in the war was Lord Haw Haw, who broadcast propaganda for the Nazis from Hamburg. Actually an Irishman by the name of William Joyce, 'Lord Haw Haw' was a nick-name based on his upper-class accent. His broadcasts began with the call 'Jairmany calling, Jairmany calling'. During the Phoney War just about all but the most patriotic radio owners listened; early in 1940 he regularly had an audience of about 6 million. His appeal was mixed; certainly many people found his broadcasts funny at a time when there was little news, but there was often also a subconscious belief that our own broadcasts were being heavily sanitised, which they sometimes were, and that there was an element of truth in what Lord Haw Haw said. Rumours ran rife that this or that claim was true, and with Dr Goebbels in charge German propaganda was often a long way from being as crude as our own propaganda has led us to believe. Lord Haw Haw's talks often harped upon social divisions and inequalities that were partly based upon truth and which struck a chord in many of his listeners. However, when the war turned real in the summer of 1940, his audience dropped dramatically.

RADIO QUIZ

From the *Brighter Blackout Book*:

Most of your radio favourites have catch-phrases by which you know them. An easy one this. Spot the owners of these radio trade marks:

'Can you hear me, mother?'
'Semi-colon.'
'I thank you.'
'Ye-e-es.'
'Play the game, you cads.'
'You see.'
'Drop me a postcard.'
'Oi!'
'Flash!'
'Shurrup!'
'It's turned out nice again.'

(Answers p. 166)

evening news and were introduced as a response to Lord Haw Haw. They became immensely popular. But Churchill, who was constantly thwarted in his efforts to bring the BBC under Government control, regarded them as dangerously left wing, advocating, as they did, that people should work not just towards victory, but also for a more socially fair post-war society. Plays were popular too, especially thriller serials such as *Paul Temple* and *Appointment with Fear*.

In February 1940 the General Forces Programme, commonly known as the Forces Programme, began broadcasting. This consisted mainly of big-band music, variety programmes and the news, and was aimed at those serving in the forces, although civilians always made up the majority of its audience. Programmes included *Forces Favourites*, *Navy Mixture* and *Calling the Forces Everywhere*. It was on the forces programme that Vera Lynn, whose voice will probably always be associated with the Second World War, earned her nickname 'the Forces' Sweetheart'.

The radio soon came to be seen as a great morale booster. During the day, programmes specifically aimed at factory workers were broadcast, often from the factories themselves: *Works Wonders*, *Workers' Playtime*, and *Music While You Work* were enormously popular.

Music, of course, made up a great part of the radio's output with singers such as Gracie Fields, George Formby, Hutch – real name Leslie Hutchinson, Jack Hubert and Cecily Courtneidge, and dance bands led by the likes of Billy Cotton, Henry Hall, Geraldo and Victor Sylvester, whose programme *Dancing Club*, was part of the continuing British obsession with ballroom dancing

The wireless did not entirely escape the shortages; like all other magazines, newspapers and comics, *Radio Times* was affected by paper shortages, shrinking to an average of twenty pages. Its previously lavish multi-coloured covers became two colour or even monochrome. After sales initially dropped in the first half of the war, they began to climb again, reaching 3½ million in 1944.

Girls enjoying a dance with American GIs; note the Stars and Stripes, and the live band on stage in the background. (Imperial war Museum)

Television

Regular public broadcasting began in November 1936 to the London area only; one year later the area capable of receiving regular broadcasts was described in *Ideal Home* magazine as a ring including 'Cambridge, Colchester, Whitstable, Tunbridge Wells, Horsham, Reading, Aylesbury, Wolverton and Bedford', although regular 'freak' reception could be had as far away as Brighton and Coventry. Broadcasts, on one channel only, lasted for two hours every day, except Sundays when there was no service.

Sets were far from cheap. The Marconi mirror-lid model of 1936 cost 80 guineas, the PYE 12-inch 4200 cost 135 guineas, almost as much as a family saloon, and top of the range models cost well over £100. It is perhaps no surprise that when the regular service started there were fewer than 500 sets in use. By 1939 many (smaller) sets cost under £30, and by the outbreak of war about 20,000 sets were in use. Yet television played no part in the war: broadcasting was suspended on 1 September 1939 and was not resumed until June 1946.

The Gramophone and the Piano

Electric gramophones were, of course, common by this time, but the old-fashioned, wind-up version was still much in evidence. It was especially useful in the shelter – its portability and clockwork mechanism, which needed no power supply, made it ideal.

Auxiliary Fire Service women relaxing. This shows several of the popular pastimes of the period: listening to the gramophone (a wind-up version), knitting, reading newspapers/magazines, and playing one of the many card games available. (Catherine Gilman)

Records were all 78s, and these became harder to get during the war. When the Americans came they brought with them big bands, the Jitterbug and V (for victory) discs.

The upright piano had long been a feature of the middle-class parlour, and although children suffered agonies with their weekly lessons, for many homes it provided an evening's entertainment, especially at times such as Christmas and for parties. Sheet music was sold widely, and the scores to songs made popular over the radio always did well. These included 'Lili Marlene', 'South of the Border', 'Don't Fence Me In', 'Long Ago and Far Away', 'White Christmas' and 'We'll Gather Lilacs'. Songs particularly associated with the war included 'The White Cliffs of Dover', 'The Siegfried Line', 'When the Lights Go On Again', and 'I'm Gonna Get Lit Up When the Lights Go Up In London'. One of our particular favourite titles is 'When Can I Have A Banana Again?', by Nat Mills, Gaby Rogers and Harry Roy.

CHRISTMAS

Christmas was a time when wartime shortages seemed to hit harder than ever; wood was one of the first casualties, and by Christmas 1939, it was considered far too wasteful to have a traditional fir. Those fortunate enough to have artificial trees would have to use them for at least the next five years. Others cut pieces of holly, shrub, or any available greenery to decorate with glass balls, pine cones, apples, and home-produced decorations, while the more creative made their own trees too. Otherwise, apart from some members of many families being 'somewhere in France', Christmas 1939 was fairly normal.

Last year, thanks to the warning we issued about the shortage of books—and thanks to the heed that was paid to it—most of our customers were able without undue difficulty to make a satisfactory selection for their Christmas presents.

This year we issue an even more urgent warning, for not only are there fewer books available, but, because of the greater scarcity of other types of gifts, more people than ever will be choosing books. Therefore, we urge those of our customers who have always realized the advantages of books as presents, to shop early—and by shopping early we do not mean in the early days of December or even November. **You cannot start too soon. Start now.**

W.H. SMITH & SON, Ltd. Head Office: STRAND HOUSE, LONDON, W.C.2

SANTA CLAUS _— a la mode !_

Here I am—in war time kit—with my sack of gifts in one hand and a Stirrup Pump in the other!

Not quite the sort of Christmas I've been used to. But still it's Christmas, and still there's the same spirit of good will—even if there has to be a little less "good cheer".

Toffee and Chocolate were my time-honoured stand-bys for Christmas. In fact, Christmas wouldn't be Christmas without them.

So I'm glad that *some* of those good things are still to be had—even although there is only half as much as usual.

Mackintosh's 'Quality Street'

OFFICIAL PRICES
"Quality Street" and "Double Centre" Assortments - - - 8d. per qr. lb.
½-lb. Box 1s. 4d. - - Handy Packet 6d.
"Rolo" & "Butt-o-Scotch" 2½d. per pkt.
"MAX" Chewing Gum - ½d. per pkt.

With paper shortages, decorations became makeshift. People cut shapes from coloured paper and strung them together on cotton; tissue paper or sweet wrappers were favourite (if you could get them). Commercially produced cards could sometimes be found, but many people chose to make their own. Those for friends or relatives serving abroad might have to be sent as early as August.

Immediately after the first wartime Christmas, food rationing was introduced and, from then until the war was over, catering at Christmas was a problem every year. In 1943 it was estimated that only 10 per cent of the population would, that year, eat a traditional Christmas dinner. Months before each wartime Christmas, people started to save their coupons or items of food, and there was a flood of recipes for alternatives to the hard-to-get, traditional fare.

One suggestion for Christmas presents was marzipan fruits, rolled into the shape of apples, pears and so on, coloured with food colouring, with cloves used as stalks or their heads pressed in to form the dried flower head. Arranged in a basket, they would make a fine gift.

Wartime Christmases were rather restrained; shortages and rationing meant that traditional Christmases were impossible but, as these adverts show, people did what they could.

STUFFING

Wash and grate three large carrots, mix with two teacups of breadcrumbs, 3 oz of chopped suet or margarine, one teaspoon of sultanas, a pinch of grated nutmeg, a pinch of ginger and one tablespoon of dried egg. When well mixed, add just enough milk and water to bind. Use as a stuffing for turkey, goose or chicken.

Woman, December 1944

FOOD FACTS

HOW TO GET YOUR CHRISTMAS EXTRAS

Here are the details of the extra rations and how to get them:

FOR HOLDERS OF ADULT BUFF RATION BOOK RB.1, CHILD'S GREEN RATION BOOK RB.2, JUNIOR BLUE RATION BOOK RB.4 AND RB.8X AND RB.8R.

SUGAR 8 oz. Obtainable once only between 10th December and 6th January. Preserves may *not* be taken instead. Coupon K for week 22 will be used. (Coupon 'Spare One' on some ration documents.)

MARGARINE 8 oz. Obtainable once only between 10th December and 6th January. Fats coupon for week 22 will be used.

MEAT Ration increased from 1/2 to 1/10, i.e., value of each coupon increased from 7d. to 11d. The value of each extra meat ration authorized on form RG.48 will also be 1/10. (Child's, 11d.) Obtainable between 17th and 23rd December. In Scotland, between 24th and 30th December instead.

Cheese for Vegetarians who are authorized to get cheese in place of meat—6 oz. (12 oz. if authorized to have two special rations). Obtainable once only between 10th December and 6th January. Cheese coupon for week 22 will be used. (In Scotland the coupon for week 23 instead.)

CHOCOLATE AND SWEETS 8 oz. (for young people only, holders of green or blue ration books). Obtainable between 10th December and 6th January. Personal points coupons (printed in red or blue) on a page in or taken from ration books RB.2 and RB.4 only: D coupons will still be worth one point each but E coupons will be worth 4 points each. Boys and girls under 18 who hold other kinds of personal points coupons (including those given in replacement of lost coupons) may obtain additional coupons on application to Food Office. A boy who holds the British Seaman's Identity Card should apply to a Mercantile Marine Office.

HOLDERS OF TEMPORARY RATION CARD RB.12. Where necessary, the extra rations may be obtained against form RB.12 valid in week 22 (in Scotland week 23 instead).

HOLDERS OF WEEKLY SEAMAN'S RATION BOOK RB.6. The extra rations of sugar and margarine (but not meat) may be obtained against ration book RB.6 (full or modified), if the counterfoil for week 22 (in Scotland 23 instead) has been signed.

HOLDERS OF DUTY RATION CARD RB.8A will not be eligible for extra sugar, margarine, meat or cheese.

LISTEN TO THE KITCHEN FRONT ON TUESDAY, WEDNESDAY, THURSDAY AND FRIDAY at 8.15 a.m.

ISSUED BY THE MINISTRY OF FOOD, LONDON, W.I.   FOOD FACTS No. 211

MOCK MARZIPAN

½ lb haricot beans
4 tablespoons sugar
2 tablespoons ground rice
1 teaspoon almond essence
1 tablespoon margarine

Soak the beans for 24 hours, then cook until tender in fresh, unsalted water. Put them on a tin in a warm oven to get dry and floury. Rub them through a sieve. Beat the sugar into the bean puree, add the ground rice, warmed margarine and, finally, the flavouring. Beat until smooth. Any flavouring or colouring may be added.

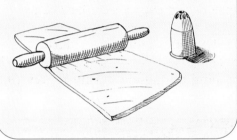

CHRISTMAS CAKE FOR THE CHILDREN

½ lb flour
6 oz margarine
6 oz fine flour
1 cup sieved stewed apples
¾ teaspoon baking soda
1 tablespoon warm water
4 tablespoons treacle

3 oz chopped, stoned raisins
3 oz cleaned currants
pinch of salt
¼ teaspoon ground cloves
¾ teaspoon ground cinnamon
pinch of grated nutmeg

Beat the margarine to a cream in a basin. Stir in the sugar by degrees, and beat till fluffy. Dissolve soda in the water, mix with apples, and add to sugar and fat. Add treacle. If liked, use half treacle and half golden syrup or clear honey. Sift the flour with the salt and spices, then stir in the prepared fruit. Add to the wet mixture. Stir lightly till well blended. Bake in a greased loaf tin for 40 minutes in a rather slow oven.

To decorate. Spread with glacé icing, and decorate with eskimos, polar bears, and silver balls, or simply with coloured sweets, or glacé cherries, or quartered pink marshmallows.

EASTER

Easter eggs were soon a rarity and chocolate was out once sweet rationing was introduced. An Easter cake was often the answer. The traditional Simnel cake was recommended, as were 'Bird's Nests', a recipe from 'Food Facts' which used soya marzipan.

PARTIES

For some, parties were vaguely unpatriotic, an excuse to eat and drink when both food and drink were scarce. For others the maxim 'Eat, drink and be merry for tomorrow you die' applied, and parties were held as often as possible. For most, parties at Christmas, children's birthdays, weddings or when a loved one came home were an essential part of keeping up morale during a grey time. As the war progressed and

BIRD'S NESTS

Make pastry tartlet cases in the usual way, and when cold fill with tiny soya marzipan eggs, some plain, some rolled in cocoa. Little cress baskets, filled with small marzipan eggs and chicks, and tied with ribbon, also make attractive nests.

SOYA MARZIPAN

2 oz margarine
2 tablespoons water
1–2 teaspoons almond
  essence
4 oz soya (flour)
4 oz sugar

Melt margarine in water. Draw saucepan off heat, stir in almond essence, sugar and soya. Turn out, knead well and shape into little eggs and chicks.

A VE-Day street party in Bromley, with make-shift benches and a stage. (Bromley Local Studies Library)

COCKTAILS

Cocktails had been very popular in the inter-war years, though they were smaller than modern cocktails and consisted almost entirely of alcohol. One particularly potent example is the Bunny Hug from the *Savoy Cocktail Book*, first published in 1929 but reprinted again and again since.

Cocktails remained popular as they were a wonderful way to use up the various bits and pieces that might be found at the back of the cocktail cabinet, or the assorted drinks people would bring to a party, or whatever was available. In truth, they were not all alcoholic, as demonstrated in the publication *Health-giving Foods and How to Prepare Them*, which gave a list of fruit and vegetable cocktails, including some admittedly rather bizarre concoctions: apple juice, strawberry and lemon; carrot and orange; spinach, parsley and orange; celery with a dash of lemon; red cabbage and pineapple; watercress and parsley.

THE BUNNY HUG

One third Gin
One third Whisky
One third Absinthe

Shake well and strain
into cocktail glass.

shortages began to bite, people brought not only a bottle, but also whatever food they could, and magazines offered tips for party food.

Here's a tip for quick party sandwiches. Use a square loaf and cut it in thickish slices lengthwise – not the usual way. You should get four or five lengthwise slices. Spread these slices first with a thin layer of margarine. Then spread one slice with mashed, seasoned pilchards, one with mixed, chopped watercress and tomato, one with cold, chopped, poached, dried egg, one with vegetable or

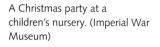

A Christmas party at a children's nursery. (Imperial War Museum)

meat extract and one with grated, raw, sour apple, well seasoned. Put the loaf together again, remove the outside crusts, tie up very securely in two places with scarlet ribbon, sprinkle the top with chopped parsley and to serve, cut the loaf downwards in the usual way, only in rather thick slices.

Woman, December 1944

Besides private parties, groups all over the country, including the fire brigades, ARP, Women's Institutes, gave Christmas parties for children. Sometimes these would be for local children, and sometimes for evacuees. Food and decorations would be begged from all and sundry.

WEDDINGS

The local food office would grant a small amount of extra rations for a wedding, for which the organisers had to apply giving details of the number of guests and so on. Once again, friends and family would chip in to help lay on food and drink. Wedding cakes were very small, the amount given to each guest being tiny; icing was non existent – in August 1940, the Government specifically banned icing on wedding cakes.

PRESENTS

Finding presents for birthdays, Christmas and weddings became a problem as consumer goods became more and more rare as factories increasingly moved over to war work. Alcohol, for entertaining and gifts, was difficult to find, as were cigarettes, cigars and tobacco, and if you could procure whisky, some cigarettes, nylons or even hair clips, you saved them for a very special occasion . . . or for yourself! Sweets and soap, traditional fall-back gifts, were rationed, and even where off-ration gifts could be bought it was considered unpatriotic to buy too much. A patriotic gift might be a National Savings Certificate, or a savings book with a few stamps attached.

One solution was to make or revamp presents. In the lead-up to December, magazines were full of ideas, and books such as *Gifts You Can*

BUTTERED NUTS

Cob, Filbert or walnuts
Butterscotch or toffee mix

Shell the nuts and lay out on a baking sheet. Place in the oven and heat slightly until it is possible to rub off the brown skins. With the aid of a fork dip these nuts into the toffee and let them cool on waxed paper.

TOFFEE MIX

4 oz sugar
2½ tablespoons water
½ oz margarine
pinch of cream of tartar

Dissolve the sugar in the water, add the margarine and cream of tartar. Bring to the boil and cook until little dropped in cold water turns brittle.

Make Yourself were popular. An old doll could be cleaned up and provided with a home-made costume, or a crib with blankets. A hand-knitted sweater or scarf was always welcome, as was something for the garden – gardening tools, books, bottling jars, and seeds could be given, and some gardening magazines even recommended a bag of fertiliser. Bouquets of flowers became rare. 'Is your journey really necessary?', the slogan asked. The Government decided that for flowers, the answer was no! In late 1942 it became illegal to send flowers by rail.

Gifts of food were also popular, especially home-made sweets or preserves.

Below: An advertisement for Hall's Wine – 'For those who cannot take a holiday'. By 1940 holidays had become a thing of the past for many workers. Those who did get time off were encouraged to take holidays at home.

Below. right: One holiday away from home that was encouraged was to 'Lend a hand on the Land', spending a week or so in the country helping on a farm.

HOLIDAYS

The traditional summer holiday to the seaside certainly suffered during the war. Within the first year, south and east coast beaches were covered in barbed wire and notices warning of mines, as the country readied itself for invasion. Travel was restricted; parents of evacuated children could get a cheap eight-day excursion ticket once a year to visit their children, and if they were lucky the foster parents (the family with whom the

children were billeted) might be able to put them up or arrange alternative accommodation for them in the area.

During 1940 annual leave for many was cancelled as war production became a question of national survival. By 1942, many people were at breaking point, and the Government introduced the Stay-at-Home Holiday Scheme, under which industrial workers were given a week's leave, which they were encouraged to spend at home. This, of course, meant no holiday and more work for the housewife. As small compensation, suggestions were made for picnic and snack meals – the Ministry of Food produced a leaflet entitled 'Suggested Menus for Holidays at Home' – and local councils organised band concerts and shows to provide entertainment.

Other entertainments were laid on during a series of fund-raising weeks that took place in most areas; the first of these were the local Spitfire Funds. These began at the height of the Battle of Britain (1940) and local communities were encouraged to 'buy their own Spitfire' at £5,000 each. Those who managed to save that much would have the aircraft named after the town or village. Many villages and small towns soon found that the target was too much, and were forced to club together. Also in 1940, War Weapons week was held. Like the other 'weeks' to come, these were local affairs and the dates were set by the local council. In 1941 Tanks for Attack week was held, 1942 brought Warship week, and Wings for Victory week was launched by National Savings in 1943 to buy bombers. Salute the Soldier week was held in 1944, and in 1945 came Thanksgiving week.

Pupils of Blean School, near Canterbury, proudly show off their War Weapons week noticeboard,. Many schools were enthusiastically saving, as well as collecting salvage. (Imperial War Museum)

A Wings for Victory auction, Deptford, March 1943. Such auctions were a regular part of fund-raising weeks. (Lewisham Local Studies Library)

Typical events during these weeks were parades – often featuring the local Home Guard, Civil Defence and youth groups such as the Boy Scouts or Boys Brigades, who would sometimes provide the band – fire-fighting or anti-gas displays by the local fire brigade or ARP; sports days, football and cricket matches; and, mainly for children, fancy dress competitions. Another interesting item was the auction; lots might include the traditional bottle of whisky but there were also wartime rarities such as pairs of silk stockings or a banana.

A concert usually provided the high spot, such as the Coventry Wings for Victory 'Grand Gala' Concert held on 23 May 1943 and featuring the bands of the WAAF, the RAF and the Hippodrome Broadcasting Orchestra. Guest artistes would be invited, and this particular event starred Jack Warner and Dorothy Summers (*ITMA*'s Mrs Mop).

Answers to Radio Quiz

'Can you hear me, mother?' – Sandy Powell   'Drop me a postcard.' – Syd Walker
'Semi-colon.' – Stainless Stephen   'Oi!' – Flanagan and Allen
'I thank you.' – Arthur Askey   'Flash!' – Vic Oliver
'Ye-e-es.' – Claude Dampier   'Shurrup!' – George Robey
'Play the game, you cads.' – Western Brothers 'It's turned out nice again.' – George Formby
'You see.' – Cyril Fletcher

TEN

RECONSTRUCTION

A NEW BEGINNING

The precise turning point of the war is difficult to pin down. Some would suggest the entry of America in December 1941, or the battles of Stalingrad and El Alamein in 1942; yet on the British home front there was a distinct sea-change during the winter and spring of 1940/1. Before this, all that counted was survival; to win the Battle of Britain, to endure the Blitz, to counter the threatened invasion. But that spring, any doubt about the war's outcome seemed to disappear. With the assumption that victory was inevitable, the main topic of interest was planning for the post-war period. At first this took the form of committees, parliamentary and others, who were asked to look into post-war reconstruction, and the creation of the post of Minister of Reconstruction, filled by Lord Woolton in 1943.

The shape of the post-war world, and more particularly that of Britain, was the cause of huge debates. For some, the ways in which British life had been changed by the war – the rationing, Utility, price controls, regulations of industry and manpower – these were necessary evils that would end with the return to peace. For others, these measures were the

Once the early threat of invasion began to disappear in mid-1941, people began to look towards the end of the war. Post-war plans abounded and these were reflected in adverts.

This advert from December 1943 looks forward to peacetime and a return to normality when work on the house could start again.

beginnings of a new egalitarian society. Many had always opposed their introduction. Not unexpectedly, many retailers had opposed price controls, believing them to be an attack on fair profits. Rationing was seen by some as an attack on the rich, who had worked hard for their money and, once they had paid their taxes, deserved to be able to spend it how they liked; others still were appalled at the tax increases of the war, believing them to be an attack on everything the country stood for.

As early as 1941, the Board of Education started to look at reforms in the education system and in July 1943 the White Paper on Educational Reconstruction was published. R.A. Butler, President of the Board, had commissioned the Ministry of Information to assess public reaction to the proposals. It found that public opinion was particularly in favour of plans to raise the school leaving age to sixteen and abolish fees in the state sector. The Butler Education Act, as it became known, became law in August 1944.

Also in 1941, the Government asked the economist, Sir William Beveridge, to chair a committee to look into the provision of improved social insurance. Among its recommendations were the introduction of disability benefit, sickness benefit, unemployment benefit, child allowance, retirement pensions and national assistance. The Beveridge Report, as the committee's findings became known, was almost a one-man affair. Most of the committee members were civil servants, and were therefore banned from making public statements about contentious issues. One of the core elements of the Beveridge Report – the formation of a National Health Service – was accepted by the Government in February 1943 (in fact, it was to be over five years before the NHS finally arrived, on 5 July 1948). One of the last acts of the Coalition Government was to introduce non-means tested family allowances: the first child allowance of 5s a week for the second and subsequent children under the school leaving age was paid in August 1946 (this was 3s less than Beveridge had recommended).

THE LABOUR GOVERNMENT

On 23 May 1945 the Coalition that had steered Britain through the war came to an end, to be succeeded by Churchill's caretaker Government, which resigned in June. On 5 July 1945 the general election took place; with so many men still in the forces, in every part of the world, the voting and the counting took three weeks. When the results were announced on the 26th, the Labour Party was elected with a massive majority of 146. Clement Attlee, Churchill's deputy in the wartime Coalition Governemnt, was the new Prime Minister, and Hugh Dalton, who had done so much while at the Board of Trade to introduce the Utility schemes, was Chancellor of the Exchequer.

It seemed incredible to many outside Britain at the time, and still so to many inside Britain today, that the people of Britain had rejected Churchill, their great wartime leader. But this was a rejection of the politics of Conservatism, not of one man, even if that man was Churchill. People were determined that the war had to mean something – all that suffering and dying had to be for a reason, and that meant a different world afterwards, starting with a new government.

With the peace, the task of rebuilding began in earnest; two stamps were specially issued for VE-Day, the more expensive 3*d* violet showed, with the dove of peace, a trowel, square and dividers representing rebuilding. In his VJ-Day broadcast on 15 August, King George VI said, 'In every country men may now turn their industry, skill and science to repairing its [the war's] frightful devastation.'

The new Labour Government needed no convincing of the need for housing. It foresaw that the majority of house building in the immediate post-war period would be carried out by local authorities. In a repeat of the post-First World War housing strategy, the 1946 Housing Act guaranteed housing subsidies and grants for new houses, and the Government set itself a target of 240,000 new houses a year.

A special booklet designed to be of real help to all ranks in the Services

THAT HOUSE IN CIVVY STREET

How to set about YOUR post-war housing problem

Post free — Threepence — from the

SERVICES INFORMATION BUREAU

ABBEY NATIONAL BUILDING SOCIETY

Abbey House, Baker Street, London, N.W.1

However, progress was slow, and by February 1951 the total of houses built had reached only 900,000. Housing became a major topic in the next general election, and it is generally accepted that the failure to provide enough new houses was one of the main reasons why Labour lost. The Conservatives promised 300,000 new houses a year, and the new Conservative Government actually achieved this target in 1953 and '54, partly through increased subsidies and partly because of a loosening of the rules over who was allowed to build houses. Unfortunately, the figure soon began to fall again and the shortage of houses was never fully dealt with. Even today, it is still one of the first casualties of any government spending cuts.

Not 'Homes Fit for Heroes', but 'post-war housing problems' are foreseen in this ad from February 1945.

BUILDING BRITAIN UP

It was clear that the country would emerge from the war with a reduced building force, many men from the building trades having gone to war, and, of course, not all returned. Also, where men had retired during the six years of the war, no one had been available to replace them. It was equally clear that Britain would need a large re-building programme. Received wisdom was that the problems of re-building Britain's housing stock could only be dealt with by some form of central planning. As early as 1941, Lord Reith, then Minister of Works and Planning, had asked the London County Council to prepare a plan for post-war development

without paying overmuch respect to existing town planning law and all the other laws affecting building and industry but with a reasonable belief that if a good scheme was put forward it would provide reasons – indeed more than

WHAT'S IN A NAME?

Post-war planning was not confined to the Government. In 1943 *Housewife* magazine ran a competition to choose the name of a post-war house; this is their summary of the responses they received:

Many readers wrote expressing positive horror at such names as Kosicot and Dunfitin (Done fighting), and *Housewife* heartily agrees with them. A good many post-war houses, we are afraid, will rejoice in names like Eisenhouse, Montyville and Winstonia, and many more will combine the Christian names of their owners – Robethel, Doneth and Jovera.

Names like Strata and Parallels for sweeping modern houses with horizontal lines were good, so was Party Walls.

'reasons' – the impulse and determination to bring about whatever changes in law are needed to carry the plan into effect.'

Always an ambitious scheme, 'The County of London Plan' was drawn up and published in 1945.

In 1941 the Minister of Health estimated that there would be a need to build a total of between 3 and 4 million houses post-war, and this was before the V- weapon attacks, one of the most destructive phases of the enemy assault. By June 1945, it was estimated that 4½ million houses would be needed over the next ten years – an average of 450,000 to be built each year. To put this in context, the highest number of houses built in any of the ten years before the war was 350,000.

Worse even than the manpower shortages was the shortage of materials. A report at the time by the Royal Institute of British Architects concluded that: 'with proper organisation and the adequate release of labour, there should be sufficient supplies of well-tried materials, with the probable exception of timber, to meet the requirements of a building programme of approximately 200,000 completed houses in two years after the European war.' The figures just did not add up. Aware of this, the Government looked at alternatives; first at the idea of temporary housing, and then at prefabricated buildings.

The people, meanwhile, saw the problem and a possible solution quite clearly; if we, as a nation, could respond to the call to supply funds for aircraft in 1940, we could do the same for houses. In the wartime flag-waver *Dawn Guard*, one of the characters says, 'We've made a fine big war effort and after it's all over, we've got to make a fine big peace effort.' In this, many saw the necessity for a new ministry, the Ministry of Housing, which would co-ordinate the efforts of Britain's 83,000 building firms rather than replace them. There were, of course, those who argued strongly for a laissez-faire approach, but too many people remembered the aftermath of the First World War; as one commentator wrote:

It will not be enough, after the war, to say to the ex-serviceman that we are 'doing our best' to provide him with a house. If, as the anti-control fanatics suggest, we were to de-control building, labour, and the cost of materials, it would provoke a housing famine such as this country has never before experienced, not even in 1919. Only by a general plan which has as its beneficiary the consumer, that is to say, the man who wants a house, can we solve the housing problem – the first great problem of the peace.

So, reconstruction was the order of the day, and this began on a massive scale. The destruction and damage to housing stock was huge; in September 1944, when the worst of the bombing was over, the official figures showed over 200,000 houses destroyed throughout Britain (half of these were in London), with a further 4 million damaged but repairable. A slightly later figure put the number destroyed or damaged beyond reasonable repair at a little under ½ million. On the other hand,

2 million marriages had taken place since the outbreak of war, and the birth rate, which had dropped to a low point in 1941, was rising again. Therefore, a vast programme of re-building was needed; for example, the LCC and outer London boroughs set a target of 100,000 new homes, but time was of essence. Certainly, as the end of the war was in sight, evacuees and service personnel would be returning home, but to what? A wide variety of temporary housing was brought out that could be erected quickly. Much of it was assembled from sections pre-fabricated in factories, sometimes in the USA.

Types of Housing

The new planners of the 1940s looked back on the previous decade and did not like what they saw; ribbon development had led to rapid and uncontrolled expansion of the towns, transforming nearby country towns and villages into suburbs with endless rows of near-identical semi-detached houses built in dull, straight lines. Certainly, the blitzing of the city centres had opened the way for development inwards instead of outwards, but it also meant that planning could be done on a grand scale; social engineering as opposed to mere local planning.

In 1944 it was still assumed that the most common form of post-war house would be the three or four-bedroomed semi. There was some experimentation with the use of new materials such as steel frames with concrete or expanded clay cladding, but the vast majority of houses were built in brick with 11-inch cavity walls. As the reality of post-war economic controls took over, so the number of semis being built declined; terraces were revived and there was an increasing use of maisonettes in small four-storey blocks.

The planners' new thinking also took several other forms, including city centre redevelopment and neighbourhood units (integrated local

Below, left: As the end of the war approached, people's aspirations for peace became more specific than just getting 'lit up when the lights go up in London'. They wanted new homes and modern kitchens.

Below: Post-war housing, Lewisham, 1947. Like many inner-city blocks erected at the time, this was built on a site cleared by German bombing. Most, like this, were low rise – five- or six-storey affairs. High-rise buildings became commonplace in the sixties. (Lewisham Local Studies Library)

planning of shops, houses, schools, etc., as with the County of London plan). Mixed estates sprang up, combining houses and flats and designed to support a reasonably dense population without creating new slums. The planners began to see that a mixture of the two types of dwelling would offer the advantages of each, and attract a far more varied community. The first began to be built in the early fifties; one of the the best example of this post-war design is the Alton Estate at Roehampton.

Green Belt land and planning restrictions meant that land for development was scarce and expensive. An obvious answer, therefore, was to build upwards. The low-rise flats of the inter-war years were succeeded by ever taller high-rise estates. Another development in flat-building saw variations in the ground plan of these blocks, which changed from the standard rectangular to the Y and T section. However, by the mid-1960s the drawbacks of high-rise building were all too plain to see. Planning mistakes and restricted budgets had meant a dearth of facilities; now broken lifts and vandalism brought despair to residents, and, perhaps worse of all, the loss of any community spirit led to isolation, loneliness and misery.

THE PRE-FAB

The huge demand for new houses, and the dearth of skilled building labour, made many minds turn to the factory system; if aircraft could be built in pieces in factories, the argument ran, why not housing? The plan was to turn the armaments factories, and their workers, over to producing pre-fabricated houses. They were cheap, easy and quick to put up, and required little in the way of skills at a time when craftsmen were at a premium. These pre-fabs, as they were soon generally known, began to be put up in 1944, the earliest being built in London where the raiding had been heaviest. The very first to be erected was completed on 30 April; it was built in three days and cost £550.

By December 1944, Aneurin Bevan, the Minister of Health, reported that pre-fabs were being put up at a rate of about 500 to 600 per week. One example was the flat-roofed 'box bungalow'. Built of wood and asbestos, it had a living room 19 feet by 12 feet, a built-in kitchen recess containing a cooker, sink, and boiler, and two bedrooms, each 11 feet by 10 feet. Another common style was the semi-tubular Nissen hut type; nearly all had built-in kitchens and bathrooms. Pre-fabs were designed to last just ten years but many examples are still in use around the country, and most of their occupants are very fond of them.

Pre-fabs photographed in the 1960s. The one in the right foreground has a thirties-style garage and, in typical post-war style, an Anderson shelter being used as a shed.

Appearances

One new factor in house building was a trend towards uniformity in size. The average working-class family was rapidly decreasing in size to match that of the middle-class family. Very few houses, private or council, were being built with more than two or three bedrooms – by the early sixties, the figure was less than 4 per cent.

One of the biggest shifts in the external appearance of private housing was that garages were by now standard and were normally connected to the house. A feature of this collection of styles was the disappearance of both the bay and the sash window.

The combined dining-room and kitchen, or the kitchen diner, as it was later known, was another new trend. This evolved as a direct result of the war, as people found heating two rooms wasteful and eating in the kitchen made much more sense. A by-product of this was the single, large living-room, or 'through lounge', as opposed to separate lounge and dining-room.

REBUILDING THE ECONOMY

Of course, reconstruction meant more than just rebuilding the physical structure of the country; it also meant the reconstruction of the economy, and of Britain's factories and overseas markets. The war had left the country with huge debts, and the Government went all-out in an export drive to pay this off. Production for the home market was frowned upon, and this led to greater shortages than had been witnessed even during the war.

In September 1946 the 'Britain Can Make It' exhibition opened in the Victoria & Albert Museum. Many of the designs on show were for export only, giving rise to the alternative title: 'Britain Can't Have It'.

Rationing

Food rationing had meant neither less to eat, nor poorer food for everyone. Indeed, for those whose diet had been restricted pre-war by poverty, rationing had provided them with their first adequate diet. Diseases related to dietary deficiencies, and infant mortality fell markedly during the war. Yet rationing was one of the most hated facets of the home front. Still, it was seen as necessary – 'Don't you know there's a war on?'.

Perhaps quite naturally, rationing became truly hated once the war was over; people could not understand why it had to be continued. However, Britain's wartime debt had to be paid off, and Attlee's Government applied 'Austerity measures', including rationing, in order to do so. These measures were rigidly enforced, and the President of the Board of Trade, Sir Stafford Cripps, himself a very austere figure, became widely known as 'Austerity Cripps'.

On 17 August 1945, just two days after VJ-Day, America ceased its supply of Lease–Lend food. In February 1946 coal was in such short

THE OLYMPIC GAMES AND THE FESTIVAL OF BRITAIN

In 1948 Britain hosted the Olympic games, the first since the Berlin Olympics of 1936. Two years earlier, the first session of the United Nations General Assembly had opened in London.

In 1951 an exhibition and season of activities were launched on the south bank of the Thames, complete with Skylon, a futuristic obelisk. Called the Festival of Britain, it marked the centenary of the Great Exhibition and, like its predecessor, it was used as a showcase for British goods. In a precursor of the Millennium Dome, one of the exhibits was called the Dome of Discovery; another, one which is still standing today, was the Royal Festival Hall.

supply that the whole of London had enough for only about one week. Butter, margarine and fat rations were cut. In July, bread was rationed, followed by potatoes in November 1947, neither of which had been rationed at all during the war. This was not entirely down to the Government; in the immediate aftermath of the war there was a world food shortage, which only began to ease in 1948. On 5 November of that year the then President of the Board of Trade, Harold Wilson, lit what he called his Bonfire of Controls, when he removed restrictions on more than sixty commodities. In 1949 clothes rationing was abolished, although at about the same time, milk rations were cut to two pints a week.

By 1950, most of the shortages had been dealt with. In February 1953 sweet rationing was abolished, and the last two items of food – butter and meat – were eventually taken off rations in 1954. So food rationing was finally at an end, although rationing itself was not entirely dead: it would be four more years before coal was freely available.

FURNITURE

During 1946, a Government working party produced a report on furniture; the shortage of available new furniture – which had led to the introduction of the Utility furniture scheme, was still widespread – and was even added to by the return of the servicemen and subsequent marriages. The working party's proposals, most of which were taken up, included the retention of price control until furniture production could at least equal demand. Until then, production of furniture should remain tied to specified designs and materials, but the range of Utility furniture should be increased and it should be available generally, and not just to those with permits.

A priority docket for a Utility mattress, 1946. Rationing of furniture continued until 1948.

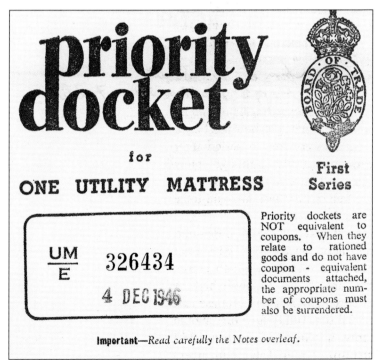

priority docket

BOARD OF TRADE

for

ONE UTILITY MATTRESS   First Series

UM/E   326434

4 DEC 1946

Priority dockets are NOT equivalent to coupons. When they relate to rationed goods and do not have coupon - equivalent documents attached, the appropriate number of coupons must also be surrendered.

Important—*Read carefully the Notes overleaf.*

In March 1946 the Design Council held another exhibition of prototype Utility furniture designs. This time there were three different ranges of furniture: the Chiltern, an extension of the basic, solid range; the Cotswold, lighter and more expensive than the Chiltern; and the Cockaigne, designed for mass production and therefore cheaper. The three ranges were exhibited at the *Daily Herald* Modern Homes Exhibition, after which the Chiltern and Cotswold ranges went into full production. For a variety of reasons, the Cockaigne range was renamed the Cheviot, and then immediately discontinued.

Other major changes included the increasing use of metal, especially aluminium, and the production of some Utility furniture abroad.

Exhibition living/dining room
1947, with later pattern Utility
furniture. (Design Council)

In 1946 it was proposed that a new Utility symbol be designed to
replace the old 'cheeses'. Enid Marx, who had designed several Utility
fabrics, was asked to prepare some designs. She came up with seven, but
none of them were taken up.

In 1947 the second Utility furniture catalogue was published. This
included the Cotswold and Chiltern ranges and Lloyd Loom type
furniture, which was now off ration. By the end of the year, it had been
announced that production of the Cotswold range would cease, to be
replaced by a new 'Diversified' range (like the Cockaigne range, this never
saw the light of day).

In June 1948 rationing of furniture came to an end; this did not mean
that Utility furniture came to an end, however, although the rules began
to be relaxed. From December manufacturers were free to design their
own furniture within the tight specifications of Utility, although many
chose to continue with the production of the Chiltern range. The work
continued to carry the Utility stamp, to be free of purchase tax, and to be
price controlled.

When the end came for Utility furniture it was somewhat drawn-out.
Many members of the Conservative Government viewed Utility with great
contempt, as one of the leftovers of wartime socialism, which could,
unlike the phenomenally popular Welfare State, be abolished. A
committee was set up to look into Utility's exemption from purchase tax.
Somewhat predictably, the committee decided that Utility furniture should
be treated the same as non-Utility furniture, and in mid-December 1952
the Government revoked the Utility Furniture Order. Labour members

A post-war flat, with Utility Lloyd loom chair, dining table and chairs. Continued shortages meant that the furnishings were rather sparse. (Lewisham Local Studies Library)

'WOMAN'S HOUR'

AT 2 p.m.

A daily programme of music, advice, and entertainment for the home

Today, Alan Ivimey introduces Mary Manton on 'Mother's Midday Meal'; Kay Beattie on 'Putting Your Best Face Forward'; 'Housewives' Choice' of gramophone records; and the current serial story, Stanley Weyman's 'Under the Red Robe'

Woman's Hour, first broadcast in 1946, is still going strong today.

forced a parliamentary debate on 21 January 1953, but when the house divided the vote was lost by thirty-seven votes – the great social experiment of Utility furniture was over.

RADIO AND TELEVISION

Regional broadcasting returned on 25 July 1945, with the choice of the Home Service and the Light Programme (actually the de-mobbed Forces Programme, still mainly big bands, variety and news). These stations were joined in 1946 by the Third Programme, which produced minority and cultural programmes.

New programmes in the post-war period included *Dick Barton – Special Agent*, a weekly serial, famous for its cliff-hanger endings and a great favourite with children and adults. The soap opera *Mrs Dale's Diary* was the story of a doctor's wife who constantly 'worried about Jim'. Having established that women made up the majority of daytime listeners, the BBC broadcast a new programme in 1946, the first edition of *Woman's Hour*.

Perhaps more importantly in terms of the 'modern world', television began broadcasting again in June 1946, although it was not until the Coronation in 1953 that it really established itself as a mass-medium.

CONCLUSION

'We're all middle class now' is a sentiment voiced by many politicians, reflecting the common perception of an homogenised society. This is the result not so much of a continued growth of the middle classes, but of a blurring of the differences that distinguished the various strata of British society, which was at least accelerated if not created by the Second World War.

Rationing of food, clothes, and even furniture meant that, by and large, people had shared similar experiences, and the country was further drawn together by the common threats of bombing and invasion. Evacuation of children, and conscription of women and men into the forces, Civil Defence and the factories had thrown people together from vastly different regional and cultural backgrounds, while the rigid class structure in the forces that had so markedly separated the officers and other ranks in the First World War, was of necessity beginning to break down.

These advances continued in the post-war period. It has been said that slum clearance in the inner cities owed more to Hitler than to any British political leader. But, not to be outdone, the post-war planners did far more damage to areas such as London's Elephant and Castle than the Luftwaffe. Yet planning acts severely limited the random growth of the suburbs, turning the middle classes back to the city so that previously working-class areas such as Fulham became 'des. res.'.

The new Welfare State, itself a product of the war, and the affluence of the fifties and sixties blurred old class boundaries further as many in traditional working-class occupations saw their income overlap that of the middle classes.

Before the war, a minimum school-leaving age of fourteen and university fees meant that higher education was the preserve of the middle and upper classes. The Butler Education Act of 1944 meant that education up to and including university level became available to all. Increasingly, those in traditional working-class occupations bought their own homes and by the sixties they began to send their children to private schools, a trend that has grown rapidly since.

The Second World War did not so much change the social face of Britain as accelerate a movement which had been discernible since the middle of the previous century. It is far too simplistic to claim that 'we're all middle class now'; but middle-class mores, especially the desire to be a homeowner, and the importance of education, have become the norm in a way that our 1930s antecedents could never have foreseen.

BIBLIOGRAPHY

Addison, Paul. *The Road to 1945*, Pimlico, 1994

Bennet-Levy, Michael. *Historic Televisions and Video Recorders*, MBL Publications, 1993

Briggs, Susan. *Keep Smiling Through*, Weidenfeld & Nicholson, 1975

Brown, Mike. *A Child's War*, Sutton Publishing, 2000

——. *Put That Light Out*, Sutton Publishing, 1999

Budden, Barbara. *The Home Decorator*, Odhams, 1937

Burnett, John. *A Social History of Housing*, Routledge, 1986

Chase, Joanna. *Sew and Save*, The Literary Press, 1943

Cole & Postgate. *The Common People 1746–1946*, Methuen, 1961

Cottington Taylor, D.D. *Fruit and Vegetable Preserving*, The Country Life, 1940

——. *Practical Home Making*, Oetzmann, 1937

Craig, Elizabeth. *Cooking in Wartime*, The Literary Press, 1940

Davies, Jennifer. *The Wartime Kitchen and Garden*, BBC Books, 1993

Diener, I. *Kitchen Parade*, W.H. Allen, 1941

Duncan, Alastair. *Art Deco Furniture*, Thames & Hudson, 1984

Evelyn Thomas, S. *ARP Practical Guide for the Householder and Air Raid Warden*, J. Askew & Son, 1939

Evelyn Thomas, S., *The Handy Wartime Guide*, S. Evelyn Thomas, 1940

Harris, Carol. *Collecting Fashion & Accessories*, Millers, 2000

Izzard, Percy. *Food from the Garden in Wartime*, Daily Mail, 1940

Patten, Marguerite. *We'll Eat Again*, Hamlyn, 1985

Rowlands. *The West Midlands from AD 1000*, Longman, 1987

Simpson, Helen. *The Happy Housewife*, Hodder & Stoughton, 1934

Weightman & Humphries. *The Making of Modern London*, Sidgwick & Jackson, 1984

The Art of Radio Times, BBC, 1981

The BBC Handbook 1928, BBC, 1928

The County of London Plan, Penguin, 1945

Food Facts for the Kitchen Front, MoF, Collins, 1941

Gifts You Can Make Yourself – Woman Magazine, Odhams Press, 1944

The Handyman & Home Mechanic, Odhams, 1936

Health Giving Foods and How to Prepare Them, Health Stores, 1940

The Home of Today, Daily Express, 1935

The Home Mechanic, Newnes, 1937

The Home Workshop, Odhams, 1940

House Painting & Decorating, Cassell & Co., 1922

The Housewife's Book, Daily Express, 1937

Manpower, HMSO, 1944

Modern Make and Mend – News Chronicle, George Newnes, 1939
Pictorial Guide to Modern Home Dressmaking, Odhams, 1940
Practical Family Knitting Illustrated, Odhams, 1941
Practical Knitting Illustrated, Odhams, 1940
Rag-bag Toys, Dryad Press, 1943
The Savoy Cocktail Book, Constable & Co., 1930
Utility furniture and fashion 1941–1951, ILEA, 1974

BOOKLETS

ARP Home Storage of Food Supplies, The Canned Foods Advisory Bureau,
    1939
Health Giving Foods and How to Prepare Them, Health Stores Ltd, 1940
The 1942–1943 Clothing Quiz, HMSO
Potato Pete's Recipe Book, Ministry of Food
Preserves from the Garden, Growmore No. 3, Ministry of Agriculture

TRADE CATALOGUES

Baxendale's Plumbing and Sanitary Catalogue, 1936
Bolsoms Quality Furniture, 1936
Cavendish Furniture Company, 1934
Peerless Built-in Furniture, 1939
Slonetric, Sloan & Co., 1935

LEAFLETS

Civil Defence leaflets 1 to 5, July/August 193
Dig for Victory leaflets
Ministry of Agriculture and Fisheries Growmore leaflets
Ministry of Food War Cookery leaflets
New World Round the Corner, British Rubber Development Board, 1938
Stay Where You Are, MoHS, June 1940
What is this Beveridge Report?, The Social Security League, 1943

MAGAZINES

Home Making Magazine, April 1933
The Homeowner, September 1934
Housewife, August 1943
The Ideal Home Magazine, various, 1936–9
Illustrated, various, 1939–45
Picture Post, various, 1939–45
Practical Motorist, August 1936
The Second Great War, various, 1939–45
The War Weekly, various, 1939–45
Woman's Magazine, January 1938

INDEX